ENGLISH STYLISTICS: A BIBLIOGRAPHY

ENGLISH STYLISTICS: A BIBLIOGRAPHY

RICHARD W. BAILEY and DOLORES M. BURTON, S.N.D.

THE M.I.T. PRESS

Massachusetts Institute of Technology
Cambridge, Massachusetts, and London, England

Library of Congress catalog card number: 67-27343

PREFACE

In compiling this bibliography, we have conceived of the field of stylistics as the linguistic study of literary texts. But we do not use the term "linguistic" to refer exclusively to those approaches to language promulgated by linguists of the twentieth century. Nor would all the authors whose works are listed here be happy to be called "linguists." Whenever a scholar—whatever he may call himself—turns to the literary uses of language qua language, he is concerned with what we have defined as stylistics. Although he may attempt to communicate his intuition about a piece of language by such diverse means as graphs and diagrams, in terms of technical jargon or elegant metaphor, we feel that he is engaged in a common pursuit with others, whether they be linguists or literary critics, psychologists or aestheticians, computer specialists or teachers of literature. A shared concern for the language of literature unites the many and varied authors whose works we have included—a concern not recognized by existing bibliographies. We hope that this similarity will become apparent to those who use this bibliography and that their own investigations will be enriched by the insights contained in those works that they find here.

We have arranged the items by topics, because we assume that the person consulting this bibliography will be concerned with general questions such as "What has been done in the study of prose style? or poetic rhythms? or statistical approaches to style?" A glance at the table of contents ought to bring the user immediately to the section that interests him, and, by scanning through the list and the annotations, he can begin to answer his question. More specific questions such as "What has been said about Milton's blank verse? or Hemingway's prose style?" can be approached through the first index, as inquiries

v

64671

concerning the work of particular critics (such as Croll, Spitzer, and Jakobson, among many others) can be through the second. The period of our concern is the literature of England and America from 1500 to the present, though we have extended our range to other languages and other literatures where such work seems to us to have important theoretical or heuristic value. Of particular interest, we feel, are the items listed in Chapter II, which enable the critic to approach through both primary and secondary material those currents in the theory of style that may have influenced authors in the period from 1500 to 1900.

Stylistics, we feel, is one of the most international of literary and linguistic disciplines. Just as Russian Formalism and French *explication de texte* underlie many American and British literary theories and approaches, so too the study of style in its broadest aspects unites scholars of diverse nationalities and backgrounds. Though no work of this kind can claim to be complete, we feel that both the novice and the experienced critic of style will find important works here that might otherwise have escaped his attention.

We wish to thank John Hollander of Hunter College for his advice and assistance during the Summer Linguistic Institute held at Indiana University in 1964 where we prepared the first edition of *English Stylistics*. We are grateful for the encouragement we have received since then from Kenneth G. Wilson of the University of Connecticut, Peter Alan Taylor of the University of British Columbia, W. Nelson Francis of Brown, Raoul N. Smith of Northwestern, Harold C. Martin of Union College, Louis T. Milic of Columbia, Archibald A. Hill of Texas, James Sinclair of the University of Birmingham (England), Lubomír Doležel of the Institute for the Study of the Czech Language (Prague), Warner G. Rice and S. J. Hanna of Michigan, and Krystyna Pomorska of the Department of Modern Languages and Linguistics, M.I.T. We owe particular thanks to Professor Roman Jakobson of Harvard and M.I.T. for his suggestions on revising our format and for drawing our attention to many valuable books and articles.

September 1967   RICHARD W. BAILEY
                                         DOLORES M. BURTON, S.N.D.

INTRODUCTION:
ENGLISH STYLISTICS
IN THE MID-TWENTIETH CENTURY

The wealth and variety of the many studies represented in *English Stylistics* makes the task of surveying current trends in style analysis a difficult one. On the surface, an article devoted to specifying the rhetorical figures in, say, Sidney's *Apology* seems to have little in common with a discussion of the structure of a folktale from some little known culture. Yet the critic concerned with accounting for his intuition about the structure of either sort of text may profit from what others in seemingly remote fields have had to say, in spite of the apparent disparity of their subject matter. Stylistics in the mid-twentieth century, then, is at a point in its development where eclecticism is a healthy sign of intellectual vigor. As linguists and critics become more and more aware of the complexity of human languages, and as psychologists and aestheticians face the staggering difficulties of accounting for artistic creativity, so stylistics in its concern for creative uses of language must explore the theories and practices of a wide variety of disciplines if the traditional problems are to yield meaningful solutions. To further this end, we have compiled *English Stylistics* as a classified bibliography; the paragraphs that follow are an attempt to lay bare the unity in diversity of the sections we have established in Chapter III, "English Stylistics in the Twentieth Century."

DEFINING CREATIVITY AND "STYLE"

A dozen years ago most linguists who wrote for those outside their field felt compelled to explain that a linguist is not necessarily a polyglot, that primitive peoples do not speak "primitive" languages with tiny vocabularies and uncomplicated grammars, and that description neither denies nor endorses prescription. The state of the art of stylistics reflects a similar compulsion today, and a recurrent strategy of style critics is to begin with a short history of the word *style:* how it arose in antiquity to denote the sharp instrument used for writing on wax tablets, that it has twenty-seven main senses in the *Oxford English Dictionary*, and so on.[1] But after this ritualistic bow to etymology, most critics redefine *style* to suit their immediate purposes. The slogan of the British linguistic philosophers—"The meaning of a term is its use in the language"— points to the often tenuous "family resemblance" in uses of the term *style*. It seems to some, in fact, that the many members of the *style* family of usage have suffered from an academic Diaspora, and, though the name suggests kinship, the records attesting to the unity of the family have been destroyed or mutilated. But the common interests of those who are engaged in the study of *style* will eventually emerge if the work of others is acknowledged and if solipsism is rejected. Today, as Leo Rockas points out in his analysis of four studies of style, "one's notion of style is logically tied up with one's notion of stylistics. . . . Critics will define style in such a way as to rationalize whatever stylistic activity they choose later to indulge." [2]

Style may, of course, not be explicitly defined, but certain assumptions about it are contained in all style studies. In general, contemporary critics have abandoned the use of the term as an honorific to be applied to such pieces of writing the critic approves of for aesthetic or moral reasons. *Style* is most commonly thought of as a property of all expressions, though there are enormous disagreements concerning just what "properties" are stylistic. For the most part, those critics represented in the first section of Chapter III confront the abstract and theoretical problems inherent in the definition of *style*.

THEORIES AND STRATEGIES OF TREATING A TEXT

Until the end of the eighteenth century, the criticism of style was mainly concerned with an analysis of the way a writer embellished and ornamented his thoughts in writing. Figures of thought and figures of expression, it seemed, were well understood; it was the critic's job to

---

[1] The etymological development of the word is most thoroughly discussed by André Sempoux, "Notes sur l'histoire des mots 'style' et 'stylistique,' " *Revue Belge de Philologie et d'Histoire*, XXXIX (1961), 736–746. Contemporary uses of "style" in French periodicals are catalogued by Heinz Schödel and Roselind Reimann, "Observations sur l'usage contemporain du mot 'style,' " *Bulletin d'Information du Laboratoire d'Analyse Lexicologique* (Besançon), no. 5 (1961), 43–53; a similar survey of English uses of the word might well prove interesting.

[2] Leo Rockas, "The Description of Styles: Dr. Johnson and His Critics." Unpublished Ph.D. dissertation, The University of Michigan, 1959, p. 7.

label such figures and evaluate their aptness in the structure of the whole work. In those halcyon days the critic named the author's tools and guided his reader through the "beauties" of the text. A rejection of the view of style as ornament is inherent in the psychological bias of Buffon's famous remark, *le style est l'homme même*. While some aspects of style were still codified in terms of literary and rhetorical tradition, the literary critic, fostered by the climate of opinion that gave rise to Buffon's aphorism at the end of the eighteenth century, turned more and more to the psychology of authors and the reflection of nonliterary experience in the work as the field of his interest. Coleridge and then Croce argued for a style criticism directly focused on the creative process and emphasized the indivisible, organic unity of form and content.

In reaction to what seemed to be an irresponsible "mentalism" in the remarks about language made by linguists and critics of the nineteenth century, Leonard Bloomfield asserted that a change in the form of any utterance necessarily reflects a change in its meaning. From this point of view, *style* seemed best defined as the furthest refinement of the meaning of a work of art. The logical implication of such a definition was for the critic to postulate various "meanings" that the author might have used and to specify why a particular one was chosen. But the standards by which alternate meanings could be seen as relevant were extremely unclear. Thus, following Wellek and Warren, American New Critics suggested that broad speculations about "meaning" and the author's possible intentions in his work be put aside and attention concentrated on the form of the language in which meaning and intentions were embodied. Though such critics claimed a healthy respect for the integrity of the linguistic "organism," so much attention was devoted to minute matters of language that others found it easy to attack the resulting criticism for "monism" and neglect of matters of real literary interest.

Despite the ferment inspired by nineteenth-century psychologism or twentieth-century formalism, the concept of style as ornament of thought has never been wholly abandoned. Some linguists and critics have postulated "norms" for the language as a whole and have discussed style in terms of deviations from "normal" linguistic usage. Others have postulated norms for particular genres or style "registers." For these critics, like their Renaissance forebears, *style* is manifested by marked or unusual linguistic features set on a ground of stylistically neutral or nondeviant elements of language. *Style* is regarded as a process of choice and the critic seeks to specify those devices which are expressive of the character of the artist and the meaning of his work.

The history of literary criticism is thus clearly reflected in the stylistics of both past and present. Some critics whose work is represented in the section called "Theories and Strategies of Treating a Text" draw their inspiration from literary theorists like Aristotle or Coleridge. Others are more directly influenced by trends in the study of language inspired by such men as de Saussure, Sapir, Bloomfield, and Chomsky. Of these latter it can be said that too little attention has been devoted to the special problems of the literary language. Linguistic theories are constructed to deal with language system—*langue* in de Saussure's terminology, *competence* in Chomsky's—and for this reason much of the information they seek to account for may be inconsequential in the study of matters of language use—*parole* or *performance*. Linguistic critics encounter texts with the whole mechanism of Trager-Smith's phonology or Chomsky's generative grammar and too seldom consider the necessity of constructing an articulated and precise theory of language use. This is not to say that linguistic theory and stylistic criticism are unrelated, but rather that the relation between system and use needs more attentive examination than has been devoted to it by most critics concerned with theories and strategies of treating literary texts. At the same time, essays and speculations have too seldom been followed into the heartland of stylistics—not how the analysis is to be done, but doing it.

SELECTION AND MANIPULATION OF WORDS

Diction

The study of style as manifested in an author's choice of words is perhaps the most common form of style analysis and the one with the longest tradition. The study of literary diction in the West began with the Alexandrian School of the third century B.C.; the work of these early scholars in explicating the texts of Greece's Golden Age was highly developed. In the twelfth century A.D. Bible concordances began to appear as the logical outcome of the assumption that a comparison of word usages in scripture could give valuable insights into the unity of divine inspiration. Similar work on religious texts continues to this day to inspire scholars working with secular literature, instanced, for example, in the work of Robert Busa, S.J., who, with his colleagues at the Aloisianum, pioneered the use of electronic data-processing equipment in the study of diction and opened the way for the production of the many computer-made concordances and glossaries that have appeared in the last decade. The articles and books listed in "Diction" are only a representative sample of the many and varied studies in this field, but a representation of major studies of literary vocabulary is provided.

Tropes

"A metaphor is the transfer of a word belonging to something else," says Aristotle in his *Poetics*, and this definition has informed most studies of this figure for centuries. Critics have proposed a scale of "transfer" ranging from commonplace or unconscious metaphors to a transfer which yokes two concepts together by violence. The recent interest in metaphor in the field of philosophy of language, as well as the imminent development of a formal semantic theory of language, will doubtless suggest new ways of establishing this scale of metaphoric relations. As in other fields of stylistics, a coherent theory is needed to advance studies of metaphoric usage from the region of description and taxonomy to a level of deep understanding. The work of such philosophers as Croce, Langer, and Black and that of such literary critics as Brooke-Rose, Richards, and Wheelwright suggest the direction that such a theory might follow.

Though metaphor has received more attention than the other tropes listed in florilegia and rhetorical handbooks, traditional linguistic ornaments have not been wholly neglected in recent criticism. Northrop Frye is prominent among the critics who have called for a wholesale revival of the lexicon of Renaissance rhetoric, and a variety of studies listed in the section on tropes attests to the relevance of this effort in the discussion of literature both ancient and modern. Where these figures have been defined in terms of linguistic features rather than their affective force, as in the work of Frederick Burwick on the associationist rhetoric of eighteenth-century Scotland, they have proved to be a potent tool in the study of literary style.

STATISTICAL APPROACHES TO STYLE

Despite the overt hostility of many critics to statistical methods in literary scholarship, counting seems to be an essential part of the experimental design of many stylistic studies. When Harry Levin says that "we need make no word-count to be sure that [Hemingway's] literary vocabulary, with foreign and technical exceptions, consists of relatively few and short words," [3] he reveals that he has made some sort of intuitive word-count, though he may choose not to support it by formulae and tables. It has become increasingly apparent in recent stylistic studies that counts of one sort or another have real value in style analysis and critics seem less inclined to apologize for making them. In addition, as studies like Milic's have demonstrated, the widening availability of computers to literary critics makes possible statistical studies of a sophistication and magnitude unknown before the advent of these machines.

A large number of statistical investigations have been directed toward problems of disputed authorship. T. C. Mendenhall's little-known work at the end of the nineteenth century on such authors as Dickens, Thackeray, Mill, Shakespeare, and Bacon pioneered the use of modern statistical methods in literary problems, but the first influential studies were devised by G. U. Yule in the late 1930's. Yule's analysis of the conflicting evidence supporting Thomas à Kempis and Jean Gerson as probable authors of *The Imitation of Christ* revealed the potential of statistics in such problems and has had considerable effect on subse-

[3] Harry Levin, "Observations on the Style of Ernest Hemingway," *KR.* XIII (1951), 596.

quent work with similar disputes. Whereas Yule was mainly concerned with content words, more recent studies—such as that performed by Mosteller and Wallace on *The Federalist Papers*—have concentrated on function words since such words appear as a "fingerprint" independently of the subject matter of the text. Other critics represented in the section on statistical approaches to style have studied works that have been assigned to Chaucer, Swift, Dr. Johnson, Sir Philip Francis, and Mark Twain.

Though statistical techniques have usually been applied in authorship or chronology controversies, some consideration has also been given to the use of such methods in discussing other literary problems. Most often, this work has concentrated on an author's vocabulary, and many studies that purport to examine syntactic structures could be more accurately described as concerning themselves with such functional signals as conjunctions or determiners. The combination of generative grammatical analysis and statistics in George Landon's work and the computer parsing routines devised by Burwick suggest new uses for statistical methods. In addition, workers in computational linguistics are beginning to supply valuable background data on language statistics that will doubtless prove relevant to the study of style. Such information has long been needed to enrich stylistic investigations of all kinds; as R. S. Crane wrote in 1927, "evidences of style or language" are virtually impossible to evaluate "until we know a great deal more than we do now about the limits of individual variation in style and vocabulary." [4]

PROBLEMS IN TRANSLATION

Successful translations depend not only upon the translator's knowledge of the language systems involved but also upon his sensitivity to the nuances of language use. In Werner Winter's apt comparison, the translator is like "an artist who is asked to create an exact replica of a marble statue, but who cannot secure any marble." [5] The implications of this comparison lead inevitably to the familiar view that *style* is that which cannot be translated. Style is thus more than the use of language by a single author and must include something vaguely defined as the "style of the language." That is, the translator is forced to deal not only with the stylistic features characteristic of his author but also with the linguistic repertory that the author takes as given. The translator must confront this "style of the language" at all levels—sound, syntax, vocabulary, and cultural values. Translation can thus be regarded as

[4] R. S. Crane, Preface to *New Essays by Goldsmith*, pp. xx; quoted by Jacob Leed and Robert Hemenway, "Use of the Computer in some Recent Studies of Style," *The Serif*, II, ii (1965), 16.

[5] Werner Winter, "Impossibilities of Translation," in *The Craft and Context of Translation*, eds. William Arrowsmith and Roger Shattuck (Garden City, N.Y., 1964), p. 93.

a close relative of stylistics, in spite of the obvious disparity of their products. Though large numbers of literary critics have consulted the theories and techniques offered by linguists, only a few seem to have attempted to draw upon the wisdom of the translator. The scholars whose works are collected in the section "Problems in Translation" in Chapter III invite the style critic to remedy this defect.

PROSE STYLISTICS

Structures of Sound in Prose

The analysis and discussion of "prose rhythm" has profited less from the insights of modern linguistic techniques than have other areas of concern to style critics. Virtually all existing studies of such rhythm depend upon the perception and scansion of poetic meters in prose; mannered writing such as that found in Lyly or Pater is usually selected as the field for the exercise. Since a consistent regularity is seldom to be found in even the most artificial prose, the application of metrical feet to such material seems doomed to failure. Yet rhythm *is* a property of such language, though its own special properties are obscured by techniques of elucidation appropriate to music or poetry. A rigorous definition of the nature of the phenomenon still awaits formulation, and the limited successes of scholars of the past may inspire new ways of approaching prose rhythm. Rhythm, it would seem, is not only a matter of the sound of the language but also a result of syntactic and semantic features. An integrated theory of prose style must take the rhythm perceived by readers into account and show how it is manifested in the total linguistic complex that is the work of art.

Other Linguistic Aspects of Prose

A great variety of means are available to the critic who would discuss the style of an author, for, as has already been noted, style studies come close to becoming microgrammars of the language on the one hand and verge on the broadest theoretical speculation about an author's worldview on the other. Getting to know an author and being able to identify the provenance of an unknown piece of prose is an experience that all readers have had, but one that is extremely difficult to explain. Clearly the experience is related to language—the stuff from which literature is shaped—but whether the clues lie in a turn of phrase to be specified by linguistic techniques or in the shaping of experience to be explained by the tools of rhetoric is difficult to say. The authors represented in the section "Other Linguistic Aspects of Prose" have all tried to answer the challenging question of what the style of particular prose writers consists of. Their work is of interest not only to those with a particular interest in the author under scrutiny but also to those who would see how a critic's job of explaining his intuition can be carried out.

STYLE IN POETRY

Structures of Sound in Poetry

While such sound patterns as alliteration, assonance, and rhyme have received relatively little attention from critics of style, metrical studies constitute the single most active area in stylistic criticism. After having prepared his extensive bibliography of studies of English prosody, Karl Shapiro expressed his vexation with the work of this sort that he had examined:

> One of the most distressing aspects of the study of English prosody, whether as theory of forms or as versification, is the necessity of beginning with absolute fundamentals and working up through an enormous copia of *unscientific scholarship*, analyses which have not even premises in common, and the prejudices of the poets, critics and students of the past three and a half centuries.[6]

As part of an anniversary observance a decade later, some distinguished readers were asked to list the three most valuable essays in their fields that had appeared in *PMLA*. One anonymous commentator expressed himself in language quite like that Shapiro had used:

> The great disappointment of the articles on metrics in *PMLA* is their lack of relation to each other. No body of accepted fact or even of critical opinion has been built up over the years. Seldom does one scholar refer to the findings of another. The result is a field obscure and uncertain in its various emphases.[7]

Today, the situation cannot be said to be much improved. After a flurry of interest in the uses of Trager-Smith phonology, metrical criticism has fallen back on the old ways. Some clarification of the issues resulted from the controversy stimulated by Wimsatt and Beardsley's "Concept of Meter," and Keyser's recent work may initiate yet another discussion of the rules of English meters.

A constant re-examination of principles and reconsideration of data is characteristic of scientific investigation. The great variety of opinion in the field of metrical studies would be heartening were it not for the fact that prosodic analysts do not feel themselves part of a common pursuit, a scholarly dialogue whose aim is to increase the understanding of the function of sound and rhythm in poetry. But the extreme subjectivity of many of the studies of prosody may give way to a clearer vision of metrical facts if critics are willing to profit from the currently increasing knowledge of the operation of English sounds as part of the over-all system of the language.

Twentieth-century metrical studies are oriented either toward

[6] Karl Shapiro, "English Prosody and Modern Poetry," *ELH*, XIV (1947), 77.

[7] Maynard Mack *et al.*, "A Mirror for the Lamp," *PMLA*, LXXIII (Dec. 1958), 51.

"temporal prosody" or toward "stress prosody." Supporters of temporal scansion regard English sounds—or at least the sounds of verse—as having fixed durations. A line of poetry, they say, is made up of a pattern of syllables with varying temporal lengths; the poet arranges the sounds in patterns of metrical repetition. Although American linguists have vigorously rejected the notion of syllabic quantity as part of the English language system, convinced temporalists like Sheridan Baker have recently received support from the British phonetician David Abercrombie, whose view of English tends to endorse their opinion.

Stress prosody is based on the assumption that poets organize the suprasegmental features of ordinary language (i.e., stress, pitch, and juncture) in such a way that rhythmical expectations are aroused in the reader. These expectations, say the stress prosodists, constitute the meter of the poem, though the poet may also deviate from the expectations to confront the reader with unexpected "tensions." A considerable amount of confusion has arisen in recent prosodic studies from the failure of analysts to provide a clear definition of poetic meter and to show the relation of poetic and nonpoetic rhythms. While beleaguered by the temporalists supporting the representation of meter by means of the musical staff, the stress prosodists have been attacked for the simplicity of their notation by supporters of various phonetic transcription schemes. The issues have been further clouded by the proclamations of some linguists that classical stress scansion is merely an old-fashioned and inept way of accounting for the facts of English intonation. Though some recent work on stress prosody has helped to clarify the dispute, both linguists and literary critics do not yet seem disposed to profit by the presuppositions or techniques that each group can offer the other.

Other Linguistic Aspects of Poetry

The material gathered in the section entitled "Other Linguistic Aspects of Poetry" represents a wide variety of techniques for explaining the style of particular authors. Critics of poetry, of course, have a long tradition of concern for forms of language, and their critical vocabulary for explicating structures both large and small is highly developed. Even so, such problems as rhetorical organization, the nature of poetic syntax, and the emblematic function of printing conventions certainly demand more detailed study. But though much has been done, much remains unexplored and unexplained.

CONCLUSION

Finally, a word about the compilation of a bibliography like *English Stylistics* may not be wholly out of place in an account of the activities of critics of style. Though the need for such a work has been apparent for at least a decade, it has not been filled because of the eclecticism of the field. Several physicists, many social scientists, and scholars from every branch of the humanities are represented in the collection that follows. Major annual bibliographies like the *Linguistic Bibliography for the Year* and the June number of *PMLA*, or those lists that appear from time to time in collections of essays, neglect to subdivide all and only those items of interest to stylistics or to include work in those fields that are ostensibly remote from the special interests of the prospective user. For at least a decade, farsighted academics have predicted the advent of a computerized library or some kind of central bibliographic clearing-house unrestricted as to scholarly discipline. Even now, physicians have such facilities available to them. If there is a demand for a remote access bibliographic service in the humanistic community directed not toward published reference works but toward the user and his question, it can easily be supplied with the technology now available. May it be so.

September 1967   RICHARD W. BAILEY

CUE TITLES AND ABBREVIATIONS

AL   *American Literature*

AS   *American Speech*

BCRE   University Microfilms has issued sixteen reels of microfilm of rare books under the title *British and Continental Rhetoric and Elocution.* The roman numeral following the abbreviation indicates the reel number and the arabic numeral the sequence of the item in the entire series.

BNYPL   *Bulletin of the New York Public Library*

Bobbs-Merrill Reprint   We have included the catalogue number of those items available in the reprint series from Bobbs-Merrill publishers.

CCC   *College Composition and Communication*

CE   *College English*

Chatman and Levin   *Essays on the Language of Literature,* eds. Seymour Chatman and Samuel R. Levin (Boston, 1967).

Critical Essays of the Seventeenth Century   *Critical Essays of the Seventeenth Century,* ed. Joel E. Spingarn. 3 vols. Oxford, 1908–1909.

Critical Essays of the Eighteenth Century   *Critical Essays of the Eighteenth Century, 1700–1725,* ed. Willard H. Durham. New York, 1961.

Critics and Criticism   R. S. Crane, *et al. Critics and Criticism.* Chicago, 1952.

DA   *Dissertation Abstracts*

EIC   *Essays in Criticism* (Oxford)

Eighteenth-Century Critical Essays   *Eighteenth-Century Critical Essays,* ed. Scott Elledge. 2 vols. Ithaca, N.Y., 1961.

ELH   *Journal of English Literary History*

Elizabethan Critical Essays   *Elizabethan Critical Essays,* ed. George Gregory Smith. 2 vols. Oxford, 1902.

English Examined   *English Examined: Two Centuries of Comment on the Mother Tongue,* ed. Susie I. Tucker. Cambridge, 1961.

Essays on Style and Language   *Essays on Style and Language: Linguistic and Critical Approaches to Literary Style,* ed. Roger Fowler. London, 1966.

Georgetown Monographs   *Georgetown University Monograph Series on Languages and Linguistics.*

HLB   *Huntington Library Bulletin*

IJAL   *International Journal of American Linguistics*

JAAC   *Journal of Aesthetics and Art Criticism*

KR   *Kenyon Review*

Langue et littérature   *Langue et Littérature: Actes du VIIIe Congrès de la Fédération Internationale des Langues et Littératures Modernes.* Paris: Bibliothèque de la Faculté de Philosophie et Lettres de L'Université de Liége, Fascicule CLXI, 1961.

Mathematik und Dichtung.   *Mathematik und Dichtung,* eds. Helmut Kreuzer and Rul Gunzenhäuser. München: Nymphenburger Verlagshandlung, 1965.

MLN   *Modern Language Notes*

MLQ   *Modern Language Quarterly*

MLR   *Modern Language Review*

MP   *Modern Philology*

Ninth Congress Papers.   *Proceedings of the Ninth International Congress of Linguists,* ed. Horace G. Lunt. The Hague, 1964.

N&Q   *Notes and Queries*

On Translation   *On Translation,* ed. Reuben A. Brower. Cambridge, Mass., 1959.

PMLA   *Publications of the Modern Language Association of America*

Poetics   *Poetics: Proceedings of the First International Conference of Work-in-Progress Devoted to the Problems of Poetics, Warsaw, August 18–27, 1960.* Warszawa and 's-Gravenhage, 1961.

PQ   *Philological Quarterly* (Iowa City)

QJS   *Quarterly Journal of Speech*

Readings I   *Readings in Applied English Linguistics,* ed. Harold B. Allen. New York, 1958.

Readings II   *Readings in Applied English Linguistics,* ed. Harold B. Allen. New York, 1964.

REL   *Review of English Literature*

RES   *Review of English Studies*

SEL   *Studies in English Literature, 1500–1900* (Rice University)

Shapiro   Items so labeled are described in Karl Jay Shapiro's *Bibliography of Modern Prosody* (Baltimore, 1948).

SIL   *Studies in Linguistics*

Sound and Poetry   *Sound and Poetry: English Institute Essays 1956,* ed. Northrop Frye. New York, 1957.

SP   *Studies in Philology*

Stil- und Formprobleme   *Stil- und Formprobleme in der Literatur: Vorträge des VII. Kongresses der internationalen Vereinigung für moderne Sprachen und Literaturen in Heidelberg,* hrsg. Paul Böckmann. Heidelberg: Winter, 1959.

Studies Otsuka   *Studies in English Grammar and Linguistics: A Miscellany in Honour of Takanobu Otsuka,* eds. Kazuo Araki, *et al.* Tokyo, 1958.

Style in Language   *Style in Language,* ed. Thomas A. Sebeok. Cambridge, Mass., New York, and London, 1960.

Style in Prose Fiction   *Style in Prose Fiction: English Institute Essays 1958*, ed. Harold C. Martin. New York, 1959.

TLS   *The Times Literary Supplement* (London).

TPS   Philological Society, London, *Transactions*

Trends in Content Analysis   *Trends in Content Analysis*, ed. Ithiel de Sola Pool. Urbana, Ill., 1959.

TSLL   *Texas Studies in Literature and Language*

UTQ   *University of Toronto Quarterly*

CONTENTS

xxi

ENGLISH STYLISTICS: A BIBLIOGRAPHY

I. BIBLIOGRAPHICAL SOURCES

1   ALLEN, HAROLD B. *Linguistics and English Linguistics.* New York, 1967.

Allen lists some 2000 items in all fields of general and applied linguistics, though items in languages other than English are generally excluded. A list of forty-one items on stylistics and English metrics appears on pp. 86–87.

2   ALSTON, R. C. *A Bibliography of the English Language from the Invention of Printing to the Year 1800.* Leeds, 1965–.

Alston compiles a systematic record of all writings relevant to the historical study of the English language, based on the collections of the principal libraries in Europe and the United States.

3   BENNETT, JAMES R. "An Annotated Bibliography of Selected Writings on English Prose Style," *CCC,* XVI (1965), 248–255.

Bennett arranges some 127 items by historical period. About a third of the items are briefly annotated.

4   BURSILL-HALL, G. L. "Bibliography: Theories of Syntactic Analysis," *SIL,* XIV (1962), 100–112.

5   COOPER, LANE. *Theories of Style.* New York and London, 1912.

Cooper lists a large selection of works on the theory of style and on the stylistic analysis of prose (pp. xiii–xxii).

6   DINGWALL, WILLIAM ORR. *Transformational-Generative Grammar: A Bibliography.* Washington, D. C., 1965.

"It has been the aim of the author to compile as complete a bibliography as possible from public sources of linguistic works incorporating rules that relate sentences" (p. v).

1   GUIRAUD, PIERRE. *Bibliographie critique de la statistique linguistique.*
    Utrecht-Anvers, 1954.
    Guiraud includes a selection of statistical approaches to literature.
    Of particular interest to the student of stylistics are his sections on
    "Métrique et versification," "Rimes et strophes (anglais et français),"
    "L'harmonie," and "La Prose rythmée (grec et latin et quelques
    langues modernes)."

2   HAMP, ERIC P. "General Linguistics—The United States in the
    Fifties," in *Trends in European and American Linguistics: 1930–1960,*
    eds. Christine Mohrmann, Alf Sommerfelt, and Joshua Whatmough.
    Utrecht and Antwerp, 1961. Pp. 164–195. Bobbs-Merrill Reprint,
    Language-37.
    Hamp's article serves to explicate a bibliography of 469 items pub-
    lished by American linguists. Some items concerned with English
    stylistics are included.

3   HATZFELD, HELMUT. *A Bibliography of the New Stylistics.* Chapel
    Hill, N.C., 1952.
    Hatzfeld's bibliography is limited to items concerned with stylistics
    in the Romance languages; it covers the field from 1900 to 1952.

4   ———. *Bibliografía crítica de la nueva estilística aplicada a las literaturas
    romanicas.* Madrid, 1955.
    A somewhat fuller collection than the Chapel Hill edition.

5   ———, et YVES LE HIR. *Essai de bibliographie critique de stylistique
    française et romane (1955–1960).* Paris, 1961.

6   KENNEDY, ARTHUR G. *A bibliography of Writings on the English Lan-
    guage.* Cambridge, Mass., and New Haven, 1927.
    Kennedy's bibliography has recently been reissued (New York: Hafner
    Publishing Co., 1961), but it has not been revised to cover material
    after the original cutoff date, 1922. Of particular interest for stylistics
    is the list of early rhetorics (items 12772–12817)

7   KING, H. H., AND H. CAPLAN. "Pulpit Eloquence: A List of
    Doctrinal and Historical Studies in English," *Speech Monographs,*
    XXII (1955), 1–159.

8   LAFOURCADE, FRANÇOISE. "Contribution à une bibliographie
    chronologique pour l'étude des théories sur la versification anglaise
    de 1550 à 1950," in *Hommage à Paul Dottin (–Caliban,* no. 3, n. s. II,
    fasc. 1) (Toulouse, 1966), pp. 271–317.

9   *Linguistic Bibliography for the Year.* Utrecht and Antwerp, 1949–.
    The *Linguistic Bibliography,* covering the period from 1939 to the
    present, is published by the Permanent International Committee of
    Linguistics. It is very thorough in its coverage of materials on linguis-
    tics, general stylistics, and English language study.

1   MAROUZEAU, JULES (ed.). *L'Année Philologique: bibliographie critique et analytique de l'antiquité greco-latine*. Paris, 1924–.

2   MARTIN, HAROLD C., AND RICHARD M. OHMANN. "A Selective Bibliography," in *Style in Prose Fiction*, pp. 191–200.
Martin and Ohmann collect a list of items published between 1920 and 1958 by both linguists and literary critics. For studies of prose style and particularly style in prose fiction, their list is very valuable.

3   MILIC, LOUIS T. *Style and Stylistics: An Analytical Bibliography* (New York, 1967).
Milic supplies a list of some 800 items arranged in chronological order, thoroughly cross-referenced by means of an index of key words.

4   MURPHY, JAMES. "The Medieval Arts of Discourse: An Introductory Bibliography," *Speech Monographs*, XXIX (1962), 71–78.
For an analysis of Murphy's bibliography, see Section II, p. 13.

5   OMOND, THOMAS STEWART. *English Metrists*. Oxford, 1921.
Omond includes a bibliography of comments on meter from the sixteenth through the nineteenth centuries.

6   PIKE, KENNETH L., AND EUNICE V. PIKE. *Live Issues in Descriptive Linguistics*. Santa Ana, California, 1966. 41 pp.
The Pikes gather bibliographical information in such areas as: Linguistic Structure; Phonology; Grammar; Lexicon, Meaning, and Culture; Language Teaching; Descriptive Linguistics in Relation to Historical Comparative Studies; Communication Theory; Linguistics and the Analysis of Literature; and Translation.

7   *PMLA*. The annual bibliography of *PMLA* lists work on style under the headings of "General Language and Linguistics," "Themes and Types," "Aesthetics," and "Literary Criticism and Literary Theory," as well as under individual authors.

8   REID, RONALD F. "Books: Some Suggested Readings on the History of Ancient Rhetorical Style," *Central States Speech Journal*, XI (1960), 116–122.

9   ROBERTS, THOMAS J. "Literary-Linguistics: A Bibliography, 1946–1961," *TSLL*, IV (1962), 625–629.
Roberts prepared his bibliography while at the American University in Cairo and was somewhat hampered by the limited library resources there. However, his bibliography contains many important items and has been useful in preparing our list.

10 SHAKESPEARE. The subject of Shakespeare's style has been treated by so many scholars that we have selected only a few items for our bibliography. Section VII ("The Art of Shakespeare," pp. 79–95) of *A Shakespeare Bibliography* (compiled by Walter Ebisch and Levin L. Schücking, Oxford, 1931) contains material on Shake-

speare's language, vocabulary, prosody, and style. Their *Supplement for the Years 1930–1935* (Oxford, 1937) lists such material on pages 29–33. *A Classified Shakespeare Bibliography, 1936–1958* (compiled by Gordon Ross Smith, University Park, Pa., 1963) deals with Shakespeare's style from pages 217 to 241 (items A5124–A5748). All three bibliographies contain material on Elizabethan and Jacobean style and language in addition to studies of Shakespeare.

1   SHAPIRO, KARL JAY. *A Bibliography of Modern Prosody.* Baltimore, 1948.

Shapiro lists 71 books and articles on prosody; by "modern" he means the period from 1880 to 1947. Since he describes and evaluates each work in 100–200 words, we refer the reader to his work by the use of the cue title "Shapiro" after the title of each item he annotates.

2   *Style in Language*, pp. 435–449. Though limited to those items cited by the participants in the 1958 Style Conference, the collection of 462 items covers a broad range of the concerns of students of stylistics.

3   WELLEK, RENÉ, AND AUSTIN WARREN. *Theory of Literature.* New York, 1956.

Wellek and Warren list items from many areas of literary study. Of particular interest for English stylistics is the bibliography of studies of euphony, rhythm, and meter (pp. 329–333) and style (pp. 333–336).

II. LANGUAGE AND STYLE BEFORE 1900

THE CLASSICAL PERIOD

Major Works and Commentary

1   **Isocrates.** *Antidosis*, tr. George Norlin. New York, 1929.

2   HUBBELL, H. M. *The Influence of Isocrates on Cicero, Dionysius, and Aristides.* New Haven, 1914.

3   **Plato.** *'Cratylus' and 'Parmenides,'* tr. H. N. Fowler. Cambridge, Mass., 1953.

4   ———. *Epistoles,* tr. R. G. Bury. Cambridge, Mass., 1952.

5   ———. *Gorgias,* tr. W. R. M. Lamb. Cambridge, Mass., 1953.

6   ———. *Phaedrus,* tr. H. N. Fowler. Cambridge, Mass., 1953.

7   ———. *'Theaetetus' and 'Sophist,'* tr. H. N. Fowler. Cambridge, Mass., 1952.

8   BLACK, EDWIN. "Plato's View of Rhetoric," *QJS*, XLIV (1958), 361–374.

9   DEMOS, RAPHAEL. "Plato's Theory of Language," *Journal of Philosophy*, LXI (1964), 595–610.

10 FLESHLER, HELEN. "Plato and Aristotle on Rhetoric and Dialectic," *Pennsylvania Speech Annual*, XX (1963), 11–17.

11 HUNT, EVERETT LEE. "Plato and Aristotle on Rhetoric and Rhetoricians," in *Studies in Rhetoric and Public Speaking in Honor of James Albert Winans.* New York, 1925. Pp. 3–60.

1 LECERF, JEAN. "Remarques sur le *Cratyle* de Platon et la grammaire générale," in *Mélanges Louis Massignon*. Damas, 1957. Vol. III, pp. 37–43.

2 LEVINSON, R. B. "Language and the *Cratylus:* Four Questions," *Review of Metaphysics*, XI (1957), 29–41.

3 NEHRING, A. "Plato and the Theory of Language," *Traditio*, III (1945), 13–48.

4 PAGLIARO, ANTONINO. "Struttura e pensiero del *Cratilo* di Platone," in his *Nuovi saggi di critica semantica*. Messina e Firenze, 1956. Pp. 49–61.

5 **Aristotle.** *The Art of Rhetoric*, tr. J. H. Freese. Cambridge, Mass., 1949.

6 ———. '*Categories*,' '*On Interpretation*,' *and* '*Prior Analytics*,' tr. H. P. Cooke and H. Tredennick. Cambridge, Mass., 1938.

7 ———. *Poetics*, tr. W. Hamilton Fyfe. Cambridge, Mass., 1953.

8 ———. '*Posterior Analytics*' *and* '*Topica*,' tr. H. Tredennick and E. S. Forster. Cambridge, Mass., 1960.

9 ———. '*Problems*' *and* '*Rhetorica ad Alexandrum*,' tr. W. S. Hett and J. Rackham. Cambridge, Mass., 1957.

10 ———. *On Sophistical Refutations*, tr. E. S. Forster. Cambridge, Mass., 1955.

11 BUTCHER, SAMUEL H. *Aristotle's Theory of Poetry and Fine Art*. London, 1907.

12 COOPER, LANE. *The Poetics of Aristotle: Its Meaning and Influence*. London, 1923.

13 ———, AND A. GUDEMAN. *A Bibliography of the Poetics of Aristotle*. New Haven, 1928.

14 DIETER, OTTO. "Stasis," *Speech Monographs*, XVII (1950), 345–369.

15 HERRICK, M. T. "The Early History of Aristotle's *Rhetoric* in England," *PQ*, V (1926), 242–257.

16 ———, *The Poetics of Aristotle in England*. New Haven, 1930.

17 KING, H. R. "Aristotle's Theory of *Topos*," *Classical Quarterly*, XLIV (1950), 76–96.

18 ŁUKASIEWICZ, J. *Aristotle's Syllogistic: From the Standpoint of Modern Formal Logic*. Oxford, 1951.

19 McKEON, RICHARD. "Aristotle's Conception of Language and the Arts of Language," *Classical Philology*, XLI (1946), 193–206; XLII (1947), 21–50; reprinted in *Critics and Criticism*, pp. 176–231.

1   PAGLIARO, ANTONINO. "Il capitolo linguistico della *Poetica* di
    Aristotele," in his *Nuovi saggi di critica semantica*. Messina e Firenze,
    1956. Pp. 70–151.

2   POMEROY, RALPH. "Aristotle and Cicero: Rhetorical Style,"
    Western Speech (Los Angeles), XXV (1961), 25–32.

3   ROSENFELD, LAWRENCE WILLIAM. "Aristotle and Information
    Theory: A Comparison of the Influence of Causal Assumptions on
    Two Theories of Communication," *DA*, XXV (1964), 698–699.

4   ROSS, W. D. *Aristotle*. London, 1923.

5   WILEY, EARL W. "Aristotle's *Topoi:* Patterns of Persuasion," *Ohio
    Speech Journal*, II (1963), 5–14.

6   **Demetrius, (?) Phalereus.** *On Style*, tr. W. Rhys Roberts. Cam-
    bridge, Mass., 1953.

7   WEINBERG, BERNARD. "Translations and Commentaries of Deme-
    trius's *On Style* to 1600: A Bibliography," *PQ*, XXX (1951),
    353–380.

8   **Varro, Marcus Terentius.** *On the Latin Language*, tr. R. G. Kent.
    2 vols. Cambridge, Mass., 1951.

9   COLLART, JEAN. *Varron grammairien latin*. Paris: Publications de la
    Faculté des Lettres de l'Université de Strasbourg, fasc. 121, 1954.

10 **Rhetorica ad Herennium,** tr. H. Caplan. Cambridge, Mass.,
    1954.

11 **Cicero, Marcus Tullius.** '*Brutus*' and '*Orator*,' tr. G. L. Hendrickson
    and H. M. Hubbell. Cambridge, Mass., 1952.

12 ———. '*De Inventione*,' '*De Optimo Genere Oratorum*,' and '*Topica*,'
    tr. H. M. Hubbell. Cambridge, Mass., 1959.

13 ———. '*De Oratore*,' '*De Fato*,' '*Paradoxa Stoicorum*,' and '*De Parti-
    tione Oratoria*,' tr. E. W. Sutton and H. Rackham. 2 vols. Cam-
    bridge, Mass., 1942.

14 CAUSERET, C. *Etude sur la langue de la rhétorique et de la critique
    littéraire dans Cicéron*. Paris, 1886.

15 DOUGLAS, A. E. "A Ciceronian Contribution to Rhetorical The-
    ory," *Eranos*, LV (1957), 18–26.

16 GRUBE, G. M. A. "Educational, Rhetorical and Literary Theory
    in Cicero," *The Phoenix*, XVI (1962), 234–257.

17 LAURAND, L. *Etudes sur le style des discours de Cicéron avec une esquisse
    de l'histoire du "cursus"*. Paris, 1928.

1   SLURR, WILLIAM. "Cicero and English Prose Style," *Classical
     Bulletin*, XXXVII (1961), 49–50.

2   SPROTT, S. E. "Cicero's Theory of Prose Style," *PQ*, XXXIV
     (1955), 1–17.

3   **Dionysius, of Halicarnassus.** *On Literary Composition*, tr. W. Rhys
     Roberts. London, 1910.

4   ———. *The Three Literary Letters*, tr. W. Rhys Roberts. Cambridge,
     1901.

5   EGGER, MAX. *Denys d'Halicarnasse: Essai sur la critique littéraire et la
     rhétorique chez les Grecs au siècle d'Auguste*. Paris, 1902.

6   SMILEY, CHARLES N. *Latinitas and Ellenismos: The Influence of the
     Stoic Theory of Style as Shown in Writings of Dionysius, Quintilian,
     Pliny the Younger, et al.* Madison, Wis.: University of Wisconsin
     Bulletin, No. 143, 1906.

7   **Seneca, Lucius Annaeus, "Rhetor".** *The Suasoriae of Seneca the
     Elder, being the 'Liber suasoriarum' of the work entitled L. Annaei Senecae
     Oratorum et rhetorum sententiae, divisiones, colores*, tr. W. A. Edward.
     Cambridge, 1928.

8   BORNECQUE, HENRI. "Les Déclamations et les déclamateurs d'après
     Sénèque le Père," *Travaux et Mémoires de l'Université de Lille*, n.s. I, i
     (1902).

Seneca, Lucius Annaeus, "Philosopher"

9   BOURGERY, A. *Sénèque prosateur: Etudes littéraires et grammaticales sur
     la prose de Sénèque le Philosophe*. Paris, 1922.

10   MERCHANT, FRANK IVAN. "Seneca the Philosopher and his Theory
     of Style," *American Journal of Philology*, XXVI (1905), 44–59.

11   SMILEY, CHARLES N. "Seneca and the Stoic Theory of Literary
     Style," in *Classical Studies in Honor of Charles Forster Smith*. Madison,
     Wis., 1919. Pp. 50–61.

12   **Tacitus, Publius Cornelius.** *Dialogus*, tr. Sir William Peterson.
     Cambridge, Mass., 1932.

13   PERRET, J. "La Formation du style de Tacite," *Revue des Etudes
     Anciennes*, LVI (1954), 90–120.

14   ULLMANN, R. *La Technique des discours dans Salluste, Tite Live, et
     Tacite*. Oslo, 1927.

15   **Quintilianus, Marcus Fabius.** *Institutio oratoria*, tr. H. E. Butler.
     4 vols. Cambridge, Mass., 1933.

1   COLEMAN, ROBERT. "Two Linguistic Topics in Quintilian," *Classical Quarterly*, XIII (1963), 1–18.

2   HARDING, H. F. "Quintilian's Witnesses," *Speech Monographs*, I (1934), 1–20.
    Harding surveys the history of Quintilian's reputation in England from the sixteenth to the eighteenth centuries.

3   **Hermogenes of Tarsus.** *On Stasis*, tr. Ray Nadeau. *Speech Monographs*, XXXI (1964), 361–424.

4   **Lucian.** "How to Write History," in Vol. VI of *Dialogues of Lucian*, tr. K. Kilburn. Cambridge, Mass., 1959.

5   **Suetonius Tranquillus, Gaius.** '*The Lives of the Twelve Caesars*' and '*The Lives of Illustrious Men*,' tr. J. C. Rolfe. 2 vols. Cambridge, Mass., 1935.

6   **Sextus, Empiricus.** *Philosophical Works*, tr. J. B. Bury. 4 vols. Cambridge, Mass., 1952.

7   KRENTZ, EDGAR M. "Sextus Empiricus on Language and Literature," *DA*, XXI (1960), 1558.

8   **Longinus, Dionysius Cassius.** *On the Sublime*, tr. W. Hamilton Fyfe. Cambridge, Mass., 1953.

9   GRUBE, G. M. A. "Notes on the *Peri Hypsous*," *American Journal of Philology*, LXXVIII (1957), 355–374.

10 HENN, T. R. *Longinus and English Criticism*. Cambridge, 1934.

11 OLSON, ELDER. "The Argument of Longinus's *On the Sublime*," *MP*, XXXIX (1942), 225–258; reprinted in *Critics and Criticism*, pp. 232–259.

12 WEINBERG, BERNARD. "Translations and Commentaries of Longinus *On the Sublime*, to 1600: A Bibliography," *MP*, XLVII (1950), 145–151.

13 **Aphthonius, Aelius Festus.** "The *Progymnasmata* of Aphthonius," tr. Ray Nadeau, *Speech Monographs*, XIX (1952), 264–285.

Collected Primary Sources

14 *Artium Scriptores: Reste der voraristotelischen Rhetorik*, ed. Ludwig Radermacher. Wien, 1951.

15 *Grammatici latini*, ed. H. Keil. 7 vols. and Supplement. Leipzig, 1857–1880.

16 *Rhetores graeci*, ed. Leonhard von Spengel. 3 vols. Leipzig, 1853–1856.

1   *Rhetores latini minores*, ed. Karl Halm. Leipzig, 1863.

2   *Stoicorum vetorum fragmenta*, compiled by Hans von Arnim. 4 vols. 1903–1924.

General Secondary Sources

3   ALLEN, W. S. "Ancient Ideas on the Origin and Development of Language," *Transactions of the Philological Society*, (Oxford) (1948), 35–60.

4   ATKINS, J. W. H. *Literary Criticism in Antiquity*. 2 vols. London, 1952.

5   BALDWIN, CHARLES SEARS. *Ancient Rhetoric and Poetic Interpreted from Representative Works*. New York, 1924.

6   BARFIELD, OWEN. "Greek Thought in English Words," *Essays and Studies by Members of the English Association*, N.S. III (1950), 69–81.

7   BARWICK, KARL. "Probleme der stoischen Sprachlehre und Rhetorik," Berlin: *Abhandlungen der Sächsischen Akademie der Wissenschaften zu Leipzig*, XLIX, iii, 1957.

8   VAN BERCHEM, DENIS. "Poètes et grammairiens," *Museum Helveticum*, IX (1952), 79–87.

9   BOCHEŃSKI, I. M. *Ancient Formal Logic*. Amsterdam, 1957.

10 BOLGAR, R. R. *The Classical Heritage and Its Beneficiaries*. Cambridge, 1954.

11 BONNER, S. F. *Roman Declamation in the Late Republic and Early Empire*. Liverpool, 1949.

12 BROADHEAD, H. D. *Latin Prose Rhythm: A New Method of Investigation*. Cambridge, 1922.

13 BROWN, H. "The Classical Tradition in English Literature," *Harvard Studies and Notes in Philology and Literature*, XVIII (1935), 7–46.

14 BRYANT, DONALD C. "Aspects of the Rhetorical Tradition," *QJS*, XXXVI (1950), 169–176, 326–332.

15 CARNEY, T. F. "Plutarch's Style in the *Marius*," *Journal of Hellenic Studies*, LXXX (1960), 24–31.

16 CARRIÈRE, JEAN. *Stylistique grecque pratique: la phrase de la prose classique*. Paris, 1960.

17 CHANTREAU, PIERRE. *La Stylistique grecque*. Paris, 1951.

18 CLARK, DONALD L. "Imitation: Theory and Practice in Roman Rhetoric," *QJS*, XXXVII (1951), 11–22.

1   CLARKE, MARTIN L. *Rhetoric at Rome: A Historical Survey*. London, 1953.

2   ———. *Classical Education in Britain, 1500–1900*. Cambridge, 1959.

3   COLERO, E. *Introduction to Latin Style and Rhetoric*. Malta, 1959.

4   COOPER, C. G. *An Introduction to the Latin Hexameter*. Melbourne, 1952.

5   CURTIUS, E. R. "Die Lehre von den drei Stilen in Altertum und Mittelalter," *Romanische Forschungen*, LXIV (1952), 57–70.

6   D'ALTON, JOHN F. *Roman Literary Theory and Criticism: A Study in Tendencies*. New York, 1931.

7   DE GROOT, A. WILLEM. *A Handbook of Antique Prose Rhythm*. Groningen, 1919.

8   DENNISTON, J. D. *Greek Prose Style*. New York, 1953.

9   DIHLE, ALBRECHT. "Analogie und Attizismus," *Hermes*, LXXXV (1957), 170–205.

10   DONOGHUE, JAMES JOHN. *The Theory of Literary Kinds: I. Ancient Classifications of Literature*. Dubuque, Iowa: Loras College Press, 1943.

11   ———. *The Theory of Literary Kinds: II. The Ancient Classes of Poetry*. Dubuque, Iowa: Loras College Press, 1949.

12   EHNINGER, DOUGLAS. "The Classical Doctrine of Invention," *Gavel*, XXIX (1957), 59–62, 70.

13   EYRE, J. J. "Roman Education in the Late Republic and Early Empire," *Greece and Rome*, X (1963), 47–59.

14   GEANAKOPLOS, D. J. *Greek Scholars in Venice: Studies in the Dissemination of Greek Learning from Byzantium to Western Europe*. Cambridge, 1962.

15   GOETZL, JOHANNA. "*Variatio* in the Plinian Epistle," *Classical Journal*, XLVII (1952), 265–268, 299.

16   HALPORN, JAMES W., M. OSTWALD, AND T. ROSENMEYER. *The Meters of Greek and Latin Poetry*. London, 1963.

17   HARDIE, W. R. *Res Metrica: An Introduction to the Study of Greek and Roman Versification*. Oxford, 1920.

18   HENDRICKSON, G. L. "The Peripatetic Mean of Style and the Three Stylistic Characters," *American Journal of Philology*, XXV (1904), 125–146.

1 ———. "The Origin and Meaning of the Ancient Characters of Style," *American Journal of Philology*, XXXVI (1905), 249–290.

2 HUDSON-WILLIAMS, H. L. "Greek Orators and Rhetoric," in *Fifty Years of Classical Scholarship*, ed. M. Platnauer. Oxford, 1954. Pp. 193–213.

3 JEBB, R. C. *Attic Orators from Antiphon to Isaeos*. London, 1876.

4 KENNEDY, GEORGE. *The Art of Persuasion in Greece*. Princeton, 1963. See the review article by William R. Carmack, "A History of Greek Rhetoric and Oratory," *QJS*, XLIX (1963), 325–328.

5 KOSTER, W. J. *Traité de métrique grecque, suivi d'un précis de métrique latine*. Leiden, 1936. Revised edition, 1954.

6 KROLL, W. "Rhetorik," in *Paulys Real-Encyclopädie der klassischen Altertumwissenschaft*. Stuttgart: Supplementband VI, 1940. Pp. 1039–1138.

7 LAUSBERG, HEINRICH. *Handbuch der literarischen Rhetorik: Eine Grundlegung der Literaturwissenschaft*. 2 vols. München, 1900 and 1959.

8 LEJEUNE, M. "La Curiosité linguistique dans l'antiquité," *Conférence de l'Institut de Linguistique de l'Université de Paris*, III (1949), 45–61.

9 LINDSAY, W. M. *Early Latin Verse*. Oxford, 1922.

10 MAAS, P. *Greek Metre*, tr. H. Lloyd-Jones. Oxford, 1962.

11 MAROUZEAU, JULES. *Traité de stylistique appliquée au latin*. Paris, 1935.

12 MARRON, H. I. *A History of Education in Antiquity*, tr. G. Lamb. London, 1956.

13 McBUTNEY, JAMES H. "The Place of the Enthymeme in Rhetorical Theory," *Speech Monographs*, III (1936), 49–74.

14 McDONALD, A. H. "The Style of Livy," *Journal of Roman Studies*, XLVII (1957), 155–172.

15 McKEON, RICHARD. "Literary Criticism and the Concept of Imitation in Antiquity," *MP*, XXXIV (1936–37), 1–35; reprinted in *Critics and Criticism*, pp. 147–175.

16 NOUGARET, L. *Traié é de métrique latine classique*. Paris, 1948.

17 PARKS, E. PATRICK. *The Roman Rhetorical Schools as a Preparation for the Courts under the Early Empire*. Baltimore, 1945.

18 PLATNAUER, M. (ed.). *Fifty Years of Classical Scholarship*. Oxford, 1954.

1 POSTGATE, J. P. *Prosodia Latina: An Introduction to Classical Latin Verse.* Oxford, 1923.

2 QUADLBAUER, FRANZ. "Die *genera dicendi* bis Plinius d. J.," *Wiener Studien*, LXXI (1958), 55–111.

3 RAVEN, D. S. *Greek Metre: An Introduction,* London, 1962.

4 ROBERTS, W. RHYS. *Greek Rhetoric and Literary Criticism.* New York, 1928.

5 ROBINS, R. H. *Ancient and Medieval Grammatical Theory in Europe with Particular Reference to Modern Linguistic Doctrine.* London, 1951.

6 SANDYS, J. E. *A History of Classical Scholarship.* 3 vols. New York, 1958.

7 THOMSON, G. D. *Greek Lyric Metre.* Cambridge, 1929.

8 THOMSON, JAMES ALEXANDER KER. *The Classical Background of English Literature.* New York, 1948.

9 ———. *Classical Influences on English Poetry.* London and New York, 1951.

10 ———. *Classical Influences on English Prose.* London, 1956, and New York, 1962.

11 THORNTON, HARRY, and AGATHA THORNTON, in collaboration with A. A. LIND. *Time and Style: A Psycho-Linguistic Essay in Classical Literature.* London, 1962.

12 TISDALL, FITZGERALD. *A Theory of the Origin and Development of the Heroic Hexameter.* New York, 1889.

13 WILKINSON, L. P. *Golden Latin Artistry.* Cambridge, 1963.

THE MEDIEVAL PERIOD

Major Works and Commentary

We have not attempted to compile a list of primary and specialized secondary material on medieval rhetorical and stylistic theory since such a compilation would only duplicate the work of James J. Murphy in his "The Medieval Arts of Discourse: An Introductory Bibliography," *Speech Monographs*, XXIX (1962), 71–78. Murphy gathers a list of general works on the medieval period and offers a selection of material on the transitional period, 400–1500 A.D. The headings of his third section, "Authors and Works of the Middle Ages (1050–1400)," are: I. Transmission of Classical Texts, II. Vernacular Treatises, III. Ars Grammatica, IV. Ars Dictaminis, V. Ars Praedicandi, VI. The Disputation, and VII. Miscellaneous. Among the authors that Murphy lists are Geoffrey of Vinsauf, John of Garland, Alberic of

Monte Cassino, and Thomas of Capua. Listed below are some secondary sources that will serve to introduce the reader to the attitudes toward literary style that were held in the medieval period.

General Secondary Sources

1   ARBUSOW, LEONID. *Colores rhetorici: Eine Auswahl Rhetorischer Figuren und Gemeinplatz als Hilfsmittel für akademische Übungen an mittelalterlichen Texten.* Göttingen, 1948.

2   ATKINS, J. W. H. *English Literary Criticism: The Medieval Phase.* Cambridge, 1943.

3   AUERBACH, ERICH. *Literary Language and Its Public in Late Latin Antiquity and in the Middle Ages,* tr. Ralph Manheim. London and New York, 1965.

4   BALDWIN, CHARLES S. *Medieval Rhetoric and Poetic (to 1400) Interpreted from Representative Works.* New York, 1928.

5   BIELER, LUDWIG. *A Grammarian's Craft: Studies in the Christian Perpetuation of the Classics.* New York, 1948.

6   BOEHNER, PHILOTHEUS. *Medieval Logic: An Outline of its Development from 1250 to 1400.* Chicago, 1952.

7   BURSILL-HALL, G. L. "Medieval Grammatical Theories," *Canadian Journal of Linguistics,* IX (1963), 40–54.

8   CURTIUS, ERNST R. *European Literature and the Latin Middle Ages,* tr. Willard R. Trask. New York, 1953.

9   DE WULF, MAURICE. *A History of Medieval Philosophy,* tr. E. C. Messenger. London, 1926. Sixth edition, 1952.

10   FARAL, EDMOND. *Les Artes poétiques du XIIe et du XIIIe siècle.* Paris: Bibliothèque de l'Ecole des hautes études, fasc. 238, 1924.

11   KNOWLES, DAVID. *The Evolution of Medieval Thought.* Baltimore, 1962.

12   LAISTNER, M. L. W. *Thought and Letters in Western Europe,* A.D. *500 to 900.* New York, 1931.

13   McKEON, RICHARD. "Rhetoric in the Middle Ages," *Speculum* XVII (1942), 1–32; reprinted in *Critics and Criticism,* pp. 260–296.

14   ———. "Poetry and Philosophy in the Twelfth Century: The Renaissance of Rhetoric," *MP,* XLIII (1946), 217–234; reprinted in *Critics and Criticism,* pp. 297–318.

15   MURPHY, JAMES J. "The Arts of Discourse, 1050–1400," *Medieval Studies,* XXIII (1961), 194–205.

1   NEHRING, ALFONS. "A Note on Functional Linguistics in the
     Middle Ages," *Traditio*, IX (1953), 430–434.

2   PAETOW, LOUIS J. *The Arts Course at Medieval Universities, with
     Special Reference to Grammar and Rhetoric*. Champaign, Ill., 1910.

3   RASHDALL, HASTINGS. *The Universities of Europe in the Middle Ages*,
     eds. F. M. Powicke and A. B. Emden. Oxford, 1936.

4   ROBINS, R. H. *Ancient and Medieval Grammatical Theory in Europe,
     with Particular Reference to Modern Linguistic Doctrine*. London, 1951.

5   SANDYS, JOHN E. *A History of Classical Scholarship*. 3 vols. New York,
     1958. First edition, Cambridge, 1921.

6   TAYLOR, HENRY OSBORN. *The Classical Heritage of the Middle Ages*.
     New York, 1901. Fourth edition, 1957.

7   THUROT, M. "Notices et extraits de divers manuscrits latins pour
     servir à l'histoire des doctrines grammaticales au moyen âge,"
     Notices et extraits, XXII (1868), 1–540.

8   WYLD, HENRY CECIL. "Aspects of Style and Idiom in Fifteenth
     Century English," *Essays and Studies by Members of the English Asso-
     ciation*, XXVI (1940), 30–44.

THE RENAISSANCE (TO 1660)

Major Works and Commentary

9   **Erasmus, Desiderius.** *On Copia of Words and Ideas*, tr. Donald B.
     King and H. David Rix. Milwaukee, 1963.

10   ———. *Ciceronianus: Or, A Dialogue on the Best Style of Speaking*,
     tr. Izora Scott. New York, 1908.

11   ———. *Compendium rhetorices*, tr. H. H. Hudson, in *Studies in Speech
     and Drama in Honor of Alexander M. Drummond*. Ithaca, N.Y., 1944.
     Pp. 326–340.

12   PHILLIPS, MARGARET MANN. *The Adages of Erasmus: A Study with
     Translations*. Cambridge, 1964.

13   SCHRAM, R. HUGH, JR. "John of Garland and Erasmus on the
     Principle of Synonymy," *University of Texas Studies in English*, XXX
     (1951), 24–39.

14   SOWARDS, J. K. "Erasmus and the Apologetic Textbook: A Study
     of the *De duplici copia verborum ac rerum*," *SP*, LV (1958), 122–135.

15   **Elyot, Thomas.** *The Book of the Governor* (1531), ed. S. E.
     Lehmberg. London, 1962.

1   **La Ramée, Pierre.** *Grammatica.* Paris, 1572.

2   ———. *The Art of Logik.* London, 1626. BCRE XIV:132.

3   GRAVES, F. P. *Peter Ramus and the Educational Reformation of the Sixteenth Century.* New York, 1912.

4   HOWELL, WILBUR S. "Ramus and English Rhetoric, 1574–1681," *QJS*, XXXVII (1951), 299–310.

5   NELSON, NORMAN E. *Peter Ramus and the Confusion of Logic, Rhetoric, and Poetry.* Ann Arbor: University of Michigan Contributions in Modern Philology II, 1947.

6   ONG, WALTER J. *Peter Ramus: Method, and the Decay of the Dialogue.* Cambridge, Mass., 1958.

7   SCOTT, WILLIAM O. "Ramism and Milton's Concept of Poetic Fancy," *PQ*, XLII (1963), 183–189.

8   SMITH, A. J. "An Examination of Some Claims for Ramism," *RES*, VII (1956), 348–359.

9   **Sherry, Richard.** *A Treatise of Schemes and Tropes* (1550) and his translation of *The Education of Children* by Desiderius Erasmus. Gainesville, Florida: Scholars' Facsimiles and Reprints, 1961. BCRE XII:70.

10 ———. *A Treatise of Figures of Grammar and Rhetorike.* London, [1555]. BCRE XII:71.

11 ENGELHARDT, G. J. "The Relation of Sherry's *Treatise of Schemes and Tropes* to Wilson's *Arte of Rhetorique*," *PMLA*, LXII (1947), 76–82.

12 HILDEBRANDT, HERBERT W. "Sherry: Renaissance Rhetorician," *Central States Speech Journal*, XI (1960), 204–209.

13 **Talaeus, Audomarus.** *Rhetorica.* Lutetiae [i.e., Paris ed.], 1551.

14 NADEAU, RAY. "Talaeus versus Farnaby on Style," *Speech Monographs*, XXI (1954), 59–63.

15 **Wilson, Thomas.** *The Arte of Rhetorique* (1553), ed. Robert Hood Bowers. Gainesville, Florida: Scholars' Facsimiles and Reprints, 1962. BCRE IX:88.

16 ENGELHARDT, G. J. "The Relation of Sherry's *Treatise of Schemes and Tropes* to Wilson's *Arte of Rhetorique*," *PMLA*, LXII (1947), 76–82.

17 WAGNER, RUSSELL H. "The Text and Editions of Wilson's *Arte of Rhetorique*," *MLN*, XLIV (1929), 421–438.

18 ———. "Wilson and His Sources," *QJS*, XV (1929), 525–537.

1 ———. "Thomas Wilson's Contributions to Rhetoric," in *Papers in Rhetoric*, ed. Donald C. Bryant. St. Louis, 1940. Pp. 1–7.

2 ———. "Thomas Wilson's *Arte of Rhetorique*," *Speech Monographs*, XXVII (1960), 1–32.

3 **Webbe, William.** *A Discourse of English Poetrie* (1586), ed. Edward Arber. London: English Reprints, No. 26, 1870. A selection appears in *Elizabethan Critical Essays*, vol. I, pp. 226–302.

4 **Rainolde, Richard.** *The Foundacion of Rhetorike* (1563), with an introduction by Francis R. Johnson. New York: Scholars' Facsimiles and Reprints, 1945.

5 JOHNSON, FRANCIS R. "Two Renaissance Textbooks of Rhetoric," *Huntington Library Quarterly*, VI (1942), 427–444.
The textbooks are the *Progymnasmata* of Aphthonius and Rainolde's *The Foundacion of Rhetorike*.

6 **Lily, William.** *A Shorte Introduction of Grammar* (1567), with an introduction by Vincent J. Flynn. New York: Scholars' Facsimiles and Reprints, 1945.

7 **Ascham, Roger.** *The Schoolmaster* (1570), ed. Edward Arber. Boston, 1898. A selection appears in *Elizabethan Critical Essays*, vol. I, pp. 1–45.

8 **Rainolds, John.** *Oratio in laudem artis poeticae* (c. 1572), tr. Walter Allen and ed. William Ringler. Princeton, 1940.

9 **Lever, Ralph.** *The Arte of Reason, Rightly Termed Witcraft*. London, 1573. BCRE V:51.

10 **Gascoigne, George.** *Certayne Notes of Instruction Concerning the Making of Verse in English*, ed. Edward Arber. London, 1868. A selection appears in *Elizabethan Critical Essays*, vol. I, pp. 46–57.

11 **Peacham, Henry.** *The Garden of Eloquence*. London, 1577. A facsimile of the 1593 edition with an introduction by William G. Crane, Gainesville, Florida: Scholars' Facsimiles and Reprints, 1954. BCRE V:57.

12 **Harvey, Gabriel.** *Ciceronianus* (1577), tr. Clarence A. Forbes and ed. Harold S. Wilson. Lincoln, Nebraska: University of Nebraska Studies in the Humanities IV, 1945.

13 ———. *Marginalia*, ed. G. C. Moore Smith. Stratford-on-Avon, 1913.

14 DUHAMEL, P. ALBERT. "The Ciceronianism of Gabriel Harvey," *SP*, XLIX (1952), 155–170.

15 WILSON, H. S. "Gabriel Harvey's Orations on Rhetoric," *ELH*, XII (1945), 167–182.

1   **Spenser, Edmund, and Gabriel Harvey.** *Three Proper and Witty Familiar Letters.* London, 1580.

The first and third letters are reprinted in *Elizabethan Critical Essays,* vol. I, pp. 98–122.

2   ———. *Two Other Very Commendable Letters.* London, 1580. Reprinted in *Elizabethan Critical Essays,* vol. I, pp. 87–97.

3   **Mulcaster, Richard.** *The First Part of the Elementarie* (1582), ed. E. T. Campagnac. Oxford, 1925.

4   JONES, RICHARD FOSTER. "Richard Mulcaster's View of the English Language," *Washington University Studies,* XIII (1926), 267–303.

5   **Fenner, Dudley.** *The Artes of Logike and Rhethorike.* London, 1584. BCRE III:32.

A section of this work was incorporated into the writings of Thomas Hobbes and erroneously attributed to him until this century.

6   **King James I and VI.** *Ane Schort Treatise, Conteining Some Reules and Cautelis To Be Obseruit and Eschewit in Scottis Poesie* (1585), ed. Edward Arber. London: English Reprints, No. 19, 1869. A selection appears in *Elizabethan Critical Essays,* vol. I, pp. 208–225.

7   **Day, Angell.** *The English Secretorie: Wherein is Contayned, a Perfect Method for the Inditing of All Manner of Epistles and Familiar Letters.* . . . London, 1586. BCRE III:24.

8   **Fraunce, Abraham.** *The Arcadian Rhetorike* (1588), ed. Ethel Seaton. Oxford, 1950. BCRE IV:33.

9   **Puttenham, George.** *The Arte of English Poesie* (1589), eds. Gladys Doidge Willcock and Alice Walker. Cambridge, 1936.

10 **Cox, Leonard.** *The Arte or Crafte of Rhethoryke* (c. 1530), ed. F. I. Carpenter. Chicago, 1899.

11 **Carew, Richard.** *The Survey of Cornwall and An Epistle Concerning the Excellency of the English Tongue* (1595), ed. F. E. Halliday. London, 1953.

12 **Coote, Edmund.** *The English Schoole-Master.* London, 1596.

13 DANIELSSON, BROR. "A Note on Edmund Coote: Prolegomena for a Critical Edition of Coote's *English School-Master,*" *Studia Neophilologica,* XXXII (1960), 228–240.

14 **Blundeville, Thomas.** *The Arte of Logike Plainly Taught in the English Tongue.* London, 1599. BCRE I:9.

15 **Hoskyns, John.** *Directions for Speech and Style* (1599), ed. Hoyt H. Hudson. Princeton, 1935.

1   Osborn, L. B. *The Life, Letters and Writings of John Hoskyns, 1566–1638.* New Haven, 1937.

2   **Campion, Thomas.** *Songs and Masques: With Observations in the Art of English Poesy* (1602), ed. A. H. Bullen. London. 1903.

3   **Daniel, Samuel.** *Poems* and *A Defence of Ryme* (1603), ed. Arthur C. Sprague. Cambridge, Mass., 1930.

4   **Camden, William.** *Remaines Concerning Britaine.* London, 1605. Camden's remarks on the English language are reprinted in *English Examined*, pp. 17–21.

5   **Verstegan, Richard.** *A Restitution of Decayed Intelligence.* Antwerp, 1605. Selection in *English Examined*, pp. 21–25.

6   **Bacon, Francis.** *Works*, eds. James Spedding, Robert Leslie Ellis, and Douglas Denon Heath. 15 vols. Boston, 1857–1874.

7   Wallace, Karl R. "Bacon's Conception of Rhetoric," *Speech Monographs*, III (1936), 21–48.

8   ———. *Francis Bacon on Communication and Rhetoric: Or, The Art of Applying Reason to the Imagination for the Better Moving of the Will.* Chapel Hill, N.C., 1943.

9   ———. "Aspects of Modern Rhetoric in Francis Bacon," *QJS*, XLII (1956), 398–406.

10 **Brerewood, Edward.** *Enqviries Tovching the Diversity of Langvages and Religions through the Cheife Parts of the World.* London, 1614. Selection in *English Examined*, pp. 26–27.

11 **Robinson, Robert.** *The Art of Pronuntiation.* London, 1617. Reprinted in *The Phonetic Writings of Robert Robinson*, ed. E. J. Dobson. London, 1957.

12 Fiedler, H. G. *A Contemporary of Shakespeare on Phonetics and on the Pronunciation of English and Latin.* London, 1936.

13 **Bolton, Edmund.** *Hypercritica: Or, A Rule of Judgement for Writing or Reading Our Historys.* London [1618?]. Selection in *Critical Essays of the Seventeenth Century*, vol. I, pp. 83–115.

14 **Brinsley, John.** *A Consolation for Ovr Grammar Schooles* (1622), ed. T. C. Pollock. New York: Scholars' Facsimiles and Reprints, 1943.

15 ———. *Ludus Literarius: Or, The Grammar Schoole* (1627), ed. E. T. Campagnac. Liverpool and London, 1917.

16 **Farnaby, Thomas.** *Index Rhetoricus* (1625), tr. Raymond E. Nadeau. Unpublished dissertation presented to the University of Michigan, 1952. See abstracts: *DA*, XI (1951), 462–463; *Speech Monographs*, XIX (1952), 127–128.

1   NADEAU, RAY. "Thomas Farnaby: Schoolmaster and Rhetorician of the English Renaissance," *QJS*, XXXVI (1950), 340–344.

2   ———. "Talaeus versus Farnaby on Style," *Speech Monographs*, XXI (1954), 59–63.

3   **Richardson, Alexander.** *The Logician's School-master: Or, A Comment upon Ramus Logick.* London, 1629.

4   ———. *The Logician's School-master . . . Whereunto are Added Prelections on Ramus His Grammar, Talaeus His Rhetoric.* London, 1657.

5   **Hobbes, Thomas.** See the following in *The English Works of Thomas Hobbes*, ed. Sir William Molesworth, 11 vols. (London, 1839–1845; reprinted London, 1962): "The Whole Art of Rhetoric," vol. VI, pp. 419–510; "The Art of Rhetoric, Plainly Set Forth with Pertinent Examples for the More Easy Understanding of the Same," vol. VI, pp. 511–528; "The Art of Sophistry," vol. VI, pp. 529–536; "Concerning the Virtues of An Heroic Poem," vol. X, pp. iii–x.

   W. S. Howell in *Logic and Rhetoric in England* (q. v.) discusses the attribution to Hobbes of Fenner's section on rhetoric in the latter's *The Artes of Logike and Rethorike.* Fenner's work appears in Volume Six of Hobbes's *English Works* as "The Art of Rhetorick Plainly Set Forth."

6   KALLICH, M. "The Association of Ideas and Critical Theory: Hobbes, Locke, and Addison," *ELH*, XII (1945), 290–315.

7   THONSSEN, LESTER W. "Thomas Hobbes' Philosophy of Speech," *QJS*, XVIII (1932), 200–206.

8   THORPE, CLARENCE D. *The Aesthetic Theory of Hobbes, with Special Reference to His Contribution to the Psychological Approach in English Literary Criticism.* London, 1940 and 1964.

9   WATSON, G. "Hobbes and the Metaphysical Conceit," *Journal of the History of Ideas*, XVI (1955), 558–562.
   Reply by T. M. Gang, *ibid.*, XVII (1956), 418–421.

10 **Alexander, William.** *Anacrisis: Or, A Censure of Some Poets Ancient and Modern.* London, [1634?]. Reprinted in Charles Rogers' *Memorials of the Earl of Sterling and of the House of Alexander.* Edinburgh, 1877. Vol. II, pp. 205–210. Selection in *Critical Essays of the Seventeenth Century*, vol. I, pp. 180–189.

11 **Jonson, Ben.** *The English Grammar* (1640), ed. Alice V. Waite. New York, 1909.

12 FUNKE, O. "Ben Jonsons *English Grammar*," *Anglia*, LXIV (1940), 117–134.

1 **Hodges, Richard.** *A Special Help to Orthographie* (1643), facsimile edition, Ann Arbor, 1932.

2 ———. *The English Primrose, Being the Easiest and Speediest-Way Both for the True Spelling and Reading of English, as also the True-Writing thereof* (1644), ed. Heinrich Kauter. Heidelberg, 1930.

3 **Glanvill, Joseph.** *An Essay Concerning Preaching.* London, 1646. BCRE III:31. Selection in *Critical Essays of the Seventeenth Century*, vol. II, pp. 273–277.

4 ———. *A Seasonable Defence of Preaching, and the Plain Way of It.* London, 1678.

5 COPE, JACKSON I. *Joseph Glanvill: Anglican Apologist.* St. Louis, 1956.

6 MAZZA, JOSEPH. "Joseph Glanvill's *An Essay Concerning Preaching* and *A Seasonable Defence of Preaching:* A Facsimile Edition with Introduction and Notes." Unpublished dissertation presented to the University of Wisconsin, 1963. See abstract in *Speech Monographs*, XXXI (1964), 252.

7 **de Vaugelas, Claude Favre.** *Remarques sur la Langue Françoise . . .* (1647), facsimile edition by Jeanne Streicher. Paris, 1934.

8 STREICHER, JEANNE (ed.). *Commentaires sur les "Remarques" de Vaugelas par La Mothe le Vayer, Scipion Dupleix, . . . [et al.] . . . et l'Académie Française.* 2 vols. Paris, 1936.

9 **Wallis, John.** *Grammatica Lingvae Anglicanae.* London, 1653. Selection in *English Examined*, pp. 34–39.

10 **Wright, Abraham.** *Five Sermons in Five Several Styles or Waies of Preaching.* London, 1656.
The styles imitated are those of Lancelot Andrewes, Bishop Hall, Dr. Maine, Mr. Cartwright, and the Independents.

11 **Pellisson-Fontanier, Paul.** *Histoire de l'Académie Française,* ed. Ch.-L. Livet. Paris, 1858. The first English translation was by H. R., London, 1657.

12 **Smith, John.** *The Mystery of Rhetorick Unveil'd; Wherein above 130 of the Tropes and Figures are Severally Derived from the Greek into English.* London, 1657 BCRE VII:72.

13 **Arnauld, Antoine, and Claude Lancelot.** *Grammaire générale et raisonée, contenant les fondemens de l'art de parler expliquez d'une manière claire et naturelle . . . et plusieurs remarques nouvelles sur la langue françoise.* Paris, 1660. Reprinted, 1845.

14 ———, with **Pierre Nicole.** *La Logiqve, ov L'art de penser.* Paris, 1662.
There were over forty editions published from 1662 to 1874 and

nine English translations from *Logic, or the Art of Thinking* (London, 1685) to *The Port Royal Logic*, tr. Thomas Spencer Baynes (Edinburgh, 1851). The most recent edition is *The Art of Thinking: Port-Royal Logic*, with an introduction by James Dickoff and Patricia James. Indianapolis, 1964.

General Secondary Sources

1   ABBOTT, EDWIN A. *A Shakespeare Grammar.* London, 1869; 3rd edition of 1870 reprinted, New York, 1966.

2   ATKINS, J. W. H. *English Literary Criticism: The Renascence.* London, 1947.

3   BALDWIN, T. W. *William Shakspere's Small Latine and Lesse Greeke.* 2 vols. Urbana, Ill., 1944.

4   BENZ, ERNST. "Die Sprachtheologie der Reformationszeit," *Studium Generale*, IV (1951), 204–213.

5   BLENCH, J. W. *Preaching in England during the Late Fifteenth and Sixteenth Centuries: A Study of English Sermons, 1450–1600.* New York, 1964.

6   CLARK, DONALD L. *Rhetoric and Poetry in the Renaissance: A Study of Rhetorical Terms in English Renaissance Literary Criticism.* New York, 1922 and 1963.

7   ———. *John Milton at St. Paul's School: A Study of Ancient Rhetoric in English Renaissance Education.* New York, 1948.

8   ———. "Ancient Rhetoric and English Renaissance Literature," *Shakespeare Quarterly*, II (1951), 195–204.

9   ———. "The Rise and Fall of Progymnasmata in Sixteenth and Seventeenth Century Grammar Schools," *Speech Monographs*, XIX (1952), 259–263.
   Progymnasmata are exercises in writing and speaking; the term was first used in the *Rhetorica ad Herennium*.

10   DANIELSSON, BROR *John Hart's Work on English Orthography and Pronunciation.* Stockholm, 1955.

11   ———. "Erasmus Roterodamus and Tudor Pronunciation," *Stockholm Studies in Modern Philology*, XIX (1956), 24–27.

12   DAVIES, CONSTANCE. *English Pronunciation from the Fifteenth to the Eighteenth Century.* London, 1934.

13   DOBSON, E. J. "Early Modern Standard English," *Transactions of the Philological Society* (Oxford), (1955), 25–54.

14   ———. *English Pronunciation: 1500–1700.* 2 vols. Oxford, 1957.

1   DUHAMEL, P. ALBERT. "Sidney's *Arcadia* and Elizabethan Rhetoric," *SP*, XLV (1948), 134–150.

2   EINSTEIN, LEWIS. *Italian Renaissance in England.* New York, 1902.

3   FISHER, PETER F. "Milton's Logic," *Journal of the History of Ideas*, XXIII (1962), 37–60.

4   FLETCHER, HARRIS F. *The Intellectual Development of John Milton.* Urbana, Ill., 1956.

5   FRIDÉN, GEORG. *Studies on the Tenses of the English Verb from Chaucer to Shakespeare, with Special Reference to the Late Sixteenth Century.* Uppsala and Cambridge, Mass., 1948.

6   FRIES, CHARLES C. "Shakespearian Punctuation," in *University of Michigan Studies in Shakespeare, Milton, and Donne.* Ann Arbor, 1925. Pp. 67–86.

7   ———. "The Rules of Common School Grammars, 1586–1825," *PMLA*, XLII (1927), 221–237.

8   GRAY, HANNA H. "Renaissance Humanism: The Pursuit of Eloquence," *Journal of the History of Ideas*, XXIV (1963), 497–514.

9   HALLER, WILLIAM. *The Rise of Puritanism.* New York, 1938.
    See Chapter Four, "The Rhetoric of the Spirit."

10 ———. *Liberty and Reformation in the Puritan Revolution.* New York, 1955.

11 HERRICK, M. T. "The Place of Rhetoric in Poetic Theory," *QJS*, XXXIV (1948), 1–22.
    Herrick discusses the roles of invention, disposition, and style in oratory and poetry from classical antiquity to the end of the Renaissance.

12 HOENIGSWALD, HENRY M. "Linguistics in the Sixteenth Century," *Library Chronicle*, XX (1954), 1–4.

13 HOWELL, WILBUR S. *Logic and Rhetoric in England: 1500–1700.* Princeton, 1957.

14 HOWES, RAYMOND F. *Historical Studies of Rhetoric and Rhetoricians.* Ithaca, N.Y., 1961.

15 HULTZÉN, LEE SISSON. "Seventeenth Century Intonation," *American Speech*, XIV (1939), 39–43.

16 JOHNSON, ANNE CARVEY. "The Pronoun of Direct Address in Seventeenth Century English," *DA*, XX (1959), 1021.

17 JOHNSON, F. R. "Latin versus English: The Sixteenth Century Debate over Scientific Terminology," *SP*, XLI (1944), 109–135.

1 JONES, RICHARD FOSTER. *The Triumph of the English Language: A Survey of Opinions Concerning the Vernacular from the Introduction of Printing to the Restoration.* Stanford, 1953.

2 KING, WALTER N. "John Lyly and Elizabethan Rhetoric," *SP*, LII (1955), 149–161.

3 KÖKERITZ, HELGE. "English Pronunciation as Described in Shorthand Systems of the Seventeenth and Eighteenth Centuries," *Studia Neophilologica*, VII (1935), 73–146.

4 ———. "John Hart (d. 1574) and Early Standard English," in *Philologica: Malone Anniversary Studies*, eds. Thomas A. Kirby and Henry B. Woolf. Baltimore, 1949. Pp. 239–248.

5 ———. *Shakespeare's Pronunciation.* New Haven, 1953.

6 LECHNER, SISTER JOAN MARIE. *Renaissance Concepts of the Commonplaces: An Historical Investigation of the . . . Ideas Used in Argumentation and Persuasion.* New York, 1962.

7 LE HIR, YVES. *Rhétorique et stylistique de la Pléiade au Parnasse.* Grenoble, 1960.

8 MACLURE, M. *The Paul's Cross Sermons, 1534–1642.* Toronto, 1958.

9 MCKENZIE, D. F. "Shakespearian Punctuation—A New Beginning," *RES*, N.S. X (1959), 361–370.

10 MEYER, SAM. "The Figures of Rhetoric in Spenser's *Colin Clout*," *PMLA*, LXXIX (1964), 206–218.

11 MITCHELL, W. F. *English Pulpit Oratory from Andrewes to Tillotson: A Study of Literary Aspects.* New York, 1932.

12 MITSUI, TAKAYUKI. "Relative Pronouns in Shakespeare's Colloquial English," in *Studies Otsuka*, pp. 335–349.

13 MOORE, J. L. *Tudor-Stuart Views on the Growth, Status, and Destiny of the English Language.* Halle, 1910.

14 NELSON, WILLIAM. "The Teaching of English in Tudor Grammar Schools," *SP*, XLIX (1952), 119–143.

15 ONG, WALTER J. "Historical Backgrounds of Elizabethan and Jacobean Punctuation Theory," *PMLA*, LIX (1944), 349–360.

16 RAGSDALE, J. DONALD. "Invention in English 'Stylistic' Rhetorics: 1600–1800," *QJS*, LI (1965), 164–167.

17 ROBERTSON, J. *The Art of Letter Writing: An Essay on the Handbooks Published in the Sixteenth and Seventeenth Centuries.* Liverpool, 1942.

18 ROSIER, JAMES L. "Lexical Strata in Florio's *New World of Words*," *English Studies*, XLIV (1963), 415–423.

1   SALMON, VIVIAN. "Early Seventeenth Century Punctuation as a Guide to Sentence Structure," *RES*, N.S. XIII (1962), 347–360.

2   ————. "Joseph Webbe: Some Seventeenth Century Views on Language-Teaching and the Nature of Meaning," *Bibliothèque d'Humanisme et Renaissance*, XXIII (1961), 324–340.

3   SALTER, F. M. "John Skelton's Contribution to the English Language," *Transactions of the Royal Society of Canada*, XXXIX, iii, 2 (1945), 119–217.
Salter lists some 800 words from Skelton's translation of Diodorus Siculus' *Bibliotheca Historica* (EETS, O.S. 233 and 239, 1957), which antedate citations of them in the *OED*.

4   SANDFORD, W. P. "English Rhetoric Reverts to Classicism, 1600–1650," *QJS*, XV (1929), 503–525.

5   ————. *English Theories of Public Address, 1530–1828*. Columbus, Ohio, 1931.

6   SASEK, LAWRENCE A. *The Literary Temper of the English Puritans.* Baton Rouge, 1961.

7   SCHEURWEGHS, G., AND E. VORLAT. "Problems of the History of English Grammar," *English Studies*, XL (1959), 135–143.
The grammars discussed include those by Paul Greaves (1594), John Brightland (1711), and John Ash (1763).

8   SCHOLL, E. H. "New Light on Seventeenth Century Pronunciation from the English School of Lutenist Song Writers," *PMLA*, LIX (1944), 398–445.

9   SCOTT, I. *Controversies over the Imitation of Cicero.* New York, 1910.

10   SCOTT-CRAIG, T. S. K. "The Craftsmanship and Theological Significance of Milton's *Art of Logic*," *Huntington Library Quarterly*, XVII (1953), 1–16.

11   SHAFTER, EDWARD M., JR. *A Study of Rhetorical Invention in Selected English Rhetoricians, 1550–1600*. Unpublished dissertation presented to the University of Michigan, 1956. Abstract in *Speech Monographs*, XXIV (1957), 112.

12   SLEDD, JAMES. "A Footnote on the Inkhorn Controversy," *University of Texas Studies in English*, XXVIII (1949), 49–56.

13   SMITH, GEORGE GREGORY (ed.). *Elizabethan Critical Essays.* 2 vols. Oxford, 1904.

14   SÖDERLIND, J. "The Attitude to Language Expressed by or Ascertainable from English Writers of the 16th and 17th Centuries," *Studia Neophilologica*, XXXVI (1964), 111–126.

1   SØRENSEN, KNUD. *Thomas Lodge's Translation of Seneca's 'De beneficiis' Compared with Arthur Golding's Version: A Textual Analysis with Special Reference to Latinisms.* Copenhagen, 1960.

2   SOWTEN, IAN. "Hidden Persuaders as a Means of Literary Grace: Sixteenth-Century Poetics and Rhetoric in England," *UTQ*, XXXII (1962), 55–69.

3   SPINGARN, JOEL E. (ed.). *Critical Essays of the Seventeenth Century.* 3 vols. Oxford, 1908–1909.

4   SWEETING, ELIZABETH J. *Early Tudor Criticism, Linguistic and Literary.* Oxford, 1940.

5   TATEO, FRANCESCO. *"Rhetorica" e "Poetica" fra Medioevo e Rinascimento.* Bari, Italy, 1960.

6   TEETS, BRUCE E. "Two Faces of Style in Renaissance Prose Fiction," in *The Sweet Smoke of Rhetoric: A Collection of Renaissance Essays*, eds. Natalie Grimes Lawrence and J. A. Reynolds (Coral Gables, 1964), pp. 69–81.

7   TRNKA, BOHUMIL. *On the Syntax of the English Verb from Caxton to Dryden.* Prague, 1930.

8   VORLAT, EMMA. *Progress in English Grammar, 1585–1735: A Study of the Development of English Grammar and the Interdependence among the Early English Grammarians.* Luxembourg, 1963.

9   WALLACE, KARL R. "Early English Rhetoricians on the Structure of Rhetorical Prose," in *Papers in Rhetoric*, ed. Donald C. Bryant. St. Louis, 1940. Pp. 18–26.

10   WATSON, FOSTER. *The English Grammar Schools to 1660.* Cambridge, 1908.

11   WEINBERG, BERNARD (ed.). *Critical Prefaces of the French Renaissance.* Evanston, Ill., 1950.

12   WEISS, R. *The Spread of Italian Humanism.* London, 1964.

NEOCLASSICISM (TO 1800)

Major Works and Commentary
Newton, Isaac.

13   ELLIOTT, RALPH W. V. "Isaac Newton as a Phonetician," *MLR*, XLIX (1954), 5–12.

14   ———. "Isaac Newton's 'Of an Universall Language,'" *MLR*, LII (1957), 1–18.

"Of an Universall Language" is contained in a ms. notebook made by Newton in about 1661 and is a design for an artificial language.

1   **Evelyn, John.** See letters to Peter Wyche (1665) and Samuel Pepys (1689) in *Critical Essays of the Seventeenth Century*, vol. II, pp. 310–329.

2   **Sprat, Thomas.** *The History of the Royal Society for the Improving of Natural Knowledge* (1667), eds. Jackson I. Cope and Harold W. Jones. St. Louis, 1958.

3   Rosenberg, A. "Bishop Sprat on Science and Imagery," *Isis*, XLIII (1952), 220–222.

4   **Wilkins, John.** *An Essay Towards a Real Character, and a Philosophical Language.* London, 1668. An abstract appears in *The Mathematical and Philosophical Works of the Right Reverend John Wilkins.* 2 vols. London, 1802.

5   CLARK, EMERY. "John Wilkins' Universal Language," *Isis*, XXXVIII (1947), 174–185.

6   CHRISTENSEN, F. "John Wilkins and the Royal Society's Reform of Prose Style," *MLQ*, VII (1946), 179–187; 279–290.

7   DeMOTT, BENJAMIN. "The Sources and Development of John Wilkins' Philosophical Language," *JEGP*, LVII (1958), 1–13.

8   **Eachard, John.** *The Grounds and Occasions of the Contempt of the Clergy* (1670), ed. Edward Arber. London, 1877.

9   **Arderne, James.** *Directions Concerning the Matter and Stile of Sermons* (1671), ed. John Mackay. Oxford: Luttrell Society Reprint XIII, 1952.

10   **Dillon, Wentworth.** *An Essay on Translated Verse.* London, 1684. Selection in *Critical Essays of the Seventeenth Century*, vol. III, pp. 297–309.

11   **Bouhours, Dominique.** *La Manière de bien penser dans les ouvrages d'esprit.* Paris, 1687.
     Selections from an eighteenth-century English translation, *The Art of Criticism: or, the Method of Making a Right Judgment upon Subjects of Wit and Learning*, appear in *The Continental Model: Selected French Critical Essays of the Seventeenth Century, in English Translation*, eds. Scott Elledge and Donald Schier (Minneapolis, 1960), pp. 239–274.

12   **Temple, William.** *Miscellanea.* London, 1690. See the two essays reprinted in *Critical Essays of the Seventeenth Century*, vol. III, pp. 32–109.

13   **Locke, John.** *The Educational Writings of John Locke*, ed. John William Adamson. London, 1912.

1   GIVNER, DAVID A. "Scientific Preconceptions in Locke's Philosophy of Language," *Journal of the History of Ideas*, XXIII (1962), 340–354.

2   KALLICH, M. "The Association of Ideas and Critical Theory: Hobbes, Locke, and Addison," *ELH*, XII (1945), 290–315.

3   MACLEAN, K. *John Locke and English Literature of the Eighteenth Century*. New Haven, 1936.

4   MILLER, PERRY. "Edwards, Locke, and the Rhetoric of Sensation," in *Perspectives in Criticism*, ed. Harry Levin. Cambridge, Mass., 1950. Pp. 103–123.

5   O'HARA, JOHN BRYANT. "John Locke's Philosophy of Discourse," *DA*, XXIII (1963), 2625.

6   **Dennis, John.** *The Impartial Critick*. London, 1693. Reprinted in *The Critical Works of John Dennis*, ed. Edward Niles Hooker (Baltimore, 1939), vol. I, pp. 11–41.

7   **de Bellegarde, Jean-Baptiste Morvan.** *Réflexions sur l'élégance et la politesse du stile*. Paris, 1694. BCRE IX:99.

8   ————. *The Letters of Monsieur L'Abbé de Bellegarde, Done in English, With a Preface by the Translator of the French Manner of Writing Compar'd with the English*. London, 1705.

9   **Wotton, William.** *Reflections upon Ancient and Modern Learning*. London, 1694. *Selection in Critical Essays of the Seventeenth Century*, vol. III, pp. 201–226.

10 **Rymer, Thomas.** *Critical Works*, ed. Curt A. Zimansky. New Haven, 1956.

11 DUTTON, G. B. "The French Aristotelian Formalists and Thomas Rymer," *PMLA*, XXIX (1914), 152–188.

12 **Hughes, John.** "Of Style," (1698), reprinted in *Critical Essays of the Eighteenth Century*, pp. 79–85.

13 **Bysshe, Edward.** *The Art of English Poetry*. London, 1702.
    Bysshe's work is divided into three sections: "Rules for Making Verses," "A Dictionary of Rhymes," and "A Collection of the Most Natural Agreeable, and Noble Thoughts. . . . That are to be found in the Best English Poets." The first of these sections is to be found in *Bysshe's "The Art of Poetry"* (*1708*), ed. A. Dwight Culler (Los Angeles: Augustan Reprint Society, 1953).

14 CULLER, A. DWIGHT. "Edward Bysshe and the Poet's Handbook," *PMLA*, LXII (1948), 858–885.

15 GABRIELSON, A. *Edward Bysshe's Dictionary of Rhymes as a Source of Information on Early Modern English Pronunciation*. Uppsala, 1930.

1   **Oldmixon, John.** "Essay on the Old English Poets and Poetry," *The Muses Mercury*, I (1707), 127–133.

2   ———. *Reflections on Dr. Swift's Letter to Harley* (1712), with an introduction by Louis A. Landa. Los Angeles: Augustan Reprint Society, 1948.

3   ———. *The Arts of Logick and Rhetorick . . . Interpreted and Explain'd by that Learned and Judicious Critick, Father Bouhours.* London, 1728.

4   ———. *Essay on Criticism, as It Regards Design, Thought, and Expression in Prose and Verse.* London, 1728.

5   **Felton, Henry.** *A Dissertation on Reading the Classics and Forming a Just Style.* London, 1713.

6   **Trapp, Joseph.** *Praelectiones Poeticae.* 2 vols. Oxford, 1711–1715. Translated by W. Clarke and W. Bowyer as *Lectures on Poetry* (London, 1742). Selection in *Eighteenth-Century Critical Essays*, vol. I, pp. 229–250.

7   FREIMARCK, V. "Joseph Trapp's Advanced Conception of Metaphor," *PQ*, XXIX (1950), 413–416.

8   **Berkeley, George.** *The Works of George Berkeley*, ed. A. C. Fraser. 4 vols. Oxford, 1901.

9   GELBER, S. "Universal Language and the Sciences of Man in Berkeley's Philosophy," *Journal of the History of Ideas*, XIII (1952), 482–513.

10   GIVNER, DAVID A. "A Study of George Berkeley's Theory of Linguistic Meaning with a Discussion of Locke's Account of Language and a Consideration of the Relevance of their Philosophies of Science," *DA*, XX (1959), 1391.

11   RATTE, RENA JOSEPHINE. "George Berkeley's Theory of Language," *DA*, XX (1960), 4135.

12   **Swift, Jonathan.** "A Proposal for Correcting, Improving, and Ascertaining the English Tongue in a Letter to the Lord High Treasurer" (1712), in *The Prose Works of Jonathan Swift*, ed. Herbert Davis (13 vols. Oxford, 1939–1959), vol. IV, pp. 1–21.

13   ———. "Hints Towards an Essay on Conversation" (1710), *ibid.*, vol. IV, pp. 85–95.

14   ———. *A Complete Collection of Genteel and Ingenious Conversation* (1738), *ibid.*, vol. IV, pp. 97–201.

15   ———. "A Discourse to Prove the Antiquity of the English Tongue," *ibid.*, vol. IV, pp. 231–239.

16   ———. *The Tatler*, No. 230 (September 17, 1710), *ibid.*, vol. II, pp. 173–177.

1   ———. "Letter to a Young Gentleman, Lately Entered into Holy Orders" (1719–1720), *ibid.*, IX, pp. 61–81.

2   THORPE, ANNETTE. "Jonathan Swift's Prescriptions Concerning the English Language," *CLA Journal*, III (1959–1960), 173–180.

3   **Brightland, John.** *A Grammar of the English Tongue* [1711], *with the Arts of Logick, Rhetorick, Poetry, &c.* London, 1712. BCRE I:10. Brightland's grammar is sometimes attributed to Steele.

4   GRIFFITH, R. H. "Isaac Bickerstaff's Grammar," *N&Q*, CXCIV (1949), 362–365.

5   **Parnell, Thomas.** *An Essay on the Different Stiles of Poetry.* London, 1713.

6   **Pope, Alexander.** See his "Preface" to his *Iliad* (1715) in *Eighteenth-Century Critical Essays*, vol. I, pp. 257–278.

7   **Fénelon, François.** *Dialogues on Eloquence* (1718), tr. Wilbur S. Howell. Princeton, 1951.

     "Fénelon's *Dialogues*, one hundred pages in translation, present in most ways the clearest and best modern French restatement and modification of the classic position of the *De oratore* and the *Institutes*. Professor Howell's introduction of fifty-three pages sets the *Dialogues* in lucid perspective, contemporary and historical, and offers the best exposition to date of the Ramean logic-rhetoric in relation to its continental successors, notably the *Port Royal Logic*" (note by Donald C. Bryant in *Speech Monographs*, "Annual Bibliography for 1951").

8   **Gildon, Charles.** *The Complete Art of Poetry.* 2 vols. London, 1718. Selection in *Critical Essays of the Eighteenth Century*, pp. 18–75.

9   LITZ, F. E. "The Sources of Charles Gildon's *Complete Art of Poetry*," *ELH*, IX (1942), 118–135.

10   **Welsted, Leonard.** "Dissertation concerning the Perfection of the English Language, the State of Poetry, *etc.*," prefixed to his *Odes, Epistles, etc., Written on Various Subjects.* London, 1724. Selection in *Eighteenth-Century Critical Essays*, vol. I, pp. 320–348.

11   **Watts, Isaac.** "Preface" to his *Horae Lyricae.* London, 1706. Reprinted in *Eighteenth-Century Critical Essays*, vol. I, pp. 148–163.

12   ———. *Logick: Or, The Right Use of Reason in the Enquiry after Truth.* London, 1725.

13   ———. *The Improvement of the Mind: Or, A Supplement to the Art of Logick.* London, 1741.

14   **Spence, Joseph.** *An Essay on Pope's "Odyssey."* London, 1728. Selection in *Eighteenth-Century Critical Essays*, vol. I, pp. 387–405.

15   ———. *An Essay on Wit.* London, 1748.

1   **Constable, John.** *Reflections upon Accuracy of Style.* London, 1731. BCRE III:22.

2   **Hayward, Thomas.** *The British Muse: Or, A Collection of Thoughts, Moral, Natural, and Sublime, of Our English Poets. . . .* 3 vols. London, 1738.

3   SALMON, VIVIAN. "Thomas Hayward, Grammarian," *Neophilologus,* XLIII (1959), 64–74.

4   **Flint, Mather.** *Prononciation de la Langue Angloise.* Paris, 1740. Reprinted with a commentary by Helge Kökeritz, *Mather Flint on Early Eighteenth-Century English Pronunciation.* Uppsala and Leipzig, 1944.

5   **Arbuthnot, Pope, Swift, Gay, Parnell, Harley.** *Memoirs of the Extraordinary Life, Works, and Discoveries of Martin Scriblerus,* ed. Charles Kerby-Miller. New Haven, 1950.

6   **Manwaring, Edward.** *Of Harmony and Numbers, in Latin and English Prose, and in English Poetry.* London, 1744.

7   **Ogilvie, John.** *Philosophical and Critical Observations on the Nature, Characters, and Various Species of Composition.* London, 1744. BCRE VI:56.

8   **Say, Samuel.** *Poems on Several Occasions: And Two Critical Essays, viz. the First, on the Harmony, Variety, and Power of Numbers, whether in Prose or Verse, the Second, on the Numbers of "Paradise Lost."* London, 1745.

9   **Wesley, John.** *Directions Concerning Pronunciation and Gesture.* Bristol, 1749.

10   GOLDEN, JAMES L. "John Wesley on Rhetoric and Belles Lettres," *Speech Monographs,* XXVIII (1961), 250–264.

11   **Mason, John.** *Three Essays, viz., On Elocution, On the Principles of Harmony in Poetic Composition, and the Power of Harmony in Prosaic Numbers.* London, 1749.

12   **Warton, Joseph.** *An Essay on the Genius and Writings of Pope.* London, 1756. Selection in *Eighteenth-Century Critical Essays,* vol. II, pp. 717–763.

13   **Johnson, Samuel.** *The Rambler.* London, 1750–1752. Nos. 94, 121, 140, 168.

14   ————. *Dictionary of the English Language.* London, 1755.

15   ————. *The Idler.* London, 1761. Nos. 36, 63, 68, 69, 70, 77, 91.

16   DOWNES, RACKSTRAW. "Johnson's Theory of Language," *REL,* III, iv (1962), 29–41.

1   FLEMING, LINDSAY. "Dr. Johnson's Use of Authorities in Compiling
     His Dictionary of the English Language," *N&Q*, N.S. I (1954),
     254–257, 294–297, 343–347.

2   FUSSELL, PAUL. "A Note on Samuel Johnson and the Rise of
     Accentual Prosodic Theory," *PQ*, XXXIII (1954), 431–433.

3   GILBERT, VEDDER M. "The Altercations of Thomas Edwards with
     Samuel Johnson," *JEGP*, LI (1952), 326–335.
     Gilbert discusses Edwards' criticisms of the *Dictionary*.

4   MAYS, M. J. "Johnson and Blair on Addison's Prose Style," *SP*,
     XXXIX (1942), 638–649.

5   McCUE, G. S. "Sam. Johnson's Word-Hoard," *MLN*, LXIII
     (1948), 43–45.

6   MOORE, W. E. "Samuel Johnson on Rhetoric," *QJS*, XXX (1944),
     165–168.

7   NOYES, GERTRUDE E. "The Critical Reputation of Johnson's *Dic-
     tionary* in the Latter Eighteenth Century," *MP*, LII (1954), 175–
     191.

8   SHERBO, ARTHUR. "Dr. Johnson's Revision of His *Dictionary*,"
     PQ, XXXI (1952), 273–282.

9   SLEDD, JAMES H., AND GWIN J. KOLB. *Dr. Johnson's Dictionary:
     Essays in the Biography of a Book*. Chicago, 1955.

10   **Harris, James.** *Hermes: Or, A Philosophical Inquiry Concerning Uni-
     versal Grammar*. London, 1751. Selection in *English Examined*,
     pp. 77–85.

11   **Buffon, George-Louis Leclerc.** "Discours sur le style" (1753),
     in *Buffon: Oeuvres Choisies*, ed. Félix Hémon (Paris, 1925), pp. 463–
     484.

12   **Warton, Thomas.** *Observations on the Faerie queene of Spencer* [sic].
     London, 1754. Selection in *Eighteenth-Century Essays*, vol. II, pp.
     764–786.

13   ———. *The History of English Poetry, from the Close of the Eleventh to
     the Commencement of the Eighteenth Century*. 4 vols. London, 1774–1781.
     Selection in *Eighteenth-Century Critical Essays*, vol. II, pp. 787–803.

14   **Newbery, John.** *Letters . . . by Writers of Distinguished Merit . . .
     [with] a Dissertation on the Epistolary Style*. London, 1756.

15   **Sheridan, Thomas.** *British Education*. London, 1756.
     See "Dissertation on Rime," Book II, Chapter 9.

1   ————. *A Course of Lectures on Elocution: Together with Two Dissertations on Language, and Some Other Tracts Relative to Those Subjects.*
London, 1762. BCRE VII:67–68.

2   ————. *A General Dictionary of the English Language, One Main Object
of which, is to Establish a Plain and Permanent Standard of Pronunciation,
to which is Prefixed a Rhetorical Grammar.* 2 vols. London, 1780.

3   BACON, WALLACE A. "The Elocutionary Career of Thomas
Sheridan," *Speech Monographs*, XXXI (1964), 3–53.

4   FRITZ, C. A. "Sheridan to Rush: The Beginnings of English Elocution," *QJS*, XVI (1930), 75–88.

5   Harper, Richard D. "The Rhetorical Theory of Thomas Sheridan."
Unpublished dissertation presented to the University of Wisconsin,
1951. See the abstract in *Speech Monographs*, XIX (1952), 125–126.

6   NEUMANN, J. H. "Eighteenth-Century Linguistic Tastes as Exhib-
ited in Sheridan's Edition of Swift," *AS*, XXI (1946), 253–263.

7   **Bayly, Anselm.** *An Introduction to Languages, Literary and Philosophical.*
London, 1758.

8   ————. *The Alliance of Musick, Poetry and Oratory.* London, 1789.
BCRE I:4.

9   **Smith, Adam.** *The Theory of Moral Sentiments. To which is added a
Dissertation on the Origin of Languages.* London, 1759.

10   ————. *Lectures on Rhetoric and Belles Lettres* (1762–1763), ed.
John M. Lothian. New York, 1963.

11   **Priestley, Joseph.** *The Rudiments of English Grammar, with Observations on Style.* London, 1761.

12   ————. *A Course of Lectures on the Theory of Language and Universal
Grammar.* London, 1762.

13   ————. *A Course of Lectures on Oratory and Criticism.* London, 1777.
BCRE VI:62.
All these three works are reprinted in volume 23 of *The Theological
and Miscellaneous Works of Joseph Priestley*, ed. John T. Rutt (London,
1817–1832).

14   NORTH, ROSS S. "Joseph Priestley on Language, Oratory, and
Criticism," *DA*, XVII (1957), 1154.

15   **Goldsmith, Oliver.** "The Use of Metaphor," (1761), in *The
Works of Oliver Goldsmith*, ed. Peter Cunningham (4 vols., London,
1854), vol. III, pp. 314–324.

16   ————. "On Hyperbole" (1762), *ibid.*, vol. III, pp. 324–326.

1 ———. "On Versification" (1763), *ibid.*, vol. III, pp. 326–329

2 **Home, Henry, Lord Kames.** *Elements of Criticism.* Edinburgh, 1762.

3 BEVILACQUA, VINCENT M. "Lord Kames's Theory of Rhetoric," *Speech Monographs*, XXX (1963), 309–327.
   Abstract: "The theory of rhetoric presented in *Elements of Criticism* is essentially a psychological and stylistic one arising from the eighteenth-century assumptions from which Kames reasoned. . . . Kames developed a rhetoric which was concerned with grace, elegance, and force in thought and expression and which explained and justified traditional doctrines of style in terms of prevailing views of the nature of man."

4 MCKENZIE, GORDON. "Lord Kames and the Mechanist Tradition," in *Essays and Studies by Members of the Department of English.* Berkeley and Los Angeles: University of California Publications in English, 1943. Pp. 93–121.

5 RANDALL, HELEN W. *The Critical Theory of Lord Kames.* Northampton, Mass., 1944.
   See M. W. Bundy, "Lord Kames and the Maggots in Amber," *JEGP*, XLV (1946), 199–208.

6 **Lowth, Robert.** *Lectures on the Sacred Poetry of the Hebrews* (1753), tr. from Latin by G. Gregory. London, 1787. Selection in *Eighteenth-Century Critical Essays*, vol. II, pp. 687–703.
   Lowth's *Lectures* are briefly discussed by William Whallon, "Hebraic Synonymy in Sir Thomas Browne," *ELH*, XXVIII (1961), 335.

7 ———. *A Short Introduction to English Grammar.* London, 1762.

8 **Buchanan, James.** *The British Grammar.* London, 1762.

9 ———. *An Essay towards Establishing a Standard for an Elegant and a Uniform Pronunciation of the English Language.* London, 1766.

10 ———. *The First Six Books of "Paradise Lost" Rendered into Grammatical Construction.* Edinburgh, 1773.

11 EMSLEY, B. "James Buchanan and the Eighteenth Century Regulation of English Usage," *PMLA*, XLVIII (1933), 1154–1166.

12 **Percy, Thomas.** *Five Pieces of Runic Poetry Translated from the Islandic Language.* London, 1763.
   See the prefatory essay on poetic diction.

13 **Campbell, Archibald.** *Lexiphanes, a Dialogue: Imitated from Lucian, and Suited to the Present Times. Being an Attempt to Restore the English Tongue to Its Antient Purity, and to Expose the Affected Style of our English Lexiphanes, the Rambler. . . .* London, 1767.

1   **Ward, William.** *A Grammar of the English Language.* York, 1767. Ward "drew up for the first time the full set of prescriptions which underlies, with individual variations, the rules found in modern books. His pronouncements were not generally followed by other grammarians until Lindley Murray gave them greater currency in 1795. Since about 1825 they have often been repeated in English grammars" (A. C. Baugh, *A History of the English Language,* p. 346).

2   **Baker, Robert.** *Remarks on the English Language, in the Manner of Those of Vaugelas on the French.* London, 1770.

3   **Burrow, James.** *De Usu et Ratione Interpungendi: An Essay on the Use of Pointing and the Facility of Practising it.* London, 1771.

4   **Kenrick, William.** *A New Dictionary of the English Language . . . To Which is Prefixed, a Rhetorical Grammar.* London, 1773.

5   **Burnett, James, Lord Monboddo.** *Of the Origin and Progress of Language.* 6 vols. Edinburgh, 1774–1792. BCRE II:14.

6   **Campbell, George.** *The Philosophy of Rhetoric.* 2 vols. London, 1776. The introduction is reprinted in *Eighteenth-Century Critical Essays,* vol. II, pp. 932–942.

7   BENSON, FRANK T. "A Comparative Analysis of George Campbell's *Philosophy of Rhetoric,*" *DA,* XXIV (1964), 1745.

8   BITZER, LLOYD FRANK. *The Lively Idea: A Study of Hume's Influence on George Campbell's Philosophy of Rhetoric.* Unpublished dissertation presented to the State University of Iowa, 1962. Abstract in *Speech Monographs,* XXX (1963), 194–195.

9   EDNEY, CLARENCE W. "George Campbell's Theory of Logical Truth," *Speech Monographs,* XV (1948), 19–32.

10   ———. "Campbell's *Lectures on Pulpit Eloquence,*" *Speech Monographs,* XIX (1952), 1–10.

11   WAGNER, R. H. *"Lectures on Pulpit Eloquence* by George Campbell," *QJS,* XV (1929), 592–594.

12   **Beattie, James.** *Essays: On Poetry and Music as they Affect the Mind; On Laughter and Ludicrous Composition; on the Utility of Classical Learning.* Edinburgh, 1778.

13   ———. *The Theory of Language: Part I: Of the Origin and General Nature of Speech. Part II: Of Universal Grammar.* London, 1788.

14   **Steele, Joshua.** *Prosodia Rationalis: Or, An Essay Towards Establishing the Melody and Measure of Speech, to be Expressed and Perpetuated by Peculiar Symbols.* London, 1779.

15   ALLSON, PAUL. "Joshua Steele and the Melody of Speech," *Language and Speech,* II (1959), 154–174.

1 **Blair, Hugh.** *Lectures on Rhetoric and Belles Lettres.* 2 vols. London, 1783.

2 COHEN, HERMAN. "The Rhetorical Theory of Hugh Blair," *DA*, XIV (1954), 1004–1005.

3 EDNEY, CLARENCE W. "Hugh Blair's Theory of *Dispositio*," *Speech Monographs*, XXIII (1956), 38–45.

4 MAYS, M. J. "Johnson and Blair on Addison's Prose Style," *SP*, XXXIX (1942), 638–649.

5 **Barnes, Thomas.** "On the Nature and Essential Characters of Poetry as Distinguished from Prose," *Memoirs of the Manchester Literary and Philosophical Society*, I (1785).

6 **Tooke, John Horne.** *Epea Pteroenta: Or, The Diversions of Purley.* 2 vols. London, 1786.

7 RICHARDSON, CHARLES. *On the Study of Language: An Exposition of "The Diversions of Purley" by John Horne Tooke.* London, 1854.

8 **Withers, Philip.** *Aristarchus: Or, The Principles of Composition.* London, 1789.

9 **Twining, Thomas.** *Aristotle's Treatise on Poetry, Translated, with . . . Two Dissertations on Poetical and Musical Imitation.* London, 1789. Selection in *Eighteenth-Century Critical Essays*, vol. II, pp. 984–1004.

10 **Webster, Noah.** *Dissertations on the English Language* (1789), with an introduction by Harry R. Warfel. Gainesville, Fla.: Scholars' Facsimiles and Reprints, 1951.

11 **Tytler, Alexander Frazer, Lord Woodhouselee.** *Essay on the Principles of Translation* (1791), ed. Ernest Rhys. New York, 1907.

12 **Whiter, Walter.** *A Specimen of a Commentary on Shakespeare.* London, 1794. Selection in *Eighteenth-Century Critical Essays*, vol. II, pp. 1065–1103.

13 **Burrowes, Robert.** "Essay on Style in Writing Considered with Respect to Thoughts and Sentiments as well as Words," *Transactions of the Royal Irish Academy*, V (1795), 39–64.

14 **Murray, Lindley.** *English Grammar.* London, 1795, and Boston, 1800.

15 READ, ALLEN WALKER. "The Motivation of Lindley Murray's Grammatical Work," *JEGP*, XXXVIII (1939), 525–539.

16 VORLAT, E. "The Sources of Lindley Murray's *The English Grammar*," *Leuvense Bijdragen*, XLVIII (1959), 108–125.

1   **Wallace, Thomas.** "Essay on the Variations of English Prose, from the Revolution to the Present Time," *Transactions of the Royal Irish Academy*, VI (1797), 41–70.

General Secondary Sources

2   ABBOTT, ORVILLE LAWRENCE. "A Study of Verb Form and Verb Uses in Certain American Writings of the Seventeenth Century," *DA*, XIV (1954), 361.

3   ABERCROMBIE, DAVID. "Forgotten Phoneticians," *Transactions of the Philological Society* (Oxford) (1948), 1–34.

4   ——— (ed.). *G. W. Magazine: Or, Animadversions on the English Spelling* (1703). Los Angeles: Augustan Reprint Society No. 70, 1958.

5   ACTON, HENRY BURROWS. *The Philosophy of Language in Revolutionary France.* London, 1959.

6   ADAMS, ROBERT MARTIN. "The Text of *Paradise Lost:* Emphatic and Unemphatic Spellings," *MP*, LII (1954–55), 84–91.

7   ATKINS, J. W. H. *English Literary Criticism: Seventeenth and Eighteenth Centuries.* London, 1951.

8   ATKINSON, A. D. "The Royal Society and English Vocabulary," *Notes and Records of the Royal Society of London*, XII (1956), 40–43.

9   BAUMGARTNER, PAUL R. "Jonathan Edwards: The Theory behind His Use of Figurative Language," *PMLA*, LXXVIII (1963), 321–325.

10 BERGSTRÖM, FOLKE. "John Kirby (1746) on English Pronunciation," *Studia Neophilologica*, XXVII (1955), 65–104.
    A part of Bergström's article is devoted to a reprint of Chapter One of Kirby's *New English Grammar.*

11 BRYAN, W. F. "Notes on the Founders of Prescriptive English Grammar," in *Manly Anniversary Studies.* Chicago, 1923. Pp. 383–393.

12 CLARK, ALEXANDER F. *Boileau and the French Classical Critics in England.* [1660–1830], Paris, 1925.

13 COLLINS, A. S. "Language 1660–1784," in *From Dryden to Johnson*, ed. Boris Ford. Baltimore, 1957. Pp. 125–141.

14 CRANE, R. S. "Imitation of Spenser and Milton in the Early Eighteenth Century," *SP*, XV (1918), 195–206.
    Crane discusses the use of archaisms in English neoclassic poetry.

15 DOLPH, JOSEPH M. "Taste in Eighteenth-Century English Rhetorical Theory," *DA*, XXV (1964), 3164.

1   DURHAM, WILLARD H. (ed.). *Critical Essays of the Eighteenth Century, 1700–1725*. New York, 1961.

2   ELLEDGE, SCOTT, AND DONALD SCHIER (eds.). *The Continental Model: Selected French Critical Essays of the Seventeenth Century, in English Translation*. Minneapolis, 1960.

3   ELLEDGE, SCOTT (ed.). *Eighteenth-Century Critical Essays*. 2 vols. Ithaca, N.Y., 1961.

4   FREIMARCK, V. "The Bible and Neo-Classical Views of Style," *JEGP*, LI (1952), 507–526.

5   FRIES, CHARLES C. "The Rules of Common School Grammars," *PMLA*, XLII (1927), 221–237.

6   FUNKE, O. *Studien zur Geschichte der Sprachphilosophie*. Berne, 1927.

7   ———. "Sprachphilosophie und Grammatik in englischen Sprach-büchern des 17. und 18. Jahrhunderts," in *Wege und Ziele: Ausge-wählte, Aufsätze und Vorträge*. Bern, 1945. Pp. 185–199.

8   FUSSELL, PAUL. *Theory of Prosody in Eighteenth-Century England*. New London, 1954.

9   GOLDEN, JAMES L. "James Boswell on Rhetoric and Belles-Lettres," *QJS*, L (1964), 266–276.

10 GUTHRIE, WARREN. "The Development of Rhetorical Theory in America, 1635–1850," *Speech Monographs*, XIII (1946), 14–22; XIV (1947), 38–54; XV (1948), 61–71; XVI (1949), 98–113; XVIII (1951), 17–30.

11 HABERMAN, FREDERICK W. "The Elocutionary Movement in England, 1750–1850." Unpublished dissertation presented to Cornell University, 1947.

12 HANZO, THOMAS A. *Latitude and Restoration Criticism*. Copenhagen, 1961.

13 HARNOIS, GUY. *Les Théories du langage en France de 1660 à 1821*. Paris, 1928.

14 HOLMBERG, BÖRJE (ed.). *James Douglas on English Pronunciation*. Lund, 1956.

15 HONAN, PARK. "Eighteenth and Nineteenth Century English Punctuation Theory," *English Studies* (Amsterdam), XLI (1960), 92–102.

16 HORNBEAK, KATHERINE G. *The Complete Letter-Writer in English, 1568–1800*. Northampton, Mass., 1934.

1   Howes, Raymond F. *Historical Studies of Rhetoric and Rhetoricians.* Ithaca, N.Y., 1961.

2   Hudson, Roy F. "Rhetorical Invention in Colonial New England," *Speech Monographs,* XXV (1958), 215–221.

3   ———. "Richard Sibbes's Theory and Practice of Persuasion," *QJS,* XLIV (1958), 137–148.

4   Hultzén, Lee Sisson. "Seventeenth Century Intonation," *AS,* XIV (1939), 39–43.

5   Jones, Richard Foster. "The Rhetoric of Science in England of the Mid-Seventeenth Century," in *Restoration and Eighteenth-Century Literature: Essays in Honor of Alan Dugald McKillop.* Chicago, 1964. Pp. 5–24.

6   Kaye, R. B. "Mandeville on the Origin of Language," *MLN,* XXXIX (1924), 136–142.

7   Kökeritz, Helge. "English Pronunciation as Described in Short-hand Systems of the Seventeenth and Eighteenth Centuries," *Studia Neophilologica,* VII (1935), 73–146.

8   Kuehner, Paul. *Theories on the Origin and Formation of Language in the Eighteenth Century in France.* Philadelphia, 1944.

9   Landrum, G. W. "The First Colonial Grammars in English," *William and Mary College Review,* XIX (1939), 272–285.

10 Leonard, Sterling A. *The Doctrine of Correctness in English Usage, 1700–1800.* Madison, Wis., 1929; reprinted in New York, 1962.

11 Mace, D. T. "The Doctrine of Sound and Sense in Augustan Poetic Theory," *RES,* N.S. II (1951), 129–139.

12 Mann, Elizabeth. "The Problem of Originality in English Literary Criticism, 1750–1800," *PQ,* XVIII (1939), 97–118.

13 Matthews, William. "Polite Speech in the Eighteenth Century," *English,* I (1937), 493–511.

14 ———. "Some Eighteenth Century Vulgarisms," *RES,* XIII (1937), 307–325.

15 McMahon, Frederick R., Jr. "A History of Concepts of Style in English Public Address, 1600–1700." Unpublished dissertation presented to the University of Southern California, 1958.

16 Neumann, J. H. "Chesterfield and the Standard of Usage in English," *MLQ,* VII (1946), 463–475.

17 Nitchie, Elizabeth. "Longinus and the Theory of Poetic Imitation in Seventeenth and Eighteenth Century England," *SP,* XXXII (1935), 580–597.

1   PLATT, JOAN. "The Development of the English Colloquial Idiom
    during the Eighteenth Century," *RES*, II (1926), 70–81; 189–196.

2   POLITZER, ROBERT L. "A Detail in Rousseau's Thought: Language
    and Perfectibility," *MLN*, LXXII (1957), 42–47.

3   RAYBOULD, EDITH. "How Far was English Syntax Affected by
    Latin in the Age of Johnson?" *Innsbrucker Beiträge zur Kulturwissen-
    schaft*, III (1955), 221–229.

4   READ, ALLEN WALKER. "American Projects for an Academy to
    Regulate Speech," *PMLA*, LI (1936), 1141–1179.

5   ———. "Suggestions for an English Academy in the Latter Half
    of the Eighteenth Century," *MP*, XXXVI (1938), 145–156.

6   SANDFORD, W. P. *English Theories of Public Address, 1530–1828.*
    Columbus, Ohio, 1931.

7   SASEK, LAWRENCE A. *The Literary Temper of the English Puritans.*
    Baton Rouge, 1961.

8   SCHEURWEGHS, G. AND E. VORLAT. "Problems of the History of
    English Grammar," *English Studies* (Amsterdam), XL (1959), 135–
    143.
    The grammars discussed include those by Paul Greaves (1594), John
    Brightland (1711), and John Ash (1763).

9   SENGER, JULES. *L'Art Oratoire.* Paris, 1952.

10 SHAWCROSS, JOHN T. "One Aspect of Milton's Spelling: Idle
    Final 'E,' " *PMLA*, LXXVIII (1963), 501–510.

11 SHELDON, ESTHER K. "Walker's Influence on the Pronunciation of
    English," *PMLA*, LXII (1947), 130–146.

12 ———. "Boswell's English in the *London Journal*," *PMLA*, LXXI
    (1956), 1067–1093.

13 SPINGARN, JOEL E. (ed.). *Critical Essays of the Seventeenth Century.*
    3 vols. Oxford, 1908–1909.

14 STURZEN-BECKER, A. "Some Notes on English Pronunciation about
    1800," *Studia Neophilologica*, XIV (1941–43), 301–330.

15 SUGG, REDDING S., JR. "The Mood of Eighteenth-Century English
    Grammar," *PQ*, XLIII (1964), 239–52.

16 TUCKER, SUSIE I. "Christopher Smart and the English Language,"
    N&Q, N.S. V (1958), 468–469.

17 ———. *Protean Shape: A Study in Eighteenth-Century Vocabulary and
    Usage.* London, 1967.

1 WACKWITZ, BEATE. *Die Theorie des Prosastils im England des 18. Jahr-hunderts.* Hamburg: *Britannica et Americana*, Band 10, 1962.

2 WASSERMAN, EARL. "Nature Moralized: The Divine Analogy in the Eighteenth Century," *ELH*, XX (1953), 39-76.

3 WEBB, H. J. "An Eighteenth Century Semanticist," *Etc.*, VI (1948), 55-57.
Webb discusses a series of anonymous essays in the essay journal *The Connoisseur* (1754-1756).

4 WECTER, D. "Burke's Theory of Words, Images, and Emotion," *PMLA*, LV (1940), 167-181.

5 WILLIAMSON, MARGARET. *The Colloquial Language of the Common-wealth and Restoration.* Oxford, 1929.

THE NINETEENTH CENTURY

Major Works and Commentary

6 **Wordsworth, William.** "Preface" to the Second Edition of *Lyrical Ballads* (1800), in *The Poetical Works of William Wordsworth*, ed. E. de Selincourt (Oxford, 1944), pp. 384-409.

7 BARSTOW, MARJORIE L. *Wordsworth's Theory of Poetic Diction: A Study of the Historical and Personal Background of the "Lyrical Ballads."* New Haven, 1917.
This book is sometimes listed under the author's name by marriage: Marjorie Greenbie.

8 **Coleridge, Samuel Taylor.** *Coleridge on Logic and Learning*, ed. A. D. Snyder. New Haven, 1929.

9 HANFORD, JAMES HOLLY. "Coleridge as a Philologian," *MP*, XVI (1919), 119-140.

10 NEUMANN, J. H. "Coleridge on the English Language," *PMLA*, LXIII (1948), 642-661.

11 WARD, PATRICIA. "Coleridge's Critical Theory of the Symbol," *TSLL*, VIII (1966), 15-32.

12 WILEY, MARGARET L. "Coleridge and the Wheels of Intellect," *PMLA*, LXVII (1952), 101-112.

13 WILLOUGHBY, L. A. "Coleridge as a Philologist," *MLR*, XXXI (1936), 178-201.

14 **Mitford, William.** *An Inquiry into the Principles of Harmony in Language.* London (revised edition), 1804.

1   **Adams, John Quincy.** *Lectures on Rhetoric and Oratory* (1810), eds. J. Jeffrey Auer and Jerald L. Banninga. 2 vols. New York, 1962.

2   **Hazlitt, William.** *A New and Improved Grammar of the English Tongue for the Use of Schools.* Edinburgh, 1810.

3   ———. "On Familiar Style," in *The Complete Works of William Hazlitt,* ed. P. P. Howe (21 vols. London, 1930–1934), vol. VIII, pp. 242–247.

4   ———. "On the Prose Style of Poets," *ibid.,* vol. XII, pp. 5–17.

5   ———. "On Nicknames," *ibid.,* vol. XVII, pp. 44–51.

6   **Bentham, Jeremy.** *Essay on Logic,* in *The Works of Jeremy Bentham,* ed. John Bowring (11 vols. Edinburgh, 1838–1843; reprinted New York, 1962), vol. VIII, pp. 213–293.

7   ———. *Essay on Language, ibid.,* vol. VIII, pp. 295–338.

8   ———. *Fragment on Universal Grammar, ibid.,* vol. VIII, pp. 339–357.

9   BROCKRIEDE, WAYNE E. "Bentham's Criticism of Rhetoric and Rhetoricians," *QJS,* XLI (1955), 377–382.

10   ———. "Bentham's Philosophy of Rhetoric," *Speech Monographs,* XXIII (1956), 235–246.

11   OGDEN, CHARLES K. *Bentham's Theory of Fictions.* London, 1932.

12   **De Quincey, Thomas.** "The Danish Origin of the Lake-Country Dialect" (1819), in *The Collected Works of Thomas De Quincey,* ed. David Masson (14 vols. London, 1896–1897), vol. XIII, pp. 373–383.

13   ———. "English Dictionaries" (1823), *ibid.,* vol. X, pp. 430–435.

14   ———. "Rhetoric" (1828), *ibid.,* vol. X, pp. 81–133.

15   ———. "The English Language" (1839), *ibid.,* vol. XIV, pp. 146–161.

16   ———. "Style" (1840–1841), *ibid.,* vol. X, pp. 134–245.

17   ———. "Orthographic Mutineers" (1847), *ibid.,* vol. XI, pp. 437–452.

18   ———. "On Language" (first published in 1858), *ibid.,* vol. X, pp. 246–263.

19   ———. *Essays on Style, Rhetoric, and Language,* ed. F. N. Scott. Boston, 1893.

20   HOWELL, WILBUR S. "De Quincey on Science, Rhetoric, and Poetry," *Speech Monographs,* XIII (1946), 1–13.

1   JORDAN, JOHN E. "De Quincey on Wordsworth's Theory of Diction," *PMLA*, LXVIII (1953), 764–778.

2   PROCTOR, SIGMUND K. *Thomas De Quincey's Theory of Literature.* Ann Arbor: University of Michigan Publications in Language and Literature, XIX, 1943.

3   **Landor, Walter Savage.** "Conversation between Samuel Johnson and John Horne Tooke," from *Imaginary Conversations: First Series* (1824) in *The Complete Works of Walter Savage Landor*, eds. T. E. Welby and Stephen Wheeler (16 vols. London, 1927–1936), vol. IV.

4   ———. "Language and Orthography" (1835), *ibid.*, vol. XII.

5   ———. "Letter to An Author," from *Letters of Pericles and Aspasia* (1836), *ibid.*, vol. X.

6   **Whateley, Richard.** *Elements of Rhetoric: Comprising an Analysis of the Laws of Moral Evidence and of Persuasion, with Rules for Argumentative Composition and Elocution* (1828), ed. Douglas Ehninger. Carbondale, Ill., 1963.

7   PARRISH, WAYLAND M. "Whateley on Elocution," in *The Rhetorical Idiom: Essays in Rhetoric, Oratory, Language, and Drama*, ed. Donald C. Bryant. Ithaca, N.Y., 1958. Pp. 43–52.

8   PENCE, ORVILLE L. "The Concept of Logical Proof in the Rhetorical System of Richard Whateley," *Speech Monographs*, XX (1953), 23–38.

9   **Guest, Edwin A.** *A History of English Rhythms* (1838), ed. W. W. Skeat. London, 1882.

10 **Mill, John Stuart.** *A System of Logic, Ratiocinative and Inductive.* London, 1843.

11 BACKES, JAMES G. "The Relation of John Stuart Mill's Logical Theories and Rhetorical Practices," *DA*, XXIII (1963), 3543–3544.

12 **Poe, Edgar Allan.** "The Philosophy of Composition" (1846), in *The Works of Edgar Allan Poe*, eds. Edmund C. Stedman and George E. Woodberry. 10 vols. Chicago, 1894–1895, vol. VI, pp. 31–56.

13 ———. "The Rationale of Verse" (1848), *ibid.*, vol. VI, pp. 7–128.

14 NEUMANN, J. H. "Poe's Contributions to English," *AS*, XVIII (1943), 73–74.

15 WILSON, JAMES S. "Poe's Philosophy of Composition," *North American Review*, CCXXIII (1926–1927), 675–684.

1   Emerson, Ralph Waldo. "The Superlative" (1847), in *The Works of Ralph Waldo Emerson*, ed. Edward Waldo Emerson (12 vols. New York, 1904), vol. X, 161–179.

2   ———. "Art and Criticism" (1859), *ibid.*, vol. XII, pp. 283–305.

3   BASKERVILLE, BARNET. "Emerson as a Critic of Oratory," *Southern Speech Journal*, XVIII (1953), 150–162.

4   Dallas, Ernest Sweetland. *Poetics: An Essay on Poetry*. London, 1852.

5   ———. *The Gay Science*. London, 1866.

6   Patmore, Coventry. "English Metrical Critics," *North British Review*, XXVII (1857), 67–86.

7   ———. "English Metrical Law" (1875), in his *Amelia, Tamerton Church-Tower, etc.* London, 1878. Repr. and ed. N. A. Roth (Washington, D.C., 1961).

8   Müller, F. Max. *Lectures on the Science of Language*. 2 vols. London, 1861–1864.

9   Arnold, Matthew. *On Translating Homer*. London, 1862. Repr. and ed. R. H. Super in *On the Classical Tradition* (Ann Arbor, 1960), pp. 97–216.

10   Bagehot, Walter. "Wordsworth, Tennyson, and Browning; or, Pure, Ornate, and Grotesque Art in English Poetry" (1864), in *Literary Studies*, ed. Richard Holt Hutton (London, 1879), vol. II, pp. 338–390.

11   Butler, Samuel. "Thought and Language" (1872), in *The Humour of Homer and Other Essays*, ed. R. A. Streatfield. London, 1913.

12   Minto, William. *A Manual of English Prose: Literature, Biographical and Critical, Designed Mainly to Show Characteristics of Style*. London, 1872.

13   Spencer, Herbert. *The Philosophy of Style*. New York, 1873.

14   Hopkins, Gerard Manley. *The Letters of Gerard Manley Hopkins to Robert Bridges* and *The Correspondence of Gerard Manley Hopkins and Richard Watson Dixon*, ed. C. C. Abbott. 2 vols. London, 1937; revised 1956.

15   ———. *The Journals and Papers of Gerard Manley Hopkins*, eds. Humphrey House and Graham Storey. London, 1959.

16   Phelps, Austin. *English Style in Public Discourse with Special Reference to the Usages of the Pulpit*. New York, 1883. Revised with Henry A. Frink and titled *Rhetoric: Its Theory and Practice*. New York, 1895.

1   Lanier, Sidney. "The Science of English Verse" (1880) and "Essays on Music," Volume II of *The Centennial Edition of the Works of Sidney Lanier*, eds. Charles R. Anderson *et al.* 10 vols. Baltimore, 1945.

2   Bridges, Robert. *Milton's Prosody.* Oxford, 1889.

3   ————. "Poetic Diction in English," in *Collected Essays, Papers . . . of Robert Bridges* (London, 1930), pp. 59–70.

4   KELLOG, GEORGE A. "Bridges' *Milton's Prosody* and Renaissance Metrical Theory," *PMLA*, LXVIII (1953), 268–285.

5   Pater, Walter. *Appreciations, with an Essay on Style.* New York, 1889.

6   WELLEK, RENÉ. "Walter Pater's Literary Theory and Criticism," *UTQ*, XXVII (1958), 424–433.

7   Masson, David. "Essay on Milton's Versification," in his *Poetical Works of John Milton.* 3 vols. London, 1893.

8   Newman, John Henry. *Poetry, with Reference to Aristotle's "Poetics,"* ed. Albert S. Cook. Boston, 1891. Selection in *English Critical Essays of the Nineteenth Century*, ed. Edmund D. Jones (London, 1922), pp. 223–253.

9   TILLOTSON, GEOFFREY. "Newman's Essay on Poetry: An Exposition and Comment," in his *Criticism and the Nineteenth Century* (London, 1951), pp. 147–187.

10   Mallock, W. H. "Le style c'est l'homme," *The New Review*, VI (Jan.–June 1892), 441–454.

11   Courthope, William John. *Life in Poetry: Law in Taste: Two Series of Lectures Delivered in Oxford, 1895–1900.* London, 1901.

12   Raleigh, Walter. *Style.* London, 1897.
Raleigh's style lectures are interesting, though they seem a little old-fashioned today: "All style is gesture, the gesture of the mind and of the soul. Mind we have in common, inasmuch as the laws of right reason are not different for different minds. Therefore clearness and arrangement can be taught, sheer incompetence in the art of expression can be partly remedied. But who shall impose laws upon the soul?" (p. 127).

13   Whibley, Charles. "Language and Style," *Fortnightly Review*, N.S. LXV (Jan.–June 1899), 100–109.

General Secondary Sources

14   AARSLEFF, HANS. "The Study of Language in England, 1780–1860," *DA*, XXI (1960), 1944–1945.

1   ———. *The Study of Language in England, 1780–1860*. Princeton, 1967.

2   BERGENHAN, M. E. "The Doctrine of Correctness in English Usage in the Nineteenth Century," *Summaries of Doctoral Dissertations, University of Wisconsin*, IV (1941), 230–232.

3   BRONSTEIN, ARTHUR J. "Nineteenth Century Attitudes towards Pronunciation," *QJS*, XL (1954), 417–421.

4   GUTHRIE, WARREN. "The Development of Rhetorical Theory in America, 1635–1850," *Speech Monographs*, XIII (1946), 14–22; XIV (1947), 38–54; XV (1948), 61–71; XVI (1949), 98–113; XVIII (1951), 17–30.

5   HABERMAN, FREDERICK W. *The Elocutionary Movement in England, 1750–1850*. Unpublished dissertation presented to Cornell University, 1947.

6   HOBEN, JOHN B. "Mark Twain: On the Writer's Use of Language," *AS*, XXXI (1956), 163–171.

7   HONAN, PARK. "Eighteenth and Nineteenth Century English Pronunciation Theory," *English Studies* (Amsterdam), XLI (1960), 92–102.

8   READ, ALLEN WALKER. "American Projects for an Academy to Regulate Speech," *PMLA*, LI (1936), 1141–1179.

9   STEPHEN, LESLIE. *The English Utilitarians*. 3 vols. London, 1900.

10   WARREN, ALBA H., JR. *English Poetic Theory, 1825–1865*. Princeton, 1950.

III. ENGLISH STYLISTICS
IN THE TWENTIETH CENTURY

DEFINING CREATIVITY AND "STYLE"

1   ALLEN, DON CAMERON. "Style and Certitude," *ELH*, XV (1948), 167–175.

2   ALLERS, RUDOLF. "Some Reflections on the Problems of Universal Style," *Modern Aesthetics*, IV (1960), 387–394.

3   ARAGON, LOUIS. *Traité du Style*. Paris, 1928.

4   ARONSTEIN, PHILIPP. "On Style and Styles in Languages," *AS*, IX (1934), 243–251.

5   ARTS, FREDERICK B. *From the Renaissance to Romanticism: Trends in Style in Art, Literature and Music, 1300–1830*. Chicago, 1962.

6   BAILEY, JOHN CANN. "The Grand Style: An Attempt at Definition," *Essays and Studies by Members of the English Association*, II (1911), 104–132; reprinted in his *The Continuity of Letters*. Oxford, 1923.

7   BEARDSLEY, MONROE C. "Style and Good Style," in *New Rhetorics*, ed. Martin Steinmann, Jr. (New York, 1967), pp. 191–213.

8   BELLOC, HILAIRE. "On Lucidity," in *A Conversation with an Angel, and Other Essays*. New York, 1929. Pp. 180–191.

9   BERGLER, EDMUND. "Myth, Merit, and Mirage of Literary Style," *Imago*, VII (1950), 279–287.

1 BOSTWICK, ARTHUR E. *Earmarks of Literature.* Chicago, 1914.

2 BREWSTER, WILLIAM T. (ed.). *Representative Essays on the Theory of Style.* New York, 1928.
Contains essays by Newman, De Quincey, Herbert Spencer, G. H. Lewes, Stevenson, Pater, and Frederic Harrison.

3 BROWN, ROLLO WALTER. *The Writer's Art by Those Who Have Practiced It.* Cambridge, Mass., 1921.

4 BROWNELL, WILLIAM C. *The Genius of Style.* New York, 1924.
Brownell treats "style" as a value term; a work has style "when the detail, counting in itself, also contributes to the general effect" (p. 11).

5 BURKE, KENNETH. "Style," in *Permanence and Change: An Anatomy of Purpose.* Los Altos, Calif., 1954. Pp. 50–54.

6 CHASSÉ, CHARLES. *Styles et physiologie: petite histoire naturelle des écrivains.* Paris, 1928.

7 COOPER, LANE (ed.). *Theories of Style, with Special Reference to Prose Composition.* New York and London, 1912.
Contents: Lane Cooper, "Wackernagel's Theory of Prose and of Style," pp. 1–22; selections or essays by Plato, Aristotle, Longinus, Swift, Buffon, Voltaire, Goethe, Coleridge, De Quincey, Thoreau, Schopenhauer, Herbert Spencer, G. H. Lewes, Stevenson, Pater, Ferdinand Brunetière, and Frederic Harrison.

8 CRADDOCK, SISTER CLAIRE EILEEN. *Style Theories as Found in Stylistic Studies of Romance Scholars (1900–1950).* Washington, D. C.: Catholic University of America Studies in Romance Languages and Literatures, vol. XVIII, 1952.

9 CRESSOT, MARCEL. *Le Style et ses techniques.* Paris, 1947.

10 DEUTSCHBEIN, MAX. *Neuenglische Stilistik.* Leipzig, 1932.

11 DRAPER, RONALD PHILIP. "Style and Matter," in *Langue et Littérature*, pp. 319–320.
Draper asserts that "style can convey a meaning independent of matter without employing the 'special vocabulary' of poetic diction" (p. 319). The style of a Donne poem, for example, may contrast effectively with its subject.

12 ——. "Style and Matter," *Revue des langues vivantes* (Bruxelles), XXVII (1960), 15–23.

13 FERNÁNDEZ RETAMAR, ROBERTO. *Idea de la estilística.* Habana, 1958.

14 FISHER, WALTER R. "The Importance of Style in Systems of Rhetoric," *Southern Speech Journal*, XXVII (1962), 173–182.

15 FOOTE, DOROTHY NORRIS. "The Style is *Which Man?*" *CEA Critic*, XXV, i (1962), 4–5.

1   FRYE, NORTHROP. *Anatomy of Criticism.* Princeton, 1947.
     See especially pp. 267–269, 330–331.

2   FULCHER, PAUL M. (ed.). *Foundations of English Style.* New York,
     1928.

3   GALSWORTHY, JOHN. *On Expression.* London: English Association
     Pamphlet #59, 1924.

4   GEORGIN, RENÉ. *Les Secrets du style: un inventoire précis des moyens
     d'expression.* Paris, 1961.

5   ———. *L'Inflation du style.* Paris, 1963.

6   DE GOURMONT, RÉMY. "Concerning Style or Writing," in *Decadence
     and Other Essays on the Culture of Ideas.* Paris, 1921. Pp. 165–187.

7   GRADENWITZ, PETER. "Mid-eighteenth Century Transformations
     of Style," *Music and Letters,* XVIII (1937), 265–275.
     Gradenwitz is concerned with social factors that influenced eighteenth-
     century composers and led to the rise of "Viennese classicism"; literary
     style is not his concern.

8   GRAMMONT, MAURICE. *Essai de psychologie linguistique: style et poésie.*
     Paris, 1950.

9   GUIRAUD, PIERRE. *Qu'est-ce que c'est la stylistique?* Paris, 1954.

10   ———. *La Stylistique.* Paris, 1963.

11   HEARN, LAFCADIO. "On Romantic and Classic Literature in Rela-
     tion to Style," in *Interpretations of Literature,* selected and edited by
     John Erskine. New York, 1915. Vol. I, pp. 11–24.

12   HOLLANDER, JOHN. "Opening Statement: [the Style Conference]
     From the Viewpoint of Literary Criticism," in *Style in Language,*
     pp. 396–407.

13   HULME, T. E. *Notes on Language and Style,* ed. Herbert Read.
     Seattle, Washington, 1929.

14   INGARDEN, ROMAN. "The General Question of the Essence of Form
     and Content," *Journal of Philosophy,* LVII (1960), 22–23.

15   ———. "Raccourcis de perspective du temps dans la concrétisa-
     tion de l'oeuvre littéraire," *Revue métaphysique et de morale,* LXV
     (1960), 19–51.

16   "In Pursuit of Style," TLS (October 23, 1959), 609.

17   JOOS, MARTIN. "The Isolation of Styles," *Georgetown Monographs 12*
     (1961), 107–113.
     Joos presents in condensed form some of the ideas on style and usage
     variables that later appeared in *The Five Clocks.* Although the varieties

of style that he describes do not all appear in the written language, his categories provide a valuable framework for style studies.

1   ———. *The Five Clocks.* Bloomington, Ind.: Publication Twenty-two of the Research Center in Anthropology, Folklore, and Linguistics, 1962; reprinted New York, 1967.

The Five Clocks is written in a casual or even intimate style and is concerned with a variety of topics about language. Joos's remarks on literary style are fresh and sometimes unorthodox: "Literary good form is whatever keeps the reader feeling at home" (Bloomington ed., p. 41).

2   KAINZ, FRIEDRICH. "Vorarbeiten zu einer Philosophie des Stils," *Zeitschrift für Aesthetic,* XX (1926), 21–63.

3   KROEBER, A. L. *Style and Civilization.* Ithaca, N.Y., 1957.

4   KUHNS, RICHARD F. "Perception, Understanding and Style: A Study in the Foundations of Criticism Derived from an Examination of Artistic Creativity and Appreciation," *DA,* XVI (1956), 548–549.

5   KUZNEC, M. D., AND I. M. SKREBNEV. *Stilistika Anglijskogo Jazyka* [Stylistics of the English Language]. Leningrad, 1960.

Review article by R. Gläser, *Zeitschrift für Anglistik und Amerikanistik,* IX (1961), 435–438.

6   LERNER, LAURENCE D. "Style," in *Encyclopedia of Poetry and Poetics,* eds. Alex Preminger *et al.* (Princeton, 1965), pp. 814–817.

7   [LEVIN, HARRY]. "Expressive Voices: The Emergence of a National Style," *TLS* (September 17, 1954), xii–xiv.

8   LOTT, BERNARD. *Style and Linguistics.* Djakarta, 1960. Lott's lecture was delivered at the University of Indonesia on October 31, 1959.

9   LUCAS, F. L. *Style.* London, 1955.

10   MARTIN, HOWARD H. " 'Style' in the Golden Age," *QJS,* XLIII (1957), 374–382.

11   MAYENOWA, MARIE RENATA. "Zalozenia poetyke lingwistcznej" ["The principles of linguistic poetics"], Polska Akademia Nauk, *Sprawaozdania z prac naukowych wydzialu nauk spolecznych,* VI, ii (1963), 25–26.

12   McINTOSH, ANGUS. "Language and Style," *Durham University Journal,* XXIV (1963), 116–123.

McIntosh's article is the text of a lecture given by him in 1962 and attempts to serve two purposes. First, he argues that the teaching of grammar in schools should be generative (in the broad sense) and not just descriptive. Second, he shows that language in good literature contains delicate grammatical nuances. "Style, we might almost say, is a matter of the selection of particular grammatical patterns and sequences of patterns, and of particular items of vocabulary and sequences of items; and of course (by implication) the avoidance of others" (p. 120).

1 ———. "Some Thoughts on Style," in Angus McIntosh and M. A. K. Halliday, *Patterns of Language: Essays in General, Descriptive, and Applied Linguistics* (London, 1966), pp. 83–97.

2 MOREUX, T. *Science et style: conseils à un jeune écrivain.* Paris, 1930.

3 MORIER, HENRI. *La Psychologie des styles.* Genève, 1959.

4 MURRY, JOHN MIDDLETON. *The Problem of Style.* Oxford, 1922.
Murry's series of lectures on style emphasizes the notion of style as an organic aspect of writing: "style is not an isolable quality of writing; it is writing itself" (p. 77). "Style is a quality of language which communicates precisely emotions or thoughts, or a system of emotions or thoughts, peculiar to the author. . . . Style is perfect when the communication of the thought or emotion is exactly accomplished; its position in the scale of absolute greatness, however, will depend upon the comprehensiveness of the system of emotions and thoughts to which the reference is perceptible" (p. 71).

5 MYERS, HENRY ALONSO. "Style and the Man," *South Atlantic Quarterly,* XL (1941), 259–268.

6 NICHOLSON, MEREDITH. *Style and the Man.* Indianapolis, 1911.

7 ORTEGA Y GASSET, JOSÉ. "Fraseología y sinceridad," in *El Espectador.* Madrid, 1928. Vol. V, pp. 185–209.

8 ORWELL, GEORGE [pseud. of Eric Blair]. "Politics and the English Language," in *Shooting an Elephant and Other Essays.* New York, 1950. Pp. 77–92.

9 OSGOOD, CHARLES E. "Some Effects of Motivation on Style of Encoding," in *Style in Language.* Pp. 293–307.
Osgood and his associates studied stylistic variables between suicide and pseudosuicide notes; a more detailed description of the experiment appears in Charles E. Osgood and E. Walker, "Motivation and Language Behavior: A Content Analysis of Suicide Notes," *The Journal of Abnormal and Social Psychology,* LIX (1959), 58–67. Osgood begins with the assumption that "any language includes both obligatory and variable features at all levels of analysis, phonemic, morphemic, and syntactical. The study of style concerns the *variable features* of the code" (p. 293).

10 PORIER, RICHARD. "Worlds of Style," *Partisan Review,* XXXIII (1966), 509–524, 631–650.

11 RIFFATERRE, MICHAEL. "Vers la définition linguistique du style," *Word,* XVII (1961), 318–344.
Review article of *Style in Language.*

1   ROUSE, W. H. D. "Style," *Essays and Studies*, XXVII (1941), 52–65.

2   RUSSELL, GEORGE WILLIAM ERSKINE. "Style," in *Essays for Today*, ed. F. H. Pritchard. London, 1924. Pp. 238–248.

3   SAIDLA, LEO E. A. *Essay for the Study of Structure and Style*. New York, 1939.

4   SAMUEL, HERBERT. *On Style*. London, 1941.

5   SANDMANN, MANFRED. "Syntaxe verbale et style épique," in *Atti del VIII Congresso Internazionale di Studi Romanzi*. Firenze, 1960.

6   SARTRE, JEAN PAUL. *What is Literature*, tr. Bernard Frechtman. London, 1950.

7   SAYCE, R. A. "The Definition of the Term 'Style,' " in *Proceedings of the Third Congress of the International Comparative Literature Association*. The Hague, 1962. Pp. 156–166.

8   SCHAPIRO, MEYER. "Style," in *Anthropology Today: An Encyclopedic Inventory*, ed. A. L. Kroeber. Chicago, 1953. Pp. 287–312.
    Schapiro is mostly concerned with "style" as a broad cultural phenomenon but he does say a little about literature: "although some writers conceive of style as a kind of syntax or compositional pattern, which can be analyzed mathematically, in practice one has been unable to do without the vague language of qualities in describing styles" (p. 289).

9   SCHÖDEL, HEINZ, AND ROSELIND REIMANN. "Observations sur l'usage du mot 'style,' " *Bulletin d'Information du Laboratoire d'Analyse Lexicologique* (Besançon), no. 5 (1961), 43–53.

10 SEMPOUX, ANDRÉ. "Notes sur l'histoire des mots 'style' et 'stylistique,' " *Revue Belge de Philologie et d'Histoire*, XXXIX (1961), 736–746.

11 SONTAG, SUSAN. "On Style," *Partisan Review*, XXXII (1965), 543–560.

12 SYPHER, WYLIE. *Four Stages of Renaissance Style: Transformations in Art and Literature, 1400–1700*. Garden City, N.Y., 1955.

13 TILLOTSON, GEOFFREY. "*Ars Celare Artem*," *Style* (Arkansas), I (1967), 65–68.

14 WELLEK, RENÉ, AND AUSTIN WARREN. "Style and Stylistics," in their *Theory of Literature*. New York, 1956, pp. 163–174.

15 WELLEK, RENÉ. "Closing Statement: [the Style Conference] From the Viewpoint of Literary Criticism," in *Style in Language*, pp. 408–419.

1   ———. *Concepts of Criticism*, ed. Stephen G. Nichols, Jr. New Haven and London, 1963.

A chapter entitled "The Revolt against Positivism" contains a brief history of early twentieth-century literary criticism in Eastern Europe with special reference to Russian Formalism, Czech structuralism, and Polish literary theory and criticism.

2   WIMSATT, W. K., JR. "Verbal Style: Logical and Counterlogical," *PMLA*, LXV (1950), 5–20; reprinted in his *The Verbal Icon*. Lexington, Ky., 1954, and New York, 1958. Pp. 201–217.

MODES OF STYLISTIC INVESTIGATION

Theories and Strategies of Treating a Text

3   ALBALAT, ANTOINE. *Le travail du style: enseigné par les corrections manuscrites des grands écrivains*. Paris, 1903.

4   ALONZO, AMADO. "The Stylistic Interpretation of Literary Texts," *MLN*, LVII (1942), 489–496.

5   ARONSTEIN, PHILIPP. *Englische Stilistik*. Leipzig and Berlin, 1924.

6   AUERBACH, ERICH. *Mimesis: The Representation of Reality in Western Literature*, tr. Willard Trask. Princeton, 1953.

7   BAILEY, RICHARD W. "Current Trends in the Analysis of Style," *Style* (Arkansas), I (1967), 1–14.

Bailey surveys four trends in stylistics: the intuitive, the descriptive, the comparative, and the Gestalt.

8   BAKER, R. J. "A Linguistic Theory of Criticism," *Canadian Literature*, II (1960), 73–76.

Review of Jean-Paul Vinay and J. Darbelnet, *Stylistique comparée du français et de l'anglais*. Paris, 1958.

9   BARTHES, ROLAND. *Le degré zéro de l'écriture*. Paris, 1953.

10   ———. *On Racine*, tr. Richard Howard. New York, 1964.

Barthes approaches the study of Racine from the point of view of structuralism. Particular features of language are related to larger units of structure in Racine's tragedies.

11   ———. *Essais critiques*. Paris, 1964.

12   BAUMGÄRTNER, KLAUS. "Formale Erklärung poetischer Texte," in *Mathematik und Dichtung*, pp. 67–84.

13   BEARDSLEY, MONROE. "The Language of Literature," reprinted from his *Aesthetics* (1958) in Chatman and Levin, pp. 283–295.

1 BENAMOU, MICHEL. "Pour une pédagogie du style littéraire," *The French Review*, XXXVII (1963), 158–168.

Benamou presents a method of stylistic analysis based on the theory that style results from deviations from linguistic conventions. The theory is exemplified by the analysis of a sentence from Proust, and by brief studies of connectives in Voltaire, adjectives in Colette, and verbs in Camus.

2 BIERWISCH, MANFRED. "Poetik und Linguistik," in *Mathematik und Dichtung*, pp. 49–66.

3 BINNS, A. L. " 'Linguistic' Reading: Two Suggestions of the Quality of Literature," in *Essays on Style and Language*, pp. 118–134.

4 BLACKMUR, R. P. *Language as Gesture*. New York, 1952.

5 BLOCH, BERNARD. "Linguistic Structure and Linguistic Analysis," *Georgetown Monograph* 4 (1953), 40–44.

"The style of a discourse is the message carried by the frequency distributions and transitional probabilities of its linguistic features, especially as they differ from those of the same features in the language as a whole" (p. 42).

6 BLOCK, HASKELL M. "Theory of Language in Gustave Flaubert and James Joyce," in *Langue et Littérature*, p. 305.

"Flaubert's theory of *le mot juste* must be seen as both intrinsic and contextual in application: as Joyce was also to insist, the writer must study etymology and the history of his language so as to be able to use words precisely; but the appropriateness of a particular word depends on its place in the total orchestration of the whole composition. For both Flaubert and Joyce, rhythm expresses a reciprocal relationship of whole and part" (p. 305).

7 BÖCKMANN, PAUL. "Stil- und Formprobleme in der Literatur," in *Stil- und Formprobleme*, pp. 11–15.

8 BOOTH, ANDREW D., L. BRANDWOOD, AND J. P. CLEAVE. *The Mechanical Resolution of Linguistic Problems*. London, 1958.

Brandwood's experiment to discover the chronological order of Plato's work is described in Chapter Four, "Stylistic Analysis," pp. 50–65.

9 BRADBROOK, MURIEL. "Fifty Years of Criticism of Shakespeare's Style," *Shakespeare Survey*, VII (1954), 1–11.

10 BREWSTER, WILLIAM T. *Studies in Structure and Style*. New York, 1903.

11 BROWER, REUBEN A. *The Fields of Light*. New York, 1951.

12 BROWNE, ROBERT. "Grammar and Rhetoric in Criticism," *TSLL*, III (1961), 144–151.

13 BRUNEAU, CHARLES. "La Stylistique," *Romance Philology*, V (1951), 1–14.

1 BURKE, KENNETH. *A Rhetoric of Motives.* New York, 1945.

2 CANNON, GARLAND. "Linguistics and Literature," *CE*, XXI (1960), 254–260; Bobbs-Merrill Reprint, *Language-11.*

3 CASSIRER, E. A. "Structuralism in Modern Linguistics," *Word*, I (1945), 99–120.

4 CASTAGNINO, RAÚL H. *El análisis literario: Introducción metodológica a una estilística integral.* Buenos Aires, 1953.

5 CHARLESTON, BRITTA M. *Studies on the Emotional and Affective Means of Expression in Modern English.* Berne, 1960.

6 CHATMAN, SEYMOUR B. "Linguistics and Teaching Introductory Literature," *Language Learning*, VII (1956–1957), 3–10; *Readings I*, pp. 407–412; *Readings II*, pp. 500–506.

7 ———. "Linguistic Style, Literary Style and Performance: Some Distinctions," *Georgetown Monographs 13* (1962), 73–81.

8 ———. "Reading Literature as Problem Solving," *English Journal*, LII (1963), 346–352.

9 ———. "On the Theory of Literary Style," *Linguistics*, No. 27 (1966), 13–25.

Chatman attacks the theory of style held by Wimsatt and Beardsley whose attachment to meaning he finds overly comprehensive. "For 'style' to be maximally useful as a critical term, it ought to be limited even further, to refer to a literary manner which is homogeneous and recognizable. The stylists are those whose manners have a sufficient persistence of quality, a characterizing density such that no matter where one cuts the discourse he is likely to get something which is characteristically *it*" (p. 18).

10 CHATMAN, SEYMOUR, AND SAMUEL R. LEVIN. "Linguistics and Poetics," in *Encyclopedia of Poetry and Poetics*, eds. Alex Preminger *et al.* (Princeton, 1965), pp. 450–457.

11 CHATMAN, SEYMOUR, AND SAMUEL R. LEVIN (eds.). *Essays on the Language of Literature.* Boston, 1967.

The authors present a collection of thirty-one essays, most of which have appeared in the last decade. The five groups into which the essays are arranged are "Sound Texture," "Metrics," "Grammar," "Literary Form and Meaning," and "Style and Stylistics."

12 CHRISTENSEN, FRANCIS. "A Generative Rhetoric of the Sentence," *CCC*, XIV (1963); reprinted in his *Notes Toward a New Rhetoric* (New York, 1967), pp. 1–22.

13 ———. "A Generative Rhetoric of the Paragraph," *CCC*, XVI (1965), 144–156; reprinted in his *Notes Toward a New Rhetoric* (New York, 1967), pp. 52–81.

1   COTEANU, I. "Considerations upon the Stylistic Structure of Language," *Revue Roumaine de Linguistique*, VII (1962), 223–241.

2   CRANE, R. S. *The Language of Criticism and the Structure of Poetry.* Toronto, 1953.

3   CRESSOT, MARCEL. *Le style et ses techniques: précis d'analyse stylistique.* Paris, 1947.

4   CUNNINGHAM, J. V. (ed.). *The Problem of Style.* Greenwich, Conn., 1966.

"A comprehensive history of the idea of style, documented in the works of the major literary critics from Aristotle to René Wellek."

5   DANIELLS, ROY. "Baroque Form in English Literature," *UTQ*, XIV (1945), 393–408.

6   DAVIE, DONALD. *The Language of Science and the Language of Literature: 1700–1740.* London and New York, 1953.

7   DEARING, VINTON A. "The Use of a Computer in Analyzing Dryden's Spelling," *Literary Data Processing Conference: Proceedings.* Yorktown Heights, N.Y., 1964. Pp. 200–210.

8   DE GROOT, A. WILLEM. "Phonetics and Its Relations to Aesthetics," in *Manual of Phonetics*, ed. L. Kaiser. Amsterdam, 1957. Pp. 385–400.

9   DEVOTO, GIACOMO. *Studi di stilistica.* Firenze, 1950.

10   ———. *Linguistics and Literary Criticism*, tr. M. F. Edgerton, Jr. New York, 1963.

11   DOLEŽEL, LUBOMÍR. "Vers la stylistique structurale," *Travaux Linguistiques de Prague*, I (1964), 257–266.

12   ———, AND K. HAUSENBLAS. "The Interrelationship of Poetics and Stylistics," in *Poetics*, pp. 39–52. In Russian.

13   DORFLES, G. "Pro ou contre une esthétique structurale?" *Revue Internationale de Philosophie*, XIX (1965), 409–441.

14   DRESDEN, S. "Stylistique et science de la littérature," *Neophilologus*, XXXVI (1952), 193–205.

15   DRIJKONINGEN, F. F. J. "Stilistiek en het onderzoek der periodestijlen," *Forum der Letteren*, IV (1963), 207–214.

16   EATON, T. "The Semantics of Literature," *Proceedings of the Ninth Congress of the Australasian Universities' Languages and Literature Association, 19–26 August 1964.* Melbourne, 1964. Pp. 132–133.

17   EFIMOV, N. I. *Stilistika khudozhestvennoi rechi* [Stylistics of Artistic Language]. Moskva, 1961.

1 EICHENBAUM, BORIS. "The Theory of the 'Formal Method,'" in
   Russian Formalist Criticism: Four Essays, translation introduction by
   Lee T. Lemon and Marion J. Reis. Lincoln, Nebraska, 1965.
   Pp. 102–139.

2 EMPSON, WILLIAM. *Seven Types of Ambiguity*. London, 1930.
   See: Elder Olson, "William Empson: Contemporary Criticism and
   Poetic Diction," in *Critics and Criticism: Ancient and Modern*, by R. S.
   Crane *et al*. Chicago, 1952. Pp. 45–82.

3 ENKVIST, NILS ERIK, JOHN SPENCER, AND MICHAEL J. GREGORY.
   Linguistics and Style. London, 1964.
   See the review by David Crystal, *Journal of Linguistics*, I (1965),
   173–179.

4 ERLICH, VICTOR. "Russian Poets in Search of a Poetics," *Comparative Literature*, IV (1952), 54–74.

5 ――――. "Limits of the Biographical Approach," *Comparative Literature*, VI (1954), 130–137.

6 ――――. "Russian Formalism—In Perspective," *JAAC*, XIII
   (1954), 215–225.

7 ――――. *Russian Formalism—History, Doctrine*. The Hague, 1955.
   Second revised edition, 1965.
   In his first section, Erlich describes the emergence of Russian Formalism from the concern for poetic form shown by symbolist criticism.
   He outlines the concerns of the Moscow Linguistic Circle (founded in
   1915 by Roman Jakobson and G. O. Vinokur) and the parallel work
   of the Petersburg *Opojaz* (founded in 1916 by Osip Brik). The section
   ends with a description of the official rejection of formalism by the
   doctrinaire Marxist critics. In his second section, Erlich analyzes the
   literary concerns of the formalists and relates them to such Western
   critical schools as American New Criticism.

8 EUSTIS, ALVIN A., JR. "Stylistics," in *Encyclopedia of Poetry and
   Poetics*, eds. Alex Preminger *et al*. (Princeton, 1965), pp. 817–818.

9 FISCHER, HARDI. "Entwicklung und Beurteilung des Stils," in
   Mathematik und Dichtung, pp. 171–184.

10 FLEISHMAN, AVROM. "The Criticism of Quality: Notes for a Theory
   of Style," *University Review*, XXXIII (1966), 3–10.

11 FÓNAGY, IVAN. "l'Information du style verbal," *Linguistics*, No. 4
   (1964), 19–47.

12 ――――. "Form and Function of Poetic Language," *Diogenes*, LI
   (1965), 72–110.

13 ――――. "Der Ausdruck als Inhalt," in *Mathematik und Dichtung*,
   pp. 243–274.

1   FOWLER, ROGER. "Linguistic Theory and the Study of Literature," *Essays on Style and Language*, pp. 1–28.

2   ———. "Linguistics, Stylistics; Criticism?," *Lingua*, XVI (1966), 153–165.

3   ———. "Argument II. Literature and Linguistics," *EIC*, XVII (1967), 322–335.

Fowler replies to a review of his *Essays on Style and Language* by Helen Vendler and an editorial postscript by F. W. Bateson (*EIC*, XVI [1966], 457–463). In answer to Mrs. Vendler's assertion that linguists approach literature with obtuseness and insensitivity, Fowler argues "from the theoretical potential rather than the published attainment of linguistic critics" (p. 322); for the moment, he says, linguistics may serve criticism only by bringing every detail of the literary work to the attention of the critic. In a following argument (pp. 335–347), Bateson says that "the sort of co-operation that Mr. Fowler and his colleagues are pleading for is a vain hope" (p. 335). Linguistics old and new, Bateson argues, has only occasional and superficial utility for the main business of the literary critic.

4   FRANCIS, W. NELSON. "Linguistics and Literature," in his *The Structure of American English*. New York, 1958. Pp. 569–573.

"Specifically, structural linguistics can aid the study and teaching of literature in two ways. (1) It can supply a solid foundation of linguistic analysis upon which a critical analysis of the artistic structure of a work of literature can be based. (2) It can supply a method of analysis which can be extended into the metalinguistic and artistic realms where the critic works" (p. 571).

5   ———. "Syntax and Literary Interpretation," *Georgetown Monographs 13* (1962), 83–92; *Readings II*, pp. 515–522; reprinted in Chatman and Levin, pp. 209–216.

6   FRANGEŠ, IVO. "Quelques remarques sur les déviations de style," in *Langue et Littérature*, pp. 240–242.

Frangeš points out that such critics as Bally and Spitzer have viewed style in terms of deviations from the norms of everyday language. He argues that a more limited view of "deviation" is necessary: "Ainsi norme et déviation ne doivent être prises qu'en tant que termes appartenant à la stylistique descriptive ne pouvant avoir ni valeur esthétique, ni critique. Il va de soi qu'il reste encore beaucoup à faire pour déterminer ce qu'est la norme" (p. 242).

7   FRYE, NORTHROP. *The Well-Tempered Critic*. Bloomington, Ind., 1963.

8   GALINSKY, HANS. "The Overseas Writer and the Literary Language of the Mother Country: American and British English as Viewed by American Writers from Whitman through Wilder," in *Langue et Littérature*, p. 437.

Galinsky notes a generally defensive and nationalistic view of American

English until the time of T. S. Eliot when "the problem . . . lost its sharp American, traditionally American contours" (p. 438).

1 GARVIN, PAUL (ed.). *A Prague School Reader on Esthetics, Literary Structure, and Style.* Washington, D.C., 1964.
Contents: Bohuslav Havránek, "The Functional Differentiation of Standard Language," pp. 3–16; Jan Mukařovský, "Standard Language and Poetic Language," pp. 17–30; Jan Mukařovský, "The Esthetics of Language," pp. 31–70; Felix Vodička, "The History of the Echo of Literary Works," pp. 71–82; Jiří Veltruský, "Man and Object in the Theatre," pp. 83–92; Vladimír Procházka, "Notes on Translating Technique," pp. 93–112; Jan Mukařovský, "The Connection between the Prosodic Line and Word Order in Czech Verse," pp. 113–132; Jan Mukařovský, "K. Čapek's Prose as Lyrical Melody and as Dialogue," pp. 133–152; Paul Garvin, "A Critical Bibliography of Prague School Writings on Esthetics, Literary Structure, and Style," pp. 153–163.

2 GENETTE, G. "La rhétorique et l'espace du langage," *Tel Quel,* XIX (1964), 44–54.

3 ———. "Structuralisme et critique littéraire," *L'Arc,* XXVI (1965), 30–44.

4 GERHARDT, DIETRICH. "Stil und Einfluss," in *Stil- und Formprobleme,* pp. 51–65.

5 GOKAK, V. K. *The Poetic Approach to Language, with Special Reference to the History of English.* London, [1952].

6 GOLINO, E. "Dal formalismo allo strutturalismo," *Tempo Presente,* XI (1966), 60–64.

7 GÓRNY, WOJCIECH. "Text Structure Against the Background of Language Structure," in *Poetics,* pp. 25–37.
Górny examines the principles of Prague structuralism. "The text style is a structural quality of the text resulting from the choice, disposition and transformation of the speech elements" (p. 32).

8 GRAY, BARBARA B. "An Inquiry into the Problem of Style: A Negative Experiment," *DA,* XXV (1965), 5257–5258.

9 GRAY, BENNISON. "The Lesson of Leo Spitzer," *MLR,* LXI (1966), 547–555.

10 GREENFIELD, STANLEY B. "Grammar and Meaning in Poetry," *PMLA,* LXXXII (1967), 377–387.
Greenfield surveys major trends in the discussion of the grammar of poetry since 1960 with particular attention to S. R. Levin's *Linguistic Structures in Poetry,* J. McH. Sinclair's "Taking a Poem to Pieces," and M. A. K. Halliday's "The Linguistic Study of Literary Texts." He concludes with a discussion of two passages from *Beowulf* in an effort

to illustrate further the "way in which grammatical analysis of selected passages and lines can illuminate poetic meaning and effect" (p. 386).

1   GUIRAUD, PIERRE. "Stylistiques," *Neophilologus*, XXXVIII (1954), 1–12.

2   HALLIDAY, M. A. K. "The Linguistic Study of Literary Texts," in *Ninth Congress Papers*, pp. 302–307; reprinted in Chatman and Levin, pp. 217–223.
"It is part of the task of linguistics to describe texts; and all texts, including those, prose and verse, which fall within any definition of 'literature,' are accessible to analysis by the existing methods of linguistics. In talking of 'the linguistic study' of literary texts we mean, of course, not 'the study of the language,' but 'the study [of the language] by the theories and methods of linguistics.' There is a crucial difference between the *ad hoc*, personal and arbitrary selective statements offered, frequently in support of a preformulated literary thesis, as 'textual' or 'linguistic' statements about literature, and an analysis founded on general linguistic theory and descriptive linguistics. It is the latter that may reasonably be called 'linguistic stylistics' " (p. 302).

3   ———. "Descriptive Linguistics in Literary Studies," in *English Studies: Third Series*, ed. G. I. Duthie (Edinburgh, 1964), pp. 25–39; reprinted in *Patterns of Language: Papers in General, Descriptive and Applied Linguistics*, by Angus McIntosh and M. A. K. Halliday (London, 1966), pp. 42–55.

4   HAMILTON, KENNETH GORDON. *The Two Harmonies: Poetry and Prose in the Seventeenth Century*. Oxford, 1963.

5   HARKINS, WILLIAM F. "Slavic Formalist Theories in Literary Scholarship," *Word*, VII (1951), 177–185.

6   HARTMAN, GEOFFREY. "Structuralism: The Anglo-American Adventure," *Yale French Studies*, XXXVI–XXXVII (1966), 148–168.

7   HASAN, RUQAIYA. "The Linguistic Study of Literary Texts." Unpublished dissertation presented for the Diploma in Applied Linguistics, University of Edinburgh, 1961.

8   HATZFELD, HELMUT. "The Language of the Poet," *SP*, XLIII (1946), 93–120.

9   ———. "Stylistic Criticism as Art-Minded Philology," *Yale French Studies*, II (1949), 62–70.
Hatzfeld surveys the influence of such style critics as Bally, Spitzer, and Alonso on literary theory in France. "Style investigation and criticism have many if not all of their tasks in common, the finding of decisive original traits in a literary text, the coordination of these traits into a reasonable unity, the explanation of the same style principle in the whole and in the details and the evaluation of the stylistic compound as a product belonging to the esthetical order" (p. 63).

1 ———. "Two Spanish Methods of Style Investigation," in *Miscelánea filológica dedicada a Mons. A. Griera.* Barcelona, 1955. Vol. I, pp. 347–352.
On Amado Alonso and Dámaso Alonso.

2 ———. "Methods of Stylistic Investigation," in *Literature and Science: Proceedings of the Sixth Congress of the International Federation of Modern Languages and Literatures.* Oxford, 1955. Pp. 44–51.

3 ———. "Baroque Style: Ideology and the Arts," *Bucknell Review*, VII (1957), 71–79.

4 ———. *Trends and Styles in Twentieth-Century French Literature.* Washington, D.C., 1957.

5 ———. "Recent Italian Stylistic Theory and Stylistic Criticism," in *Studia Philologia et Litteraria in Honorem L. Spitzer,* eds. A. G. Hatcher and K. L. Selig. Bern, 1958. Pp. 227–243.

6 ———. "Peut-on systématiser l'analyse stylistique?" in *Langue et Littérature,* pp. 231–234.
"Il est évident que, pour faire l'analyse organique d'une oeuvre, il faut partir de son contenu, du moins de sa dominante sémantique, de son idée maîtresse en tant que perceptible de prime abord. Cette forme simple de pensée, devenue style, est le motif, souligné par sa répétition dans une distribution proportionée, et pour cela par analogie à la musique, appelé leitmotif" (p. 232).

7 HEILMAN, ROBERT B. "Poetic and Prosaic: Program Notes on Opposite Numbers," *Pacific Spectator*, V (1951), 454–463.

8 HELLINGA, W. G., AND H. VAN DER MERWE SCHOLTZ. *Kreatiewe analise van taalgebruik: Prinsipes van stilistiek op linguistiese grondslag* [Creative Analysis of Linguistic Usage: Principles of Stylistics on a Linguistic Base]. Amsterdam, 1955.

9 HILL, ARCHIBALD A. "Towards a Literary Analysis," in *English Studies in Honor of James Southall Wilson,* ed. Fredson Bowers. Charlottesville, Va., 1951. Pp. 147–165.

10 ———. "Correctness and Style in English Composition," *CE*, XII (1951), 280–285; *Readings II*, 389–395.

11 ———. "Stylistics," in his *Introduction to Linguistic Structures: From Sound to Sentence in English.* New York, 1958. Pp. 406–409.
"The function of stylistics is to reduce the area of linguistic arbitrariness by explaining as much as possible of linguistic variation" (p. 408).

12 ———. "Linguistics and the College Teacher of Language, Literature, or Composition," *CLA Journal*, II (1958), 75–86.

1   ———. "A Program for the Definition of Literature," *University of Texas Studies in English*, XXXVII (1958), 46–52; abstract in *Style in Language*, pp. 94–95.

2   ———. "Principles Governing Semantic Parallels," *TSLL*, I (1959), 356–365; *Readings II*, pp. 506–514.

3   ———. "Linguistic Principles for Interpreting Meaning," *CE*, XXII (1961), 466–473.

4   HOCKETT, CHARLES F. "Literature," in *A Course in Modern Linguistics*. New York, 1958. Pp. 553–565.

5   HOLSTI, OLE R., with the collaboration of JOANNE K. LOOMBA and ROBERT C. NORTH. "Content Analysis." To appear in *The Handbook of Social Psychology* (second edition), eds. Gardner Lindsey and Elliot Aronson (Cambridge, Mass.: Addison-Wesley).

6   HORALEK, K. "Sprachfunktion und funktionelle Stilistik," *Linguistics*, XIV (1965), 14–22.
The author discusses the theories of style propounded by Bühler, Mukařovský, and Jakobson.

7   HOWARD-HILL, TREVOR H. "Computer Analysis of Shakespearean Texts," *Shakespeare Newsletter*, XIV (1964), 79.
The author presents a more extended version of this paper in "Shakespeare, Crane, and the Computer," *Proceedings of the 1965 International Conference on Computational Linguistics* (Detroit, 1965).

8   ———. "Computer Analysis of Shakespearean Texts: II," *Shakespeare Newsletter*, XVI (1966), 7.

9   HOWELL, WILBUR SAMUEL. "Renaissance Rhetoric and Modern Rhetoric: A Study in Change," in *The Rhetorical Idiom: Essays in Rhetoric, Oratory, and Drama*, ed. Donald C. Bryant. Ithaca, N.Y., 1958. Pp. 53–70.

10   HYMES, DELL H. "On the Typology of Cognitive Styles in Language (with Examples from Chinookan)," *Anthropological Linguistics*, III (1961), 22–54.

11   HYTIER, J. "La Méthode de M. L. Spitzer," *Romantic Review*, XLI (1950), 42–59.
Review article on *Linguistics and Literary History*.

12   IVANOVÁ-SALINGOVÁ, MÁRIA. "Zakladni problemy jazykoveho stylu umeleckej literatury" ["Fundamental Questions of Literary Style from the Point of View of Linguistics"], *Slovenska Literatura*, IX (1962), 195–206.

13   ———. "The Basic Characteristics of the Category of Individual Linguistic Style," in *Asian and African Studies*, ed. Jozef Blaškovič (Bratislava, 1965), vol. I, pp. 131–138.

1   IVES, SUMNER. "A Theory of Literary Dialect," *Tulane Studies in English*, II (1950), 137–182.

2   ———. "Dialect Differentiation in the Stories of Joel Chandler Harris," *AL*, XVII (1955), 33–96; *Readings I*, pp. 413–420; *Readings II*, pp. 523–529.

3   ———. "Grammatical Analysis and Literary Criticism," *Georgetown Monographs 13* (1962), 99–107.

4   ———. "Grammar and Style," *English Journal*, LII (1963), 364–370; reprinted in Sumner Ives and Stephen O. Mitchell, *Language, Style, Ideas: The Writer's Challenge*. New York, 1964. Pp. 132–142. Ives proposes a pedagogical system of style analysis that makes use of "a procedure for symbolizing and abstracting grammatical constituents . . . which is relatively fast and easily taught, which can be used with passages of considerable length, and which leaves the original text in its original form, preserving even its punctuation and word order" (p. 132). The procedure that Ives describes is a modified IC labelled tree diagram.

5   JAKOBSON, ROMAN. "Linguistics and Poetics," in *Style in Language*, pp. 350–378; reprinted in Chatman and Levin, pp. 323–336.

6   ———. "Du réalisme artistique," *Tel Quel*, XXIV (1966), 33–41.

7   ———. "Grammatical Parallelism and Its Russian Facet," *Language*, XLII (1966), 399–429.

8   ———. "Poesie der Grammatik und Grammatik der Poesie," in *Mathematik und Dichtung*, pp. 21–32.

9   ———. *Selected Writings, Volume IV: Slavic Epic Studies*. The Hague, 1966.

10   JUILLAND, ALPHONSE G. Review of Charles Bruneau's *L'Epoque Réaliste: Première Partie: Fin du Romantisme et Parnasse, Language*, XXX (1954); reprinted in Chatman and Levin, pp. 374–384. Juilland offers thoughtful and still timely remarks on the relation of linguistics and stylistics.

11   KAYSER, WOLFGANG. *Das sprachliche Kunstwerk: eine Einführung in die Literaturwissenschaft*. Bern, 1948.

12   KLANICZAY, TIBOR. "Styles et histoire du style," in *Littérature hongroise, littérature européenne*, ed. István Sótér and Ottó Süpek (Budapest, 1964), pp. 9–50.

13   KNAUER, KARL. "Die Analyse von Feinstrukturen im sprachlichen Zeitkunstwerk," in *Mathematik und Dichtung*, pp. 193–210.

14   KOCH, WALTER ALFRED. "On the principles of stylistics," *Lingua*, XII (1963), 411–422.

1   ———. "Predictability of Literary Structure and Some Didactic Consequences: A Linguistic Approach," *Orbis*, XIV (1965), 303–311.

2   ———. *Recurrence and a Three-Modal Approach to Poetry*. The Hague, 1966.

3   KRIDL, MANFRED. "Russian Formalism," *The American Bookman*, I (1944), 19–30.

4   ———. "The Integral Method of Literary Scholarship: Theses for Discussion," *Comparative Literature*, III (1951), 18–31.

5   LABOV, WILLIAM, AND JOSHUA WALETZKY. "Narrative Analysis: Oral Versions of Personal Experience," in *Essays on the Verbal and Visual Arts: Proceedings of the 1966 Annual Spring Meeting of the American Ethnological Society* (Seattle, 1967), pp. 12–44.
From an examination of the formal and functional properties of fourteen American folk anecdotes, the authors propose a structural framework in which "the simplest and most fundamental narrative structures are analyzed in direct connection with their originating functions" (p. 12). The method is clearly amenable to the analysis of more sophisticated narratives, and, in fact, the functional segments they discern are quite similar to the subdivisions of the classical oration.

6   LaDRIÈRE, J. CRAIG. "Literary Form and Form in the Other Arts," in *Stil- und Formprobleme*, pp. 28–37.

7   LEE, BRIAN. "The New Criticism and the Language of Poetry," *Essays on Style and Language*, pp. 29–52.

8   LEHMANN, WINFRED P. "The Stony Idiom of the Brain: Symbolic Manipulation of Language in Literature," in *Literary Symbolism: A Symposium*, ed. Helmut Rehder (Austin, 1965), pp. 11–30.

9   LEVIN, SAMUEL R. "Poetry and Grammaticalness," in *Ninth Congress Papers*, pp. 308–314; reprinted in Chatman and Levin, pp. 224–230.
Levin discusses the relation of "ungrammatical" poetic sequences to a generative grammar of the language. "The important fact about sequences like *a grief ago* is that the grammar limits the framework within which the attempts to render the sequence grammatical must take place. This fact has two important effects; it makes feasible the grammaticalizing of the sequence, and it brings into association with the element(s) in the sequence a group of forms with narrow, well-defined meanings. This latter type of confrontation probably lies behind all metaphor" (p. 314).

10   ———. "On Automatic Production of Poetic Sequences," *TSLL*, V (1963), 138–146.

1 ————. "Deviation—Statistical and Determinate—in Poetic Language," *Lingua*, XII (1963), 276–290.

Levin explores the use of a generative grammar to enable a critic to define "deviations" in poetic language. ". . . the criterion of non-generability provides a determinate measure for ascertaining whether a given sequence is deviant or not. It also makes clear that the use of the grammar makes inferences possible about the manner or degree in which different sequences are deviant. I wish also to maintain that the results correspond with native-speaker intuitions about these sequences" (pp. 289–290).

2 ————. "Two Grammatical Approaches to Poetic Analysis," *CCC*, XVI (1965), 256–260.

Levin contrasts the "traditional" approach to linguistics and poetry of Josephine Miles and Leo Spitzer with that offered by a generative grammar. As in his earlier statements, Levin puts high value on poetic sequences that somehow deviate from the grammar of non-poetic language: "Many sentences occurring in poetry will, of course, be judged well-formed by the grammar. Such sequences are then either not especially poetic, or their poeticalness derives from attributes other than their particular syntactic structure" (258).

3 ————. "Internal and External Deviation in Poetry," *Word*, XXI (1965), 225–237.

4 LEVY, R. "A New Credo of Stylistics," *Symposium*, III (1949), 321–334.
Review of Spitzer's *Linguistics and Literary History*.

5 LOESCH, KATHERINE T. "Literary Ambiguity and Oral Performance," *QJS*, LI (1965), 258–267.

6 MAPES, E. K. "Implications of Some Recent Studies on Style," *Revue de Littérature Comparée*, XVIII (1938), 514–533.

7 MAROUZEAU, J. "Comment aborder l'étude du style," *Le français moderne*, XI (1943), 1–6.

8 ————. "Nature, degrés et qualité de l'expression stylistique," in *Stil- und Formprobleme*, pp. 15–18.

9 McINTOSH, ANGUS. "Patterns and Ranges," *Language*, XXXVII (1961), 325–337; reprinted in *Patterns of Language: Papers in General, Descriptive and Applied Linguistics* (London, 1966), pp. 183–199.

McIntosh posits "four obviously distinct stylistic modes: normal collocations and normal grammar, unusual collocations and normal grammar, normal collocations and unusual grammar, unusual collocations and unusual grammar" (p. 333). "In particular I have tried to deal with the factor of *range*, and to suggest that the term might profitably be used in connection with lexis in a sense whereby it then answers to what on the grammatical side, I have labeled *pattern*. Pattern has to do with structures of the sentences we make; range has to do with

the specific collocations we make in a series of particular instances"
(p. 337).

1   MESSING, G. M. "Structuralism and Literary Tradition," *Language*,
    XXVII (1951), 1–12.

2   MILIC, LOUIS T. "Against the Typology of Styles," in Chatman
    and Levin, pp. 442–450.

3   ——. "Metaphysics in the Criticism of Style," *CCC*, XVII
    (1966), 124–129; reprinted in *New Rhetorics*, ed. Martin Steinmann,
    Jr. (New York, 1967), pp. 161–175.

4   ——. "Making Haste Slowly in Literary Computation," in
    Computers in Humanistic Research, ed. Edmund A. Bowles (Englewood
    Cliffs, N.J., 1967), pp. 143–152.

5   MORGAN, BAYARD QUINCY. "Some Functions of Time in Speech,"
    AS, XX (1945), 28–33.

6   MORISON, ELTING (ed.). *American Style: Essays in Value and Perform-
    ance.* New York, 1958.

7   MORRIS, EDWARD P. "A Science of Style," *Transactions and Proceed-
    ings of the American Philological Association*, XLVI (1915), 103–118.
    In this Presidential address to the American Philological Association,
    Morris claims that language study has reached a point where stylistics
    "is now ready to be organized into a distinct science" (p. 109). He
    then goes on to suggest some of the questions that the new science must
    examine.

8   MOWATT, D. G., AND P. F. DEMBOWSKI. "Literary Study and
    Linguistics," *Canadian Journal of Linguistics*, XI (1965), 40–62.

9   MUNRO, THOMAS. "Style in the Arts: A Method of Stylistic Anal-
    ysis," *JAAC*, V (1946), 128–158.

10 MUNTEANO, B. "Constantes humaines en littérature: l'éternel débat
    de la 'raison' et du 'coeur,' " in *Stil- und Formprobleme*. Pp. 66–67.

11 NOWOTTNY, WINIFRED. *The Language Poets Use.* London, 1962.
    In chapters on diction, metaphor, ambiguity, and symbolism, the
    author examines the elements of poetic language in order "to come
    nearer, not to a tidy solution of it, but to a clearer sight of the dimen-
    sions and intricacy of the problem of talking about poetic language
    at all" (pp. 24–25). The author uses methods offered by the tradition
    of *explication de texte*, the New Critics, and descriptive linguistics.

12 PAISLEY, W. J. "Identifying the Unknown Communicator in Paint-
    ing, Literature, and Music: The Significance of Minor Encoding
    Habits," *The Journal of Communication*, XIV (1964), 219–237.
    Paisley calls for the development of a "scientific connoisseurship" to
    aid in the study of attribution problems. "To focus on objective

characteristics of the text, a concept such as 'encoding habits' should
be substituted for 'style.' Then the unique character of a work may be
defined in terms of successive decisions made by the communicator as
he chooses from his repertory of symbols (notes, words, brush strokes,
etc.)" (p. 219).

1   PARRISH, S. M. "Computers and the Muse of Literature," in
    Computers in Humanistic Research, ed. Edmund A. Bowles (Englewood
    Cliffs, N.J., 1967), pp. 124–134.

2   PASCAL, ROY. "Tense and Novel," *MLR*, LVII (1962), 1–11.
    Pascal discusses Dr. Käte Hamburger's grammatical approach to
    stylistic interpretation.

3   PERRY, MARY FRANCES. "Linguistics as a Basis for Literary Criti-
    cism," *DA*, XXV (1965), 5921.

4   PIKE, KENNETH L. "Language—Where Science and Poetry Meet,"
    CE, XXVI (1965), 283–286; 291–292.

5   PIPPING, ROLF. *Språch och Stil*. Stockholm, 1940. Second edition,
    1964.

6   *Poetika*. (Publication of the Division of the Verbal Arts at the
    Petrograd State Institute of Art History). Vol. I (1926). Reprinted
    The Hague, 1966.

7   POLLOCK, THOMAS CLARK. *The Nature of Literature: Its Relation to
    Science, Language, and Human Experience*. Princeton, 1942.

8   POMORSKA, KRYSTYNA. *Russian Formalist Theory and its Poetic Am-
    bience*. The Hague (forthcoming).

9   POSNER, REBECCA. "Linguistique et littérature," *Marche Romane*,
    XII (1963), 38–56.

10 PRIOR, M. E. *The Language of Tragedy*. New York, 1948.

11 PROPP, VLADIMIR. *Morphology of the Folktale*, tr. Laurence Scott.
    IJAL: Publication X of the Research Center in Anthropology,
    Folklore, and Linguistics (1958).
    See remarks by Roman Jakobson in *Style in Language*, p. 374; Claude
    Lévi-Strauss, "L'Analyse morphologique des contes russes," *Inter-
    national Journal of Slavic Linguistics and Poetics*, III (1960), 122–149.

12 ———. *Morfologia della fiaba*. Torino, 1966.
    This Italian translation of Propp's work is accompanied by an
    article of Lévi-Strauss, "La structure et la forme," and an answer to
    this essay from Propp.

13 *Readings in Russian Poetics*. Ann Arbor: Michigan Slavic Materials,
    No. 2, 1962.
    A reprint, in Russian, of the most valuable texts of the Russian for-

malists; included are: M. M. Batin, B. M. Eichenbaum, R. Jakobson, Ju. Tynjanov, V. V. Vinogradov, V. N. Volosinov.

1   REUM, ALBRECHT. *A Dictionary of English Style.* Munich, 1961.

2   RICHARDS, I. A. "Poetic Process and Literary Analysis," in *Style in Language*, pp. 9–23; reprinted in Chatman and Levin, pp. 323–336.

Richards discusses the creative process involved in writing poems; he uses his own poem "Harvard Yard in April/April in Harvard Yard" as an example. In the second part of the paper, Richards suggests some of the ways in which linguistics may help to discriminate relevant and irrelevant remarks about a poem.

3   ———. "Variant Readings and Misreading," in *Style in Language*, pp. 241–252.

"A sound account of interpretation must build into itself a duty to be critical. A linguistics that is properly aware of the processes through which language grows in the individual and of the effects that his attitudes to language can have upon its health in him must be concerned with pedagogy and with what sorts of assumptions are spread in the school. Poor pedagogy in the thinking of linguistic authorities is in its own way quite as alarming as bad linguistic doctrine in the classroom" (p. 252).

4   RICKERT, EDITH. *New Methods for the Study of Literature.* Chicago, 1927.

5   RIFFATERRE, MICHAEL. "Réponse à M. Leo Spitzer: sur la méthode stylistique," *MLN*, LXXIII (1958), 474–480.

6   ———. "Criteria for Style Analysis," *Word*, XV (1959), 154–174; reprinted in Chatman and Levin, pp. 412–430.

Riffaterre proposes a method of stylistic analysis whereby stylistic devices (SD's) are identified and analyzed. The "interdependence between the SD and its perception is, in short, so central to the problem that it seems to me we may use this perception to locate stylistic data in the literary discourse" (p. 162). "The stylistic context is a linguistic *pattern suddenly broken by an element which was unpredictable*" (p. 171). "Once stylistic facts have been identified, linguistic analysis, applied to them only, will be relevant; prior to their identification, it cannot alone isolate them" (p. 174).

7   ———. "Stylistic Context," *Word*, XVI (1960), 207–218; reprinted in Chatman and Levin, pp. 323–336.

As in the preceding paper, Riffaterre emphasizes the role of predictability in bringing the stylistic effect to the attention of the reader. "It should be possible to build a (stylistic) grammar of the conditions under which contrasts occur; some of their aspects are obvious enough to permit the establishment of relative measurements; for example, the effectiveness of the contrast is in direct proportion to its degree of unpredictability, that is, to the degree of predictability allowed by the internal context" (p. 209). See Riffaterre's "La durée de la valeur stylistique du néologisme," *Romantic Review*, XLIV (1953), 282–289.

1 ———. "Problèmes d'analyse du style littéraire," *Romance Philology*, XIV (1961), 216–227.

2 ———. "The Stylistic Function," in *Ninth Congress Papers*, pp. 316–322.

"Stylistics studies those features of linguistic utterances that are intended to impose the encoder's way of thinking on the decoder, i.e., it studies the act of communication not as merely producing a verbal chain, but as bearing the imprint of the speaker's personality, and as compelling the addressee's attention. In short, it studies the ways of linguistic efficiency (expressiveness) in carrying a high load of information. The most complex techniques of expressiveness can be considered—with or without esthetic intentions on the author's part—as verbal art, and stylistics also investigates literary style" (p. 209).

3 ———. "L'étude stylistique des formes littéraires conventionnelles," *French Review*, XXXVIII (1964), 3–14.

4 ———. "Describing Poetic Structures: Two Approaches to Baudelaire's *Les Chats*," *Yale French Studies*, XXXVI–XXXVII (1966), 200–242.

Riffaterre rejects the "unmodified structural linguistics" offered by Roman Jakobson and Claude Lévi-Strauss ("*Les Chats* de Charles Baudelaire," *L'Homme*, II (1962), 5–21) and argues that "a proper consideration of the nature of the poetic phenomenon will give us the vantage point required" (p. 214). Such consideration, he says, relates poetic structures to the responses—not of the Average Reader posited in his earlier essays—but of a "superreader" who combines the responses of all previous critics, Larousse lexicographers who wrote entries on the words of the poem, and "informants such as students of mine and other souls whom fate has thrown my way" (p. 215).

5 RIPPERE, VICTORIA L. "Towards an Anthropology of Literature," *Yale French Studies*, XXXVI–XXXVII (1966), 243–251.

6 ROCKAS, LEO. "The Description of Style: Dr. Johnson and His Critics," *DA*, XXI (1961), 338–339.

7 ———. *Modes of Rhetoric*. New York, 1964.

8 ROSIELLO, L. "Stilistica e strutturalismo linguistico," *Sigma*, IX (1966), 5–20.

9 ROSSI, ALDO. "Storicismo e strutturalismo," *Paragone* XIV (1963), 3–28.

10 ———. "Strutturalismo e analisi letteraria (II)," *Paragone* XV (1964), 24–78.

11 ROTHWELL, KENNETH S. "Grammar, History, and Criticism," *CE*, XXVII (1965), 27–32.

12 RUDNYCKYJ, J. B. "Functions of Proper Names in Literary Works," in *Stil- und Formprobleme*. Pp. 378–383.

1   Rus, Louis C. "Structural Ambiguity: A Note of Meaning and the Linguistic Analysis of Literature with Illustrations from E. E. Cummings," *Language Learning*, VI (1955), 62–68.

2   *Russian Formalist Criticism: Four Essays*, tr. Lee T. Lemon and Marion J. Reis. Lincoln, Neb., 1965.
     The essays on the formalist method and theory with particular application to prose fiction are written by Shklovsky, Tomashevsky, and Eichenbaum.

3   Rynell, Alarik. *Parataxis and Hypotaxis as a Criterion of Syntax and Style, Especially in Old English Poetry*. Lund, 1952.

4   Saporta, Sol, and Thomas A. Sebeok. "Linguistics and Content Analysis," in *Trends in Content Analysis*. Pp. 131–150.

5   Saporta, Sol. "The Application of Linguistics to the Study of Poetic Language," in *Style in Language*, pp. 82–93.
     "The style of a message will be described in terms of the relations of the linguistic features to one another, not in terms of the relations of linguistic features to non-linguistic features, so that questions of truth, intention, etc., will fall in a different area of literary analysis" (p. 89). Saporta endorses the notion that stylistic features are characterized by being deviations from the norms of the language.

6   Sayce, R. A. "Literature and Language," *EIC*, VII (1957), 119–133; Bobbs-Merrill Reprint, *Language-80*.

7   Schlauch, Margaret. "Modern English Style and Stylistics," in her *The English Language in Modern Times (Since 1400)*. Warszawa, 1959. Pp. 228–233.
     Schlauch reviews the contribution of Aronstein, Deutschbein, and others to the analysis of English style. "In spite of the variety of styles presented by contemporary writing and speaking, English stylistics (that is, the study of style) has not yet been discussed on the same scale as, for instance, French, German and Russian (p. 228).

8   Schmidt, Franz. "Satz und Stil," in *Mathematik und Dichtung*, pp. 159–170.

9   Scholes, Robert J. "Some Objections to Levin's 'Deviation,'" *Lingua*, XIII (1965), 189–192.

10   Schooneveld, Cornelis H. Van. "Literary Realism as a Linguistic Problem," in *Poetics*, pp. 471–474.

11   Schrader, Helen W. *A Linguistic Approach to the Study of Rhetorical Style*. Unpublished dissertation presented to Northwestern University, 1949.

12   "A Science of Literature," *TLS* (January 20, 1961), p. 40.
     An extensive article on stylistics and a review of Stephen Ullmann's *The Image in the Modern French Novel: Gide, Alain-Fournier, Proust, Camus*. Cambridge, 1960.

1   SCOTT, CHARLES T. *Persian and Arabic Riddles: A Language-Centered Approach to Genre Definition*. Bloomington, Ind.: Publication Thirty-Nine of the Indiana University Research Center in Anthropology, Folklore, and Linguistics, 1965.

Scott attempts to define and describe his collection of riddles in terms of their "stylistic structures." "Style," he writes, "is nothing if it is not an overt, conscious striving for design on the part of the artist" (p. 5). In presenting his conclusions (pp. 62–76), Scott explains the relation of his study to Pike's tagmemic model. Following Pike, he ends his study with a suggestion of how riddles fit into a broader "nonverbal matrix" within the culture.

2   SEARY, E. R. "The Place of Linguistics in Literary Study," *Journal of the Canadian Linguistic Association*, I (1955), 9–13.

3   SEBEOK, THOMAS, AND VALDIS J. ZEPS. "Computer Research in Psycholinguistics: Towards an Analysis of Poetic Language," *Behavioral Science*, VI (1961), 365–368.

4   SEBEOK, THOMAS A. "Notes on the Digital Calculator as a Tool for Analyzing Literary Information," in *Poetics*, pp. 571–590.

Sebeok presents an extensive flow chart to characterize some of the many problems facing literary-linguistic analysis.

5   SECHEHAYE, C. A. "La Stylistique et la linguistique théorique," in *Mélanges de linguistique offerts à M. Ferdinand de Saussure*. Paris, 1908. Pp. 153–187.

6   SEIDLER, HERBERT. *Allgemeine Stilistik*. Göttingen, 1953 and 1963.

7   *Shakespeare Newsletter: Special Computer Studies Issue*, XV (1965), 51–58.

8   SHERBO, ARTHUR. "The Uses and Abuses of Internal Evidence," *BNYPL*, LXIII (1959), 5–22; reprinted in *Evidence for Authorship: Essays on Problems of Attribution*, eds. David V. Erdman and Ephim G. Fogel (Ithaca, 1966), pp. 6–24.

Of the two sorts of internal evidence—style and ideas—Sherbo argues that ideas provide much the surer stay in support of attribution hypotheses.

9   SHERMAN, L. A. *Analytics of Literature*. Boston, 1893.

10   ———. "On Certain Facts and Principles in the Development of Form in Literature," *University of Nebraska Studies*, I (1888), 119–130.

11   SHKLOVSKY, VICTOR. "Art as Technique," in *Russian Formalist Criticism: Four Essays*, tr. Lee T. Lemon and Marion J. Reis. Lincoln, Neb., 1965. Pp. 3–24.

This early manifesto of Russian Formalism has been translated into French as "L'art comme procédé," by T. Todorov in *Tel Quel*, XXI (1965), 3–18.

1   SLEDD, JAMES. "A Note on Linguistics and Literary Study," *CLA Newsletter*, VIII (1956).

2   SPITZER, LEO. *Stilstudien*. 2 vols. Munich, 1928 and 1961.

3   ———. *Linguistics and Literary History: Essays in Stylistics*. Princeton, 1948.

"What [the literary scholar] must be asked to do, however, is, I believe, to work from the surface to the 'inward life-center' of the work of art: first observing details about the superficial appearance of the particular work (and the 'ideas' expressed by a poet are, also, only one of the superficial traits in a work of art); then, grouping these details and seeking to integrate them into a creative principle which may have been present in the soul of the artist; and, finally, making the return trip to all the other groups of observations in order to find whether the 'inward form' one has tentatively constructed gives an account of the whole" (p. 19). "The first step is the awareness of having been struck by a detail, followed by a conviction that this detail is connected basically with the work of art; it means that one has made an 'observation,'—which is the starting point of a theory, that one has been prompted to raise a question—which must find an answer" (pp. 26–27). The subjectivity of Spitzer's "first step" has been attacked by some stylistic theoreticians.

4   ———. *Essays in Historical Semantics*. New York, 1948.

5   ———. *A Method of Interpreting Literature*. Northampton, Mass., 1949.

6   ———. "Les Théories de la stylistique," *Le français moderne*, XX (1952), 165–168.

7   ———. "The Individual Factor in Linguistic Innovations," *Cultura Neolatina* XVI (1956), 71–89.

8   ———. "Les Etudes de style et les différents pays," in *Langue et Littérature*, pp. 23–38.

In this paper, delivered only a few days before his death, Spitzer surveys the beginnings of analytical stylistics in Germany and the rise of New Criticism in America. In discussing the "biographical fallacy," Spitzer reacts against the concern for author psychology that marked his earlier work. After a brief survey of Russian Formalism, he finishes with a sharp attack on "la carence stylistique en France."

9   ———. "Language of Poetry," in *Language: An Enquiry into Its Meaning and Function* (New York, 1957), pp. 201–231.

10   STANKIEWICZ, EDWARD. "Linguistics and the Study of Poetic Language," in *Style in Language*, pp. 69–81.

Stankiewicz discusses several approaches to literature—such as mythic and biographical criticism—besides linguistic analysis. Poets are innovators, he says, in introducing new forms into a code or language; such innovations include new metrical patterns, the use of familiar words in unexpected ways, and the creation of unusual syntactic structures. "The student of poetry is in no position to describe and to explain the nature of poetic language unless he takes into account the rules of language which determine its organization, just as the linguist cannot properly understand the forms of poetic expression unless he considers the forces of tradition and culture that affect the specific character of poetry" (p. 81).

1 STEIN, GERTRUDE. *Lectures in America.* Boston, 1935.
In her lecture on "Poetry and Grammar," Miss Stein states that "verbs and adverbs aided by prepositions and conjunctions with pronouns" possess "the whole of the active life of the writing."

2 STENDER-PETERSEN, A. "Esquisse d'une théorie structurale de la littérature," *Travaux du Cercle Linguistique de Copenhagen*, V (1949), 277–287.

3 STRADA, V. "Stile, struttura, storia," *Sigma*, IX (1966).

4 STUTTERHEIM, C. F. P. "Modern Stylistics," *Lingua*, I (1948), 410–426.
Summary: "The author has tried to unite the analysis of stylistics and the analysis of the object aimed at by dealing with a few problems which reveal themselves as such in the existing stylistic literature. After a short typification of this literature, especially in its contrast with traditional rhetoric, various opinions about the sort of style—particularly about the styles of periods, the literary genres and the style of poetry and that of prose—are discussed. The author shows what is problematical in all these aspects. A solution of these problems is impossible, if they have not been sharply outlined beforehand" (p. 410).

5 ———. "Modern Stylistics," *Lingua*, III (1952), 52–68.
Summary: "In this second article about modern stylistics the author deals with the problems by which the student of stylistics finds himself faced when—as he must—he appeals to experience in his description of concrete form-elements and style-elements. The level of awareness of theoretical reflection and the level of awareness of experience may lie far or less far apart. Sometimes it is no longer possible to reach the latter level from the former. What cannot be identified as a moment in the totality of the experience cannot be a style element" (p. 52).

6 ———. "Poetry and Prose: Their Interrelations and Transitional Forms," in *Poetics*, pp. 225–237.

7 *Style et Littérature.* The Hague, 1962.
The four essays contained in this volume are: Pierre Guiraud, "Les tendances de la stylistique contemporaine," pp. 9–23; Paul Zumthor, "Stylistique et poétique," pp. 25–38; A. Kibédi Varga, "A la recherche d'un style baroque dans la poésie française, poésie et vision du monde," pp. 39–74; J. A. G. Tans, "La poétique de l'eau et de la lumière d'après l'oeuvre d'Albert Camus," pp. 75–86.

1 *Stylistics, Linguistics and Literary Criticism.* New York, 1961.
Sol Saporta introduces three papers that were delivered at an MLA section meeting on Spanish Literature and Medieval Literature in 1961. Saporta says: "A modern linguist approaching literature brings with him a set of assumptions. For example, he distinguishes the abstract aspect of language from its physical aspect, that is, *code* from *message*. Linguistics involves the description of the code; stylistics is the description of the message" (p. 8). The three papers are by Edmund de Chasca, Heles Contreras, and Ramón Martínez-López.

2 SUIFFET BIANCHI, NORMA. "De la antigua retórica a la nueva estilística," *Revista Nacional* (Montevideo), IX (1964), 252–268.

3 TESNIÈRE, LUCIEN. "Utilisation du stemma pour l'étude de style," in his *Éléments de syntaxe structurale.* Paris, 1959. P. 632.
Tesnière claims that his method of syntactic description "a l'avantage de permettre de se rendre compte explicitement des caractéristiques de style contenues implicitement dans un passage donné et que les gens ayant le sentiment correct et délicat des finesses de leur langue maternelle sentent instinctivement" (p. 632).

4 THOMAS, OWEN. "Grammar and Literature," in his *Transformational Grammar and the Teacher of English.* New York, 1965. Pp. 220–225.
Thomas considers some of the ways in which an awareness of syntactic patterns may heighten one's appreciation of literature. Among other examples, he discusses the opening of *Genesis* in the KJV.

5 THORNE, JAMES PETER. "Stylistics and Generative Grammars," *Journal of Linguistics*, I (1965), 49–59.
Thorne argues that poems are dialectically related to the structure of the language and that the style critic would profit if he constructs a microgrammar of the poem. Such grammars would allow the critic to test his account of the work by generating a variety of poetic sentences and examining them to see if they " 'belong' to the same language as that in which the poem is written" (p. 54).

6 THORNTON, HARRY, AND AGATHA THORNTON in collaboration with A. A. LIND. *Time and Style: A Psycho-Linguistic Essay in Classical Literature.* London, 1962.

7 TODOROV, TZVETAN (ed. and tr.). *Théorie de la littérature: une révolution méconnue.* Paris, 1966.
This volume with a preface by Roman Jakobson contains articles translated from the Russian Formalists Eichenbaum, Shklovsky, Vinogradov, Tynjanov, Jakobson, Tomashevsky, and Propp on stylistics and poetics.

8 ———. "L'héritage méthodologique du formalisme," *L'Homme*, V (1965), 64–83.

1 ———. "Les poètes devant le bon usage," *Revue d'Esthétique*, III–IV (1965), 300–305.

2 *Trivium: Schweizerische Vierteljahrschrift für Literaturwissenschaft und Stilistik*. Zurich, 1942–1953.

Edited by Theophil Spoerri and Emil Staiger, *Trivium* was concerned with the methods of *Stilforschung*. Though the articles by Leo Spitzer, Karl Vossler, and others are mainly concerned with European literature, the implications of the various authors' methods are valuable for the English stylistician.

3 TSCHIŽEWSKIJ, D. "Stil und Lexik," in *Stil- und Formprobleme*. Pp. 91–95.

4 UHRHAN, EVELYN E. "A Linguistic Analysis of Style," in *Proceedings of the Linguistic Circle of Manitoba and North Dakota*, II, ii (1960), 29–32.

5 ULLMANN, STEPHEN. "Psychologie et Stylistique," *Journal de Psychologie*, XLVI (1953), 133–156.

6 ———. "Un problème de reconstruction stylistique," in *Atti del VIII Congresso Internazionale di Studi Romanzi*. Firenze, 1960. Pp. 465–469.

7 ———. "New Bearings in Stylistics," in his *Language and Style*. New York, 1964. Pp. 99–131.

"Everything that transcends the purely referential and communicative side of language belongs to the province of expressiveness: emotive overtones, emphasis, rhythm, symmetry, euphony, and also the so-called '*evocative*' elements which place our style in a particular register (literary, colloquial, slangy, etc.) or associate it with a particular milieu (historical, foreign, provincial, professions, etc.)" (p. 101). "Evocative elements" can be analyzed at the levels of phonology, lexis, and syntax. For a linguist's view of Ullmann's *Language and Style*, see the review by Fred W. Householder in *Language*, XLII (1966), 632–639: "The theme . . . is the application of the methods and results of linguistics to literary criticism. This is a familiar enough notion by now, but the schizophrenia involved has never been carefully examined. . . . Something has to give; usually it's the linguistics, I'm afraid" (p. 632).

8 ———. "Style and Personality," *REL*, VI, ii (1965), 21–31.

9 UTLEY, FRANCIS LEE. "Structural Linguistics and the Literary Critic," *JAAC*, XVIII (1960), 319–328.

10 VALESIO, P. "Problemi di metodo della critica stilistica," *Saggi linguistici dell'istituto di Glottologia*, III (1962), 9–69.

11 VERGNAUD, SIMONE M. "La Méthode en Stylistique," in *Stil- und Formprobleme*, pp. 344–351.

1   VOEGLIN, C. F. "Casual and Noncasual Utterances within Unified Structure," in *Style in Language*, pp. 57–68.

2   VOLPE, GALVANO DELLA. *Critica del gusto*. Milan, 1960. Second edition revised and enlarged. Milan, 1964.

3   VOSSLER, KARL. *Introducción a la estilística romance*. Buenos Aires, 1942.

4   WARBURG, JEREMY. "Idiosyncratic Style," *REL*, VI, ii (1965), 56–65.

5   WARFEL, HARRY R. "Syntax Makes Literature," *CE*, XXI (1960), 251–255.

6   WARNER, ALAN. *A Short Guide to English Style*. London, 1961.

7   WEINBERG, BERNARD. "Les Rapports entre l'histoire littéraire et l'analyse formelle," in *Stil- und Formprobleme*. Pp. 75–85.

8   WELLS, RULON. "Nominal and Verbal Styles," in *Style in Language*. Pp. 213–220.

Starting from the textbook advice that a high proportion of verbs makes for a better style, Wells goes on to outline an experiment for testing nominal and verbal styles. "Style is understood to be optional like vocabulary, as contrasted with grammar. So far as the writer of English has a choice, what he writes is *his* diction and *his* style; so far as he has none, it is the *English* language. A treatment that respects this optionality will somehow take account of whether, and in how many ways, a sentence with a certain degree of nominality could be replaced by one with a different degree, for example, a highly nominal by a highly verbal sentence" (p. 215).

9   WHATMOUGH, JOSHUA. *Poetic, Scientific, and Other Forms of Discourse: A New Approach to Greek and Latin Literature*. Berkeley, 1956.

10   WINTER, WERNER. "Styles as Dialects," *Ninth Congress Papers*, pp. 324–330.

11   WINTERS, YVOR. *The Function of Criticism*. Denver, 1957.

12   YOUNG, RICHARD E., AND ALTON L. BECKER. "Toward a Modern Theory of Rhetoric: A Tagmemic Contribution," in *New Rhetorics*, ed. Martin Steinmann, Jr. (New York, 1967), pp. 77–107.

13   ZACHRISSON, R. E. *Engelska stilarter*. Stockholm, 1919.

SELECTION AND MANIPULATION OF WORDS

Diction

14   AUGUST, EUGENE ROBERT. "Word Inscapes: A Study of the Poetic Vocabulary of Gerard Manley Hopkins," *DA*, XXVI (1965), 3294–3295.

1   BABCOCK, C. MERTON. "The Vocabulary of Moby Dick," *AS*, XXVII (1952), 91–101.

2   BARFIELD, OWEN. *Poetic Diction: A Study in Meaning*. London, 1925, and New York, 1964.

3   BARSTOW, M. L. *Wordsworth's Theory of Poetic Diction*. New Haven, 1917.

4   BENTMAN, RAYMOND. "Robert Burns's Use of Scottish Diction," in *From Sensibility to Romanticism: Essays Presented to Frederick A. Pottle*, eds. Frederick W. Hilles and Harold Bloom (New York, 1965), pp. 239–258.

5   BOGGS, W. ARTHUR. "Smollett's Coinages in the Win Jenkins' Letters," *Language Quarterly*, II (1963), 2–4.

6   BREDE, ALEXANDER. "Theories of Poetic Diction in Wordsworth and Others and in Contemporary Poetry," *Papers of the Michigan Academy of Science, Arts and Letters*, XIV (1930), 537–566.

7   BROWN, ROGER, AND ALBERT GILMAN. "The Pronouns of Power and Solidarity," in *Style in Language*, pp. 253–276.
    Authors' summary of the five sections of the essay: "The first section offers a general description of the semantic evolution of the pronouns of address in certain European languages. The second section describes semantic differences existing today among the pronouns of French, German, and Italian. The third section proposes a connection between social structure, group ideology, and the semantics of the pronoun. The final two sections of the paper are concerned with expressive style by which we mean covariation between the pronoun used and characteristics of the person speaking" (p. 253).

8   BRUNEAU, CHARLES. "La science de la stylistique: problèmes de vocabulaire," *Cultura Neolatina*, XVI (1956), 65–68.

9   CROSS, GUSTAV. "The Vocabulary of 'Lust's Dominion,'" *Neuphilologische Mitteilungen* (Helsinki), LIX (1958), 41–48.

10 ———. "Some Notes on the Vocabulary of John Marston," *N&Q*, CXCIX (1954), 425–427; CC (1955), 20–21, 57–58, 186–187, 335–336, 427–428, 480–482; CCI (1956), 331–332, 470–471; CCII (1957), 65–66, 221–223, 283–285, 524–526; CCIII (1958), 5–6, 103–104, 221–222; CCIV (1959), 101–102, 137–139, 254–255, 355–356; CCV (1960), 135–136; CCVI (1961), 123–126, 298–300, 388–391.

11 DAVIE, DONALD. *Purity of Diction in English Verse*. New York, 1953.

12 ELTON, OLIVER. "The Poet's Dictionary," *Essays and Studies*, XIV (1929), 7–19.

13 EMPSON, WILLIAM. *The Structure of Complex Words*. London, 1951.

1   FERRY, DAVID. "The Diction of American Poetry," in *American Poetry*, eds. John R. Brown, Irvin Ehrenpreis, and Bernard Harris (London, 1965), pp. 135–153.

2   FRANCES, G. EMBERSON. "Mark Twain's Vocabulary: A General Survey," *University of Missouri Studies*, X (1935), 1–53.

3   GOLLER, KARL HEINZ. "Die *Poetic Diction* des 18. Jahrhunderts in England," *Deutsche Vierteljahrsschrift für Literaturwissenschaft und Geistesgeschichte*, XXXVIII (1964), 24–39.

4   GROOM, BERNARD. *On the Diction of Tennyson, Browning and Arnold.* Oxford: Society for Pure English Tract, No. 53, 1939.

5   ——. *The Diction of Poetry from Spenser to Bridges.* Toronto, 1955.

6   ——. "Poetic Diction," in *Encyclopedia of Poetry and Poetics*, eds. Alex Preminger *et al.* (Princeton, 1965), pp. 628–635.

7   HALL, ROLAND. "John Locke's Unnoticed Vocabulary," *N&Q*, CCVI (1961), 186–191, 207–210, 247–250, 330–335, 432–433.

8   ——. "The Diction of John Stuart Mill," *N&Q*, XI (1964), 29–34, 102–107, 183–188, 218–223, 307–312, 379–385, 423–429; XII (1965), 51–56, 188–194, 246–254, 419–425.

9   HART, A. "Vocabularies of Shakespeare's Plays," *RES*, XIX (1943), 128–140.

10   ——. "The Growth of Shakespeare's Vocabulary," *RES*, XIX (1943), 242–254.

11   HAVENS, RAYMOND DEXTER. "The Poetic Diction of the English Classicists," in *Anniversary Papers by Colleagues and Pupils of George Lyman Kittredge* (Boston, 1913), pp. 435–444.

12   HOWARD, WILLIAM. "Emily Dickinson's Poetic Vocabulary," *PMLA*, LXXII (1957), 225–248.

13   HUMESKY, ASSYA. *Majakovskij and His Neologisms.* New York, 1964.

14   HYNES, SAMUEL. "The Uses of Diction," in his *The Pattern of Hardy's Poetry* (Chapel Hill, N.C., 1961), pp. 89–108.

15   IKEGAMI, YOSHIHIKO. "Semantic Change in Poetic Words," *Linguistics*, No. 19 (1965), 64–79.

Ikegami provides both a theory of poetic words and a list of English examples which he describes as "fairly exhaustive." He observes that "poetic words" have lost some of their sememes, i.e., they are used in a more general sense than they would have in ordinary language. "In poetic language the choice of words is often dictated by exigencies of poetic form (metre, rhyme, etc.) or by a predilection for a variety of expressions (repetitions, etc.), so that words are liable to be used in contexts that count more or less as deviations from their normal use" (p. 74).

1   KELLY, SISTER MARIA DEL REY, R.S.M. "Poetic Diction in the Non-Dramatic Works of George Chapman," *DA*, XXVI (1965), 2216.

2   KOSKENNIEMI, INNA. *Studies in the Vocabulary of English Drama, 1550–1600*. Turku, 1962.

3   LEVIN, HARRY. "The War of Words in English Poetry," in his *Contexts of Criticism* (Cambridge, Mass., 1957), pp. 208–233.

4   LEWIS, C. S. *Studies in Words*. Cambridge, 1960.

5   LINNEMAN, WILLIAM R. "Faulkner's Ten-Dollar Words," *AS*, XXXVIII (1963), 158–159.

6   MILLS, JOHN A. "Language and Laughter: A Study of Comic Diction in the Plays of Bernard Shaw," *DA*, XXII (1962), 4017–4018.

7   NEUMANN, J. H. "Jonathan Swift and the Vocabulary of English," *MLQ*, IV (1943), 191–204.

8   ———. "A Nineteenth Century 'Poetic' Prefix," *MLN*, LVIII (1943), 278–283.

9   ———. "Milton's Prose Vocabulary," *PMLA*, LX (1945), 102–120.

10 PARTRIDGE, ERIC. *Shakespeare's Bawdy*. London [1955].

11 PURDY, STROTHER BEESON. "The Language of Henry James, with Emphasis on his Diction and Vocabulary," *DA*, XXI (1960–1961), 626.

12 QUAYLE, THOMAS. *Poetic Diction: A Study of Eighteenth-Century Verse*, London, 1924.

13 RIEGEL, KLAUS F., AND RUTH M. RIEGEL. "An Investigation into Denotative Aspects of Word-Meaning," *Language and Speech*, VI (1963), 5–21.

14 ROBERTS, PAUL. "Sir Walter Scott's Contributions to the English Vocabulary," *PMLA*, LXVIII (1953), 189–210.

15 ROSIER, JAMES L. "The Vocabulary of Ralph Lever's 'Arte of Reason,'" *Anglia*, LXXVI (1953), 505–509.

16 RUBEL, VERE L. *Poetic Diction in the English Renaissance*. New York, 1941.

17 RYLANDS, GEORGE. "English Poets and the Abstract Word," *Essays and Studies*, XVI (1931), 53–84.

18 SCOTT-THOMAS, LOUIS M. "The Vocabulary of Jonathan Swift," *Dalhousie Review*, XXV (1946), 442–447.

1 TILLOTSON, GEOFFREY. "Eighteenth-Century Poetic Diction," *Essays and Studies by Members of The English Association*, XXV (1939), 59–80; reprinted in his *Essays in Criticism and Research* (Cambridge, 1941), pp. 53–85.

2 ———. *Augustan Poetic Diction*. London, 1964.

3 WIMSATT, W. K., JR. *Philosophic Words: A Study of Style and Meaning in the "Rambler" and "Dictionary" of Samuel Johnson*. New Haven, 1948.

4 WYLD, HENRY CECIL. *Some Aspects of the Diction of English Poetry*. London, 1933.

5 YAMAMOTO, TODAO. *The Growth and System of the Language of Dickens: An Introduction to a Dickens Lexicon*. [Osaka], 1954.

Tropes

6 ADAMS, BERNARD SCHRODER. "Milton and Metaphor: The *Artis Logicae* and the Imagery of the Shorter English Poems," *DA*, XXVI (1965), 1629.

7 ANDERSON, C. C. "The Psychology of Metaphor," *Journal of Genetic Psychology*, CV (1964), 53–73.

8 ANTOINE, GÉRALD. "Pour une méthode d'analyse stylistique des images," in *Langue et Littérature*, pp. 151–164.

9 ARTHOS, JOHN. "Figures of Speech," in *Encyclopedia of Poetry and Poetics*, ed. Alex Preminger *et al.* (Princeton, 1965), pp. 273–274.

10 ASCH, S. E. "On the Use of Metaphor in the Description of Persons," in *On Expressive Language*, ed. H. Werner (Worcester, Mass., 1955), pp. 29–38.

11 ———. "The Metaphor: A Psychological Inquiry," in *Person, Perception, and Interpersonal Behavior*, eds. R. Taguiri and L. Petrullo (Stanford, 1958), pp. 86–94.

12 BAYM, MAX I. "The Present State of the Study of Metaphor," *Books Abroad*, XXXV (1961), 215–219.

13 BERGGREN, C. C. "An Analysis of Metaphorical Meaning and Truth." Unpublished Ph.D. dissertation presented to Yale University, 1959.

14 ———. "The Use and Abuse of Metaphor," *The Review of Metaphysics*, XVI (1962), 237–258.

15 BLACK, MAX. *Models and Metaphors: Studies in Language and Philosophy*. Ithaca, 1962.

1 BLOOMFIELD, MORTON W. "A Grammatical Approach to Personification Allegory," *MP*, LX (1963), 161–171.
   Bloomfield sees the use of animate verbs as the most characteristic
   mode of personification because the stress is on action. The effect of
   personification lies not in the nouns chosen but in the syntax that
   drives the reader to interpret the grammatical subject as a personification.

2 BRINKMANN, F. *Die Metaphern.* Bonn, 1878.

3 BROOKE-ROSE, CHRISTINE. *A Grammar of Metaphor.* London, 1958.

4 BROOKS, CLEANTH. "Metaphor, Paradox, and Stereotype," *British
   Journal of Aesthetics*, V (1965), 315–328.

5 BROWN, ROBERT. "Metaphorical Assertions," *Philosophical Studies*,
   XVI (1965), 6–8.

6 BROWN, S. J. *The World of Imagery.* London, 1927.

7 CHATMAN, VERNON V., III. "Figures of Repetition in Whitman's
   'Songs of Parting,' " *BNYPL*, LXIX (1965), 77–82.

8 COLBRUNN, ETHEL B. "The Simile as a Stylistic Device in Elizabethan Narrative Poetry: An Analytical and Comparative Study,"
   DA, XIV (1954), 2064–2065.

9 COLEMAN, ELLIOTT. "The Meaning of Metaphor," *The Gordon
   Review*, VIII (1965), 151–163.

10 CROSTON, A. K. "The Use of Imagery in Nashe's *The Unfortunate
   Traveller*," *RES*, XXIV (1948), 90–101.
   Croston examines Nashe's prose and finds that "it is no exaggeration
   to assert that the metaphorical possibilities of language form the essential subject-matter of the prose" (p. 90). He uses the framework
   developed by Spurgeon (*q. v.*) and S. J. Brown (*The World of Imagery*,
   London, 1927) to classify Nashe's metaphorical references; the greatest
   number of metaphors is drawn from "Learning," and "Daily Life."
   "Nashe's images are not elaborated: the mind is passed on from one to
   the next with an almost bewildering rapidity, concrete and abstract
   being mingled and juxtaposed in an infinite variety, the only principle
   being the enlarging of the immediate impression" (p. 96).

11 CUTTS, JOHN P. " 'The Miserific Vision': A Study of Some of the
   Basic Structural Imagery of *Paradise Lost*," *English Miscellany*, XIV
   (1963), 57–72.

12 DEMENT, JOSEPH WILLIS, JR. "The Ironic Image: Metaphoric
   Structure and Texture in the Comedies of William Congreve,"
   DA, XXVI (1965), 6037.

13 DRAPER, JOHN W. "Prolepsis in Shakespeare's Tragedies," *Rivista
   di Letterature Moderne e Comparate.* XVII (1964), 165–177.

1 DURANT, JACK DAVIS. "The Imagery in Swift's Prose: A Descriptive Analysis of Forms and Functions," *DA*, XXIV (1964), 4677–4678.

2 DYSON, A. E. "A Note on Dismissive Irony," *English* (Oxford), XI (1957), 222–225.

3 EMBLER, WALTER. *Metaphor and Meaning*. Deland, Fla., 1966.

4 FEIDELSON, CHARLES, JR. *Symbolism in American Literature*. Chicago, 1953.

5 FÓNAGY, IVAN. *Die Metaphern in der Phonetik*. The Hague, 1963.

6 FOSS, MARTIN. *Symbol and Metaphor in Human Experience*. Princeton, 1949.

7 FRIEDMAN, MELVIN J. *Stream of Consciousness: A Study in Literary Method*. New Haven, 1955.

8 FRIEDMAN, NORMAN. "Imagery," in *Encyclopedia of Poetry and Poetics*, ed. Alex Preminger *et al.* (Princeton, 1965), pp. 363–370.

9 HAZEN, JAMES FORSYTHE. "The Imagery and Symbolism of Thomas Hardy's Major Novels," *DA*, XXIV (1963), 1616.

10 HENLE, PAUL. "Metaphor," in *Language, Thought and Culture*, ed. Paul Henle (Ann Arbor, 1958), pp. 173–195.

11 HOLDER, A. "On the Structure of Henry James's Metaphors," *English Studies* (Amsterdam), XXXI (1960), 289–297.

12 HORNSTEIN, LILLIAN HERLANDS. "Analysis of Imagery: A Critique of Literary Method," *PMLA*, LVII (1942), 638–653.

13 HUMPHREY, ROBERT. *Stream of Consciousness in the Modern Novel*. Berkeley, 1954.

14 ISENBERG, ARNOLD. "On Defining Metaphor," *Journal of Philosophy*, LX (1963), 609–622.

15 JAKOBSON, ROMAN. "The Metaphoric and Metonymic Poles," in his and Morris Halle's *Fundamentals of Language* (The Hague, 1956), pp. 76–82.

16 KALLICH, MARTIN. "Unity and Dialectic: The Structural Role of Antitheses in Pope's *Essay on Man*," *Papers on English Language and Literature*, I (1965), 109–124.

17 KENNER, HUGH. "Imagery," in *The Concise Encyclopedia of English and American Poetry*, eds. Stephen Spender and Donald Hall (New York, 1963), pp. 155–159.

18 KNIGHT, KARL FREDERICK. *Diction, Metaphor, and Symbol in the Poetry of John Crowe Ransom*. Emory Univ., 1962.

1 KONRAD, HEDWIG. *Etude sur la métaphore.* 2ᵉ éd. Paris, 1958.

2 LEECH, GEOFFREY N. "Linguistics and the Figures of Rhetoric," *Essays on Language and Style,* pp. 135–156.

3 MACKEY, LOUIS. "Aristotle and Feidelson on Metaphor: Toward a Reconciliation of Ancient and Modern," *Arion,* IV (1965), 272–285.

4 MADGE, CHARLES. "Metaphor," in *The Concise Encyclopedia of English and American Poetry,* eds. Stephen Spender and Donald Hall (New York, 1963), pp. 198–202.

5 MARGOLIS, JOSEPH. "Notes on the Logic of Simile, Metaphor, and Analogy," *AS,* XXXII (1957), 186–189.

6 McCLOSKEY, MARY A. "Metaphors," *Mind,* LXXIII (1964), 215–233.

7 McCOY, DOROTHY SCHUCHMAN. *Tradition and Convention: A Study of Periphrasis in English Pastoral Poetry from 1557–1715.* The Hague, 1965.

8 MURRAY, ROGER N. "Synecdoche in Wordsworth's 'Michael,' " *ELH,* XXXII (1965), 502–510.

9 NEMETZ, ANTHONY. "Metaphor: The Daedalus of Discourse," *Thought,* XXXIII (1958), 417–442.

10 NICULESCU, ALEXANDRU. "Sur un emploi particulier de l'éllipse du prédicat dans le style narratif," in *Poetics,* pp. 445–452.

11 OSBORN, MICHAEL McDONALD. "The Function and Significance of Metaphor in Rhetorical Discourse." Unpublished dissertation presented to the University of Florida, 1963. Abstract in Speech Monographs, XXXI (1964), 254.

12 PAGNINI, MARCELLO. "Struttura semantica del grande Simbolismo americano," in *Il Simbolismo nella letteratura Nord-Americana: Atti del Symposium tenuto a Firenze 27–29 novembre 1964,* ed. Mario Praz *et al.* (Firenze, 1965), pp. 29–52.

13 PAINTER, JACK WHITFIELD. "A Semiotic Approach to Some Problems and Theories in the Interpretation of Metaphors," *DA,* XXIII (1963), 3929.

14 PAVEL, T. "Notes pour une description structurale de la métaphore poétique," *Cahiers de linguistique théorique et appliquée,* I (1962), 185–207.

15 PECKHAM, MORSE. "Metaphor: A Little Plain Speaking on a Weary Subject," *Connotation* (Fairleigh Dickinson Univ.), I, ii (1962), 29–46.

1 PEDERSON-KRAG, G. "The Use of Metaphor in Analytic Thinking," *Psychological Quarterly*, XXV (1956), 66–71.

2 PELC, JERZY. "Semantic Functions as Applied to the Analysis of the Concept of Metaphor," in *Poetics*, pp. 305–339.
After an analysis of the basic theoretical foundations of his study, Pelc considers in detail "The Semantic Analysis of Stylistic Tropes" and "The Semantic Nature of the Concept of Metaphor."

3 PERCY, WALKER. "Metaphor as Mistake," *Sewanee Review*, LXVI (1958), 79–99.

4 PRAZ, MARIO. *Studies in Seventeenth-Century Imagery*. Rome, 1964.

5 REES, G. O. "Types of Recurring Similes in Malraux's Novels," *MLN*, LXVII (1953), 373–377.

6 ROSE, H. J. "Metaphor: Ancient and Modern," in *Studies in Honour of Gilbert Norwood* (*The Phoenix*, Supplement I). Toronto, 1952. Pp. 239–247.

7 RUGOFF, M. A. *Donne's Imagery: A Study in Creative Sources*. New York, 1939.

8 SCHOPF, FEDERICO. "La esencia de la metáfora," *Anales de la Universidad de Chile*, CXXIII, cxxxiv (1965), 125–147.

9 SHEEHAN, DONALD. "Wallace Stevens' Theory of Metaphor," *Papers on Language and Literature* (Southern Illinois Univ.), II (1966), 57–66.

10 SLAWINSKA, IRENA. "Metaphor in Drama," *Poetics*, pp. 341–346.

11 SMITH, CURTIS C. "Metaphor Structure in Swift's *A Tale of a Tub*," *Thoth*, V (1964), 22–41.

12 SPURGEON, CAROLINE F. E. *Shakespeare's Imagery and What It Tells Us*. Cambridge, 1935, and Boston, 1958.
Spurgeon uses "the term 'image' as the only available word to cover every kind of simile, as well as every kind of what is really compressed simile—metaphor" (p. 5). Section One of her book is devoted to the use of image analysis in illuminating Shakespeare's biography and psychology: "These, then, as I see them, are the five outstanding qualities of Shakespeare's nature—sensitiveness, poise, courage, humour, and wholesomeness—balancing, complementing and supporting each other" (p. 206). In her second section, she uses the results of her study to illuminate Shakespeare's works. Her remarks on *Macbeth* are discussed by Cleanth Brooks, "The Naked Babe and the Cloak of Manliness," in *The Well-Wrought Urn: Studies in the Structure of Poetry* (New York, 1947), pp. 22–49.

13 STEENBURGH, E. W. Van. "Metaphor," *The Journal of Philosophy*, LXII (1965), 678–688.

1   STEINHOFF, WILLIAM R. "The Metaphorical Texture of *Daniel Deronda*," in *Langue et Littérature*. P. 316.

Steinhoff gives a condensed survey of the relation of metaphor to the theme of conflict between individual and society in Eliot's novel.

2   TURBAYNE, COLIN. *The Myth of Metaphor*. New Haven, 1962.

3   ULLMANN, STEPHEN. *The Image in the Modern French Novel: Gide, Alain-Fournier, Proust, Camus*. Cambridge, 1960.

4   ———. "The Nature of Imagery," in his *Language and Style* (New York, 1964), pp. 174–201.

"There can be no question of an image unless the resemblance it expresses has a concrete and sensuous quality. A comparison between two abstract phenomena, however acute and illuminating it may be, will not constitute a real image. Secondly, there must be something striking and unexpected in every image: it must produce a surprise effect due to the discovery of some common element in two seemingly disparate experiences" (p. 178). See an earlier version of Ullmann's essay, "L'image littéraire: quelques questions de méthode," in *Langue et Littérature*, pp. 41–60.

5   VÄÄNÄNEN, VEIKKO. "Métaphores rajeunies et métaphores ressuscitées," in *Atti del VIII Congresso Internazionale di Studi Romanzi*. Firenze, 1960. Pp. 465–469.

6   VIANU, TUDOR. "Quelques observations sur la métaphore poétique," *Poetics*, pp. 297–304.

"Ces deux caractères nous montrent clairement que la métaphore poétique revêt une structure sémantique profonde, c'est-à-dire composée de deux plans, dont l'un est exprimé et manifeste, l'autre latent et profond" (p. 299).

7   ———. *Problemele metaforei si alte studii de stilistică*. Bucaresti, 1957.

8   WALD, H. "Métaphore et concept," *Revue de Métaphysique et de Morale*, LXXI (1966), 199–208.

9   WENTERSDORF, KARL P. "The Imagery of Wyatt," *Studia Neophilologica*, XXXVII (1965), 161–173.

10   WERNER, HEINZ. *Die Ursprünge der Metapher*. Leipzig, 1919.

11   WHEELWRIGHT, PHILIP. *Metaphor and Reality*. Bloomington, Ind., 1962.

12   YODER, SAMUEL A. "*Dispositio* in Hooker's *Laws of Ecclesiastical Polity*," *QJS*, XXVII (1941), 90–97.

STATISTICAL APPROACHES TO STYLE

13   ABERNATHY, R. "Mathematical Linguistics and Poetics," in *Poetics*, pp. 563–569.

1 ACHMANOVA, O. S., L. N. NATAN, A. I. POLTORACKIJ, AND V. I. FAT'USHCHENKO. *O principach i metodach lingvostilisticeskogo issledovanija* [Principles and Methods of Linguistic-Stylistic Investigations]. Moskva, 1966.

See especially Part II, Chapter 4.

2 ANDERSON, EDGAR. "A Botanist Looks at Poetry: The Rise and Fall of the Adjective: Five Centuries of Patterns," *Michigan Quarterly Review,* IV (1965), 177–184.

Anderson examines several graphs based on the data collected by Josephine Miles on favored grammatical devices in the history of English poems.

3 ANGELLOZ, J.-F. "Statistique et littérature," *Mercure de France,* CXVI (October 1952), 291–299.

4 ANON. "The Statistics of Style," *TLS* (Jan. 25, 1963), 67.

5 BARBER, CHARLES L. "A Rare Use of the Word *Honour* as a Criterion of Middleton's Authorship," *English Studies,* XXXVIII (1957), 161–168.

6 ———. "Some Measurable Characteristics of Modern Scientific Prose," in *Contributions to English Syntax and Philology,* ed. Frank Behre (Gothenburg, 1962), pp. 21–43.

7 BARTH, GILBERT. *Recherches sur la fréquence et la valeur des parties du discours en français, en anglais et en espagnol.* Paris, 1961.

8 BENNETT, PAUL E. "The Statistical Measurement of a Stylistic Trait in *Julius Caesar* and *As You Like It,*" *Shakespeare Quarterly,* VIII (1957), 33–50.

9 BODER, DAVID P. "The Adjective-Verb Quotient: A Contribution to the Psychology of Language," *Psychological Record,* III (1940), 309–343.

10 BOONE, LALIA PHIPPS. "The Language of Book VI, *Paradise Lost,*" in *South Atlantic Modern Language Association Studies in Milton,* ed. J. Max Patrick (Gainesville, Fla., 1953), pp. 114–127.

11 BOOTH, ANDREW D., L. BRANDWOOD, AND J. P. CLEAVE. *The Mechanical Resolution of Linguistic Problems.* London, 1958.

See especially Chapter 4, "Stylistic Analysis," pp. 50–63.

12 BRANDWOOD, L. "Analysing Plato's Style with an Electronic Computer," *Institute of Classical Studies Bulletin* (London), III (1956), 45–54.

13 BRINEGAR, CLAUDE S. "Mark Twain and the Quintus Curtius Snodgrass Letters: A Statistical Test of Authorship," *Journal of the American Statistical Association,* LVIII (1963), 85–96; reprinted in

The Practice of Modern Literary Scholarship, ed. Sheldon P. Zitner (Glenview, Illinois, 1966), pp. 352–363.

"Mark Twain is widely credited with the authorship of 10 letters published in 1861 in the *New Orleans Daily Crescent*. The adventures described in these letters, which were signed 'Quintus Curtius Snodgrass,' provide the historical basis of a main part of Twain's presumed role in the Civil War. This study applied an old, though little used, statistical test of authorship—a word-length frequency test—to show that Twain almost certainly did not write these 10 letters. The statistical analysis includes a visual comparison of several word-length frequency distributions and applications of the x^2 and two-sample t tests" (p. 85).

1   BUCHANAN, SCOTT. *Poetry and Mathematics*. New York, 1929, and Philadelphia, 1962.

2   BULL, WILLIAM E. "Natural Frequency and Word Counts," *Classical Journal*, XLIV (1949), 469–484.

3   BURWICK, FREDERICK. "Associationist Rhetoric and Scottish Prose Style," *Speech Monographs*, XXXIV (1967), 21–34.

4   CARD, WILLIAM, AND VIRGINIA McDAVID. "English Words of Very High Frequency," *CE*, XXVII (1966), 596–604.

5   CARROLL, JOHN B. "Vectors of Prose Style," in *Style in Language*, pp. 283–292.
See item 113:3 for annotation.

6   CHANDLER, ZILPHA EMMA. "An Analysis of the Stylistic Technique of Addison, Johnson, Hazlitt, and Pater," *University of Iowa Humanistic Studies*, IV, iii (1928). 110 pp.
See item 113:5 for annotation.

7   CHATMAN, SEYMOUR. "Stylistics: Quantitative and Qualitative," *Style* (Arkansas), I (1967), 29–43.

8   CHOTLOS, J. W. "A Statistical and Comparative Analysis of Individual Written Language Samples," *Psychological Monographs*, LVI (1944), 77–111.

9   CHRÉTIEN, C. DOUGLAS. "A New Statistical Approach to the Study of Language," *Romance Philology*, XVI (1963), 290–301.
A review of Herdan's *Language as Choice and Chance*.

10   DELCOURT, J. *Essai sur la langue de Sir Thomas More d'après ses oeuvres anglaises*. Paris, 1914.

11   DENES, P. B. "On the Statistics of Spoken English," *Journal of the Acoustical Society*, XXXV (1963), 892–904.

12   DOLEŽEL, LUBOMÍR. "Verojatnostnyj podchod k teorii chudozhestvennogo stil'a" ["A Probabilistic Approach to the Theory of Artistic Style"], *Voprosy jazykoznanija*, XIII, ii (1964), 19–29.

1   ———. "Zur statischen Theorie der Dichtersprache," in *Mathematik und Dichtung*, pp. 275–294.

2   ———. "Model stylistické složky jazykoveho kódování" ["A Model of the Stylistic Component of Language Encoding"], *Slovo a slovesnost*, XXVI (1965), 223–235.

3   DOYLE, LAUREN B. "The Microstatistics of Text," *Information Storage and Retrieval*, I (1963), 189–214.
     Doyle discusses some applications of statistical analysis to the problems of automatic abstracting and information retrieval.

4   ELDERTON, W. P. "A Few Statistics on the Length of English Words," *Journal of the Royal Statistical Society*, CXII (1949), 436–443.

5   ELLEGÅRD, ALVAR. "Estimating Vocabulary Size," *Word*, XVI (1960), 219–244.

6   ———. *Who Was Junius?* Stockholm, Göteborg, and Uppsala, 1962.
     Ellegård presents a nontechnical report of his work in determining the author of the "Junius" letters from a long list of possible candidates. He provides statistical evidence in support of the candidacy of Sir Philip Francis. "What distinguishes one writer from another, linguistically, is not only, and not even primarily, the use or non-use of certain words, phrases and grammatical constructions. Rather it is the differences in the *frequency* with which different expressions are used" (p. 99).

7   ———. *A Statistical Method for Determining Authorship: The Junius Letters, 1769–1772*. Göteborg, 1962.
     A technical report on the Junius investigation. The following reviews are of interest: C. Douglas Chrétien, *Language*, XL (1964), 85–90; and "The Statistics of Style," *TLS* (Jan. 25, 1963), 67.

8   ———, HANS KARLGREN, AND HENNING SPANG-HANSSEN. *Structures and Quanta: Three Essays on Linguistic Description*. Copenhagen, 1965.

9   ELLIS, ALLAN B. "The Computer and Character Analysis," *English Journal*, LIII (1964), 522–527.

10   ERDMAN, DAVID V. "The Signature of Style," *BNYPL*, LXIII (1959), 88–109; reprinted in *Evidence for Authorship*, eds. David V. Erdman and Ephim G. Fogel (Ithaca, 1966), pp. 45–68.
     "Erdman takes exception to the claim that unrelated parallelisms . . . can have cumulative force, and he maintains that 'the test of style is always crucial, at least in the negative sense.' He then illustrates the danger of trusting to strong but indirect external evidence in the absence of positive stylistic evidence; he dismisses quantitative tests briefly but places considerable emphasis on the validity of positive stylistic evidence when combined with the evidence of parallels of idea or detail. Defining Coleridge's prose style, Erdman turns to the attri-

bution of unsigned essays in the *Morning Post*—the indirect external evidence being (in part) Coleridge's known contribution of other essays during the period" (Erdman's self-characterization, *Evidence for Authorship*, p. 4).

1 ———, AND EPHIM G. FOGEL. *Evidence for Authorship: Essays on Problems of Attribution.* Ithaca, N.Y., 1966.
The editors provide an extremely thorough and copiously annotated bibliography of studies in authorship attribution (pp. 395–523).

2 FAIRBANKS, H. "The Quantitative Differentiation of Samples of Spoken English," *Psychological Monographs*, LVI (1944), 19–38.

3 FOGEL, EPHIM G. "Electronic Computers and Elizabethan Texts," *Studies in Bibliography*, XV (1962), 15–31.

4 FÓNAGY, IVAN. "Informationsgehalt von Wort und Laut in der Dichtung," in *Poetics*, pp. 591–605.

✓ 5 FRANCIS, IVOR S. "An Exposition of a Statistical Approach to the Federalist Dispute," in *The Computer and Literary Style*, ed. Jacob Leed (Kent, Ohio, 1966), pp. 38–78.
"This article describes the attempts made by Frederick Mosteller and David L. Wallace to resolve the [Federalist] controversy, not by the usual methods of historical literary analysis, but by methods of mathematical statistics" (pp. 38–39).

6 FRUMKINA, F. M. *Statisticheskije metody izuchenija leksiki* [Statistical Methods of Vocabulary Study]. Moskva, 1964.

7 FUCKS, WILHELM. "On Mathematical Analysis of Style," *Biometrika*, XXXIX (1952), 122–129.
"Every significant text of a grammatical exposition consists of certain material, the *vocabulary*, and some structural properties, the style, of its author. The passive vocabulary is formed by the totality of all words of that language, s, the author writes in; the active vocabulary is formed by a certain part, s', of that totality, the selection of which is determined essentially by the sort of literature the text belongs to and depends only in a lower degree on the peculiarity of the author. Style, however, is characteristic of the author at a certain period of his personal development. The aim of the following investigation is to formulate mathematically some of the properties constituting style, so that for a given text the application of a simple mathematical criterion allows its attribution to a particular author at a certain period of his mental development" (p. 122).

8 ———. *Mathematische Analyse von Sprachelementen, Sprachstil und Sprache.* Köln, 1955.

9 ———, AND J. LAUTER. "Mathematische Analyse des literarischen Stils," in *Mathematik und Dichtung*, pp. 107–122.

1 GAMMON, EDWARD R. "A Statistical Study of English Syntax," in *Ninth Congress Papers*, pp. 37–43.

2 GEORGE, ALEXANDER L. "Quantitative and Qualitative Approaches to Content Analysis," in *Trends in Content Analysis*, pp. 7–32.

3 GERWIG, GEORGE WILLIAM. "On the Decrease of Predication and of Sentence Weight in English Prose," *University of Nebraska Studies*, II (1894), 17–28.

4 GOUGENHEIM, G. "Statistique linguistique et histoire du vocabulaire," *Cahiers de lexicologie*, II (1960), 31–40.

5 GUBERNA, P. "La stylistique, science quantitative ou qualitative?" *Revue Roumaine de Linguistique*, IV (1959), 5–8.

6 GUIRAUD, PIERRE. *Les caractères statistiques du vocabulaire: essai de méthodologie*. Paris, 1954.
   Guiraud examines the vocabularies of Racine, Baudelaire, Mallarmé, Claudel, and Valéry.

7 ———. "A propos des caractères statistiques du vocabulaire et de l'équation de Zipf," *Bulletin de la Société de Linguistique de Paris*, LI (1955), 236–239.

8 ———. *Problèmes et méthodes de la statistique linguistique*. Dordrecht, 1959.
   In the first section of his book, Guiraud discusses the methods of statistics and their value in both linguistic and stylistic analysis. Among the chapters in this section are: "L'Evolution du style de Rimbaud et la chronologie des '*Illuminations*'" (pp. 129–140) and "La structure phonétique du vers" (pp. 141–145).
   See A. J. Greimas, "La linguistique statistique et la linguistique structurale: à propos du livre de P. Guiraud: Problèmes et méthodes de la statistique linguistique," *Le Français Moderne*, XXX (1962), 241–254, and XXXI (1963), 55–68.

9 HALLBERG, PETER. "Statistik i den litterära analysens tjänst," in *Litteraturvetenskap: Nya mål och metoder* (Stockholm: Natur och Kultur, 1966), pp. 9–36.

10 HARWOOD, F. W., AND ALISON M. WRIGHT. "A Statistical Study of English Word Formation," *Language*, XXXII (1956), 260–273.

11 HAYDEN, R. E. "The Relative Frequency of Phonemes in General American English," *Word*, VI (1950), 217–223.

12 HAYS, DAVID G. *Bibliography of Computational Linguistics*. Santa Monica: The RAND Corporation, 1965—.
   A current list of books and articles in the field of computational linguistics is given in each issue of the journal, *The Finite String*.

1   HERDAN, GUSTAV. "A New Derivation and Interpretation of Yule's Characteristic K," *Zeitschrift für angewandte Mathematik und Physik*, VI, iv (1955), 332–334.

2   ———. "Chaucer's Authorship of *The Equatorie of the Planetis*," *Language*, XXXII (1956), 254–259.

∨ 3   ———. *Language as Choice and Chance*. Groningen, 1956.
" 'Style' is therefore used in the sense of a subconscious factor which the writer cannot but obey, and this implies that linguistic expression is less a matter of deliberate choice of words than it would appear at first sight" (p. 12). Herdan concentrates on such characteristics of words as etymological origin and length. He includes tables on "Relative Frequency of English Speech Sounds" (p. 73), "Relative Frequencies of Letters in Samples from English Writing" (p. 76), "Relative Frequencies of Words According to the Number of Syllables" from Carlyle, Macaulay, Johnson, and Gibbon (p. 77).

4   ———. "An Inequality Relation between Yule's 'Characteristic K' and Shannon's 'Entropy H,' " *Journal of Applied Mathematics and Physics*, IX, i (1958), 69–73.

5   ———. "The Mathematical Relation between Greenberg's Index of Linguistic Diversity and Yule's Characteristic," *Biometrika*, XLV (1958), 268–270.

6   ———. "The Relation between the Functional Burdening of Phonemes and the Frequency of Occurrence," *Language and Speech*, I (1958), 8–13.

7   ———. "The Relation between the Dictionary Distribution and Occurrence Distribution of Word-Length and Its Importance for the Study of Quantitative Linguistics," *Biometrika*, XLV (1958), 222–228.

8   ———. "Relativity of Vocabulary Ratios," in *Proceedings of the Eighth International Congress of Linguists* (Oslo, 1958), pp. 813–815.

9   ———. *Type-Token Mathematics: A Textbook of Mathematical Linguistics*. The Hague, 1960.

10   ———. "The Statistics of Structured Meaning," in *Advances in Documentation and Library Science* (New York: Interscience, 1961), Chap. 43, vol. 3, pt. 2.

11   ———. *The Calculus of Linguistic Observations*. The Hague, 1962.

12   ———. *Quantitative Linguistics*. London, 1964.

13   ———. "Quantitative Linguistics or Generative Grammar," *Linguistics*, No. 4 (1964), 56–65.

14   ———. *The Advanced Theory of Language as Choice and Chance*. Berlin and New York, 1966.

1   HOWES, DAVID. "A Word Count of Spoken English," *Journal of Verbal Learning and Verbal Behavior*, V (1966), 572–606.

2   HRUBÝ, ANTONÍN. "Statistical Methods in Textual Criticism," *General Linguistics*, V, i (1962), 77–138.

3   KALININ, V. M. "O statistike literaturnogo teksta" ["On the Statistics of Literary Texts"], *Voprosy jazykoznanija*, XIII, i (1964), 123–127.

4   KELEMEN, BELA. "A propos des caractéristiques des styles de la langue à la lumière de la statistique linguistique," *Revue Roumaine de Linguistique*, IX (1964), 621–624.

5   KONDRATOV, A. M. *Matematika i poezija* [Mathematics and Poetry]. Moskva, 1962.

6   KRALLMANN, DIETER. *Statistische Methoden in der stilistischen Textanalyse: Ein Beitrag zur Informationserschliessung mit Hilfe elektronischer Rechenmaschinen.* Bonn, 1966.
     Krallmann provides an extensive bibliography (pp. 231–249).

7   KREUZER, HELMUT, AND R. GUNZENHÄUSER (eds.). *Mathematik und Dichtung.* München, 1965.

8   KRISHNAMURTI, S. "Dr. Johnson's Use of Monosyllabic Words," *Journal of the University of Bombay*, XIX (1950), 1–12.

9   ———. "Frequency Distribution of Nouns in Dr. Johnson's Prose Works," *Journal of the University of Bombay*, XX (1951), 1–16.

10   ———. "Vocabulary Texts Applied to [Dr. Johnson's] Authorship of the 'Misargyrus' Papers in *The Adventurer*," *Journal of the University of Bombay*, XXI (1952), 47–62.

11   ———. "Vocabulary Tests Applied to the Authorship of the 'New Essays' Attributed to Dr. Johnson," *Journal of the University of Bombay*, XXII (1953), 1–5.

12   KROEBER, A. L. "Parts of Speech in Periods of Poetry," *PMLA*, LXXIII (1958), 309–314.
     Kroeber uses a statistical examination of parts of speech in order to test the validity of the conclusions reached by Josephine Miles in her "Eras in English Poetry," *PMLA*, LXX (1955), 853–875. ". . . until nearly 1700, verbs predominated decisively over adjectives in English poetry. Then it was the other way round until soon after 1800. Since then, the ratio has been mixed, that is, indecisive: the number of poets definitely favoring either part of speech is about equal, and their distribution in time runs concurrently and evenly for a century and a half" (p. 311).

13   KROEBER, KARL. "Computers and Research in Literary Analysis," in *Computers in Humanistic Research*, ed. Edmund A. Bowles (Englewood Cliffs, N.J., 1967), pp. 143–152.

1   KURASZKIEWICZ, WŁADYSŁAW. "Etude de la paternité des textes anonymes d'après la méthode de la statistique linguistique," in *Poetics*, pp. 625–633.

2   LAMB, SIDNEY M., AND LAURA GOULD. *Concordances from Computers.* Berkeley, 1964.

3   LANDON, GEORGE M. "The Contribution of Grammar to the Poetic Style of Wilfred Owen." Unpublished Ph.D. dissertation, Indiana University, 1964.
    Landon first analyzed the syntax and some semantic categories of Owen's poetry. Using the methods of generative-transformational grammar, he then categorized the "deviations" from normal English syntax in the poems. Finally, he used a card-sorting machine to group deviant and other lines according to their syntactical relations and the categories concrete/abstract, animate/inanimate, human/nonhuman, and feminine/neuter. He concluded that the statistical information that he gathered is of relatively little value without being compared to similar analyses of other poets.

4   LEED, JACOB, AND ROBERT HEMENWAY. "Use of the Computer in Some Recent Studies of Literary Style," *The Serif* (Kent, Ohio), II, ii (1965), 16–20.

5   LEED, JACOB (ed.). *The Computer and Literary Style.* Kent, Ohio, 1966.
    Leed collects eight essays devoted to the theory of computer-aided stylistics and to such applications as the resolution of disputed authorship and diachronic poetics.

6   LESSKIS, G. A. "O zavisimosti mezhdu razmerom predlozhenij in charakterom teksta" ["On the Interdependence between Sentence Length and the Character of a Text"], *Voprosy jazykoznanija*, XIII, iii (1963), 92–112.

7   LEVIN, SAMUEL R. "Statische und determinierte Abweichung in poetischer Sprache," in *Mathematik und Dichtung*, pp. 33–48.

8   LEVISON, MICHAEL. "The Computer and Its Role in Literary Studies," *Institute of Classical Studies Bulletin* (London), XI (1964), 65–69.

9   LEVÝ, JIŘÍ. "Matematický a experimentální rozbor verše" ["A Mathematical and Experimental Analysis of Verse"], *Česká literatura*, XII (1964), 181–213.

10 ———. "Předběžné poznámky k informační analýze verše" ["Some Preliminary Remarks on the Informational Analysis of Verse"], *Slovenská literatura*, XI (1964), 15–37.

11 ———. "W sprawie ścislych metod analizy wiersza" ["On Exact Methods of Verse Analysis"], in *Poetyka i matematyka*, ed. M. R. Mayenowa (Warszawa, 1965), pp. 23–71.

1   ———. "Die Theorie des Verses—ihre mathematischen Aspekte," in *Mathematik und Dichtung*, pp. 211–231.

2   *Literary Data Processing Conference, 9–11 September 1964, Proceedings*, eds. Jess B. Bessinger, Jr., Stephen M. Parrish, and Harry F. Arader. White Plains, N.Y.: International Business Machines Corp., Data Processing Division, 1964.
Distributed by the Modern Language Association.

3   Mańczak, Witold. "La longeur de la proposition comme facteur stylistique," in *Langue et Littérature*, pp. 401–403.
Mańczak examines the "rapport de la fréquence d'emploi du verbe à mode personnel à celle des autres parties du discours dans un texte donné" as a way of characterizing style. He discovered that the second half of the nineteenth century was characterized by an emphasis on other parts of speech than the active verb in French poetic language; for example, the frequency of active verbs to other parts of speech in Rimbaud's "Voyelles" is 1:22.

√ 4   Maxwell, J. C. "Peele and Shakespeare: A Stylometric Test," *JEGP*, XLIX (1950), 557–561.
Maxwell's authorship test is based on the frequency of use of possessive adjectives or pronouns as an antecedent for a relative clause.

5   Mayenowa, M. R. "Możliwości i niebezpieczeństwa metod matematycznych v poetyce" ["Possibilities and Pitfalls of Mathematical Methods in Poetics"], in *Poetyka i matematyka*, ed. M. R. Mayenowa (Warszawa, 1965), pp. 5–20.

6   ——— (ed.). *Poetyka i matematyka* [Poetics and Mathematics]. Warszawa, 1965.

7   Mendenhall, T. C. "The Characteristic Curves of Composition," *Science*, IX, No. 214 (1887), 237–249.

√ 8   ———. "A Mechanical Solution to a Literary Problem," *Popular Science Monthly*, LX, vii (1901), 97–105.

9   Menninger, Karl. *Mathematik und Kunst*. Göttingen, 1959.

10   Miles, Josephine. *Wordsworth and the Vocabulary of Emotion*. Berkeley, 1942.

11   ———. *Major Adjectives in English Poetry from Wyatt to Auden*. Berkeley, 1946.

12   ———. *The Continuity of Poetic Language*. Berkeley, 1948–1951; reprinted New York, 1965.
I. *The Primary Language of Poetry in the 1640's*. Berkeley, 1948.
II. *The Primary Language of Poetry in the 1740's and 1840's*. Berkeley, 1950.
III. *The Primary Language of Poetry in the 1940's*. Berkeley, 1951.

1 ———. "Eras in English Poetry," *PMLA*, LXX (1955), 853–875.

2 ———. *Renaissance, Eighteenth-Century and Modern Language in English Poetry: A Tabular View*. Berkeley, 1960.

3 ———. *Eras and Modes in English Poetry*. Revised edition, Berkeley, 1964.

4 ———, AND HANAN C. SELVIN. "A Factor Analysis of the Vocabulary of Poetry in the Seventeenth Century," in *The Computer and Literary Style*, ed. Jacob Leed (Kent, Ohio, 1966), pp. 116–127.

5 ———. "A Poet Looks at Graphs: Mathematics and the History of English Poetry," *Michigan Quarterly Review*, IV (1965), 185–188. Miles comments on the graphic representation of her data in the article by Edgar Anderson, "A Botanist Looks at Poetry . . . ," *ibid.*, 177–184.

6 ———. *Style and Proportion: The Language of Prose and Poetry*. Boston, 1967.

7 MILIC, LOUIS T. *A Quantitative Approach to the Style of Jonathan Swift*. The Hague, 1966. Milic chose 3500 word samples from authenticated Swift prose and control samples from Addison, Johnson, Gibbon, and Macaulay. Using a modified set of parts of speech definitions based on the system of Charles C. Fries, he tabulated three-word sequences on Hollerith cards and analyzed the sequences with the help of an IBM 1620 computer. "This study claims to have produced: 1) a body of exact information about the structure of the literary prose of Swift, Addison, Johnson, Gibbon, and Macaulay; 2) a method of identification by internal evidence, free of the usual uncertainties, using statistical methods and computer technology; 3) the identification of a hitherto-doubtful work of Swift; and 4) the means for achieving a better sense of what Swift's style really is." See the abstract in *DA*, XXIV (1964), 3370, and a review by Karl Kroeber, *Computers and the Humanities*, I (1966), 55–58.

8 ———. "Unconscious Ordering in the Prose of Swift," in *The Computer and Literary Style*, ed. Jacob Leed (Kent, Ohio, 1966), pp. 79–106.

9 MLACEK, J. "O frekvencii jazykových prostriedkov a o jej štylistickej platnosti" ["On the Frequency of Linguistic Devices and Their Stylistic Value"], *Slovenská reč* (1965), pp. 330–335.

10 MONTENEGRO, T. H. *A análise matematica do éstilo*. Rio de Janeiro. 1956.

11 MORITZ, ROBERT E. "On the Variation and Functional Relation of Certain Sentence Constants in Standard Literature," *University of Nebraska Studies*, III (1903), 229–253.

1   MORTON, ANDREW Q. "The Structure of the New Testament," *Science News*, XLIII (1957), 19–30.

2   ———. *Christianity in the Computer Age.* New York, 1964.

3   ———. "The Authorship of Greek Prose," *Journal of the Royal Statistical Society*, series A, CXXVIII (1965), 169–224.

4   MOSTELLER, FREDERICK, AND DAVID L. WALLACE. "Inference in an Authorship Problem," *Journal of the American Statistical Association*, LVIII (1963), 275–309.
"This study has four purposes: to provide a comparison of discrimination methods; to explore the problems presented by techniques based strongly on Bayes' theorem when they are used in a data analysis of a large scale; to solve the authorship question of *The Federalist* papers; and to propose routine methods for solving other authorship problems.
Word counts are the variables used for discrimination. Since the topic written about heavily influences the rate with which a word is used, care in the selection of words is necessary. The filler words of the language such as *an*, *of*, and *upon*, and, more generally, articles, prepositions, and conjunctions provide fairly stable rates, whereas more meaningful words like *war*, *executive*, and *legislature* do not" (p. 275).

5   ———. *Inference and Disputed Authorship: The Federalist.* Reading, Mass., 1964.
The authors present an expanded and more technical account of their work on *The Federalist*. They conclude that Madison and not Hamilton wrote all twelve of the disputed papers. For a discussion of this work, see Ivor S. Francis, "An Exposition of a Statistical Approach to the *Federalist* Dispute," in *The Computer and Literary Style*, ed. Jacob Leed (Kent, Ohio, 1966), pp. 38–78.

6   MULLER, CHARLES. "Du nouveau sur les distributions lexicales: la formule de Waring-Herdan," *Cahiers de Lexicologie*, no. 6 (1965), 35–53.

7   ———. "Fréquence, dispersion et usage: à propos des dictionnaires de fréquence," *Cahiers de Lexicologie*, no. 7 (1965), 33–42.

8   *Natural Language and the Computer*, ed. Paul L. Garvin. New York, 1963.

9   NICE, MARGARET M. "On the Size of Vocabularies," *AS*, II (1926), 1–7.

10   O'DONNELL, BERNARD. "An Analysis of Prose Style to Determine Authorship: *The O'Ruddy*, A Novel by Stephen Crane and Robert Barr," *DA*, XXIV (1964), 2894.

11   ———. "Stephen Crane's *The O'Ruddy*: A Problem in Authorship Discrimination," in *The Computer and Literary Style*, ed. Jacob Leed (Kent, Ohio, 1966), pp. 107–115.

1   ORAS, ANTS. *Blank Verse and Chronology in Milton.* Gainesville, Fla., 1966.

2   OTA, SABURO. "The Statistical Method of Investigation in Comparative Literature," in *Proceedings of the Second Congress of the International Comparative Literature Association* (Chapel Hill, N.C., 1959), vol. I, pp. 88–97.

Ota studies the growing interest in James Joyce in the 1920's and 1930's in Japan by constructing graphs based on the incidence of articles concerned with Joyce in Japanese periodicals in successive years.

3   PAINTER, J. A. "Computer Preparation of a Poetry Concordance," *Communications of the Association for Computing Machinery,* III (1960), 91–95.

4   PAISLEY, WILLIAM J. "Identifying the Unknown Communicator in Painting, Literature, and Music: The Significance of Minor Encoding Habits," *The Journal of Communication,* XIV (1964), 219–237.

See item 66:12 for annotation.

5   ———. "The Effects of Authorship, Topic, Structure, and Time of Composition on Letter Redundancy in English Texts," *Journal of Verbal Learning and Verbal Behavior,* V (1966), 28–34.

6   PARKER, R. E. "Spenser's Language and the Pastoral Tradition," *Language,* I (1925), 80–87.

Parker presents a statistical treatment of archaisms in Spenser's poetry.

7   PARRISH, STEPHEN M. "Literary Data Processing," *PMLA,* LXXX, iv (1965), 3–6.

8   PHILLIPS, PATRICIA. "A Statistical Approach to Some Literary Problems." Unpublished M.S. dissertation, The University of Wales, 1964.

9   PIMSLEUR, PAUL. "Semantic Frequency Counts," *Mechanical Translation,* IV, i–ii (1957), 11–13.

10 POSNER, REBECCA. "The Use and Abuse of Stylistic Statistics," *Archivum Linguisticum,* XV (1963), 111–139.

Mrs. Posner outlines the history of stylostatistics and some discussion of major works in the field. The "study of style as *such,* that is, investigation of the techniques used by authors" has seldom employed quantitative methods, she writes. "I think this is a pity. Many estimable works are written on the language and style of Author X, without any attempt to measure how far his style differs from that of his contemporaries" (p. 118). "Syntax has up to now rarely been subjected to numerical investigation. What often appears under the heading syntax in quantitative studies is really an investigation of specialized vocabulary—like causal conjunctions" (p. 127).

1   *Readings in Automatic Language Processing,* ed. David G. Hays. New York, 1966.

2   RICKERT, EDITH. *New Methods for the Study of Literature.* Chicago, 1927.

3   ROBERTS, A. HOOD. *A Statistical Linguistic Analysis of American English.* The Hague, 1965.
     Roberts presents "a quantitative analysis of the segmental phonemes of a speaker of a North Central U.S. idiolect. With the aid of a digital computer, the 10,000-word corpus was analyzed with results that should help fill several needs in present-day linguistic study. Among these findings are the following: 1) the etymological composition of English according to proximate sources by thousands of frequency; 2) the canonical forms of the words in the language according to the classification of the phonemes as vowel, consonant, semivowel and as to places and manner of articulation; 3) the frequency of occurrence of the phonemes of the language; 4) the average word length in phonemes and in syllables by thousands of frequency; 5) the relationship between the alphabetic and phonemic systems of notation; 6) the frequencies of occurrence of initial, intervocalic and final consonants and consonant clusters; 7) the entropy of English determined by the relative frequencies of the phonemes in the corpus and by word length in phonemes and in syllables; 8) the transitional probabilities of phonemes; 9) the Standard Error of a Proportion, the Standard Error of Difference between the two proportions, and the Standard Error Deviation for consonants and vowels separately and together."

4   ROSS, A. S. C. "Philological Probability Problems," *Journal of the Royal Statistical Society,* series B, XII (1950), 19–59.

5   ROSS, DONALD, JR. "The Style of Thoreau's *Walden.*" Unpublished dissertation presented to the University of Michigan, 1967.
     Ross's study adapts statistical methods and the linguistic theory of M. A. K. Halliday to the critical examination of literary style. The primary concerns are lexis and syntax, and the distribution of functional word-classes.

6   SCHRÖDER, HARTWIG. *Quantitative Stilanalyse: Versuch einer Analyse- quantitativer Stilmerkmale unter psychologischen Aspekt.* Würtzburg, 1960.

7   SEBEOK, THOMAS A. "Notes on the Digital Calculator as a Tool for Analyzing Literary Information," in *Poetics,* pp. 571–590.

8   ———, AND VALDIS J. ZEPS. "Computer Research in Psycholinguistics: Towards an Analysis of Poetic Language," *Behavioral Science,* VI (1961), 365–369.

9   SEDELOW, SALLY YEATES, AND WALTER A. SEDELOW, JR. "A Preface to Computational Stylistics" (1964), in *The Computer and Literary Style,* ed. Jacob Leed (Kent, Ohio, 1966), pp. 1–13.

1 SEDELOW, SALLY YEATES, AND D. G. BOBROW. "A LISP Program for Use in Stylistic Analysis." Santa Monica: Systems Development Corporation Report TM-1753, 1964.

2 SEDELOW, SALLY YEATES, AND TERRY RUGGLES. "Updating the THESAUR Program." Santa Monica: Systems Development Corporation Report TM-1908/009/00, 1965.

3 SEDELOW, SALLY YEATES. "Form Recognition in Literature," in Proceedings of the IFIP Congress (Washington: Spartan Books, 1965), vol. II, pp. 626–627.

4 ———. "Stylistic Analysis: Report on the Second Year of Research." Santa Monica: Systems Development Corporation Report TM-1908/200/00, 1966.

5 ———. "Stylistic Analysis: Report on the Third Year of Research (Final Report under this Contract)." Santa Monica: Systems Development Corporation Report TM-1908/300/00, 1967.

6 SEDELOW, SALLY YEATES, AND WALTER A. SEDELOW, JR. "Stylistic Analysis," in Automated Language Processing, ed. H. Borko (New York, forthcoming), Chapter 6.

7 SHERMAN, L. A. "Some Observations upon the Sentence-Length in English Prose," University of Nebraska Studies, I, xxi (1888), 119–130.

8 ———. "On Certain Facts and Principles in the Development of Form in Literature," University of Nebraska Studies, I, iv (1892), 337–366.

9 SIMMONS, ROBERT F. "Automated Language Processing," in Annual Review of Information Science and Technology, ed. C. A. Cuadra (New York, 1966), vol. I, pp. 137–169.
In addition to a survey of the field, Simmons provides an extensive bibliography.

10 SOMERS, H. H. Analyse mathématique du langage: lois générales et mesures statistiques. Louvain, 1959.

11 ———. Analyse statistique du style: différences individuelles et facteurs psychologiques. Louvain, 1960.

12 ———. "The Measurement of Grammatical Constraints," Language and Speech, IV (1961), 150–156.

13 ———. "Statistical Methods in Literary Analysis," in The Computer and Literary Style, ed. Jacob Leed (Kent, Ohio, 1966), pp. 128–140.

14 SPANG-HANSSEN, HENNING. "Sentence Length and Statistical Linguistics," in Structures and Quanta: Three Essays on Linguistic Description, ed. Alvar Ellegård (Copenhagen, 1963), pp. 58–72.

1   STARKWEATHER, J. A., AND J. B. DECKER. "Computer Analysis of
    Interview Content," *Psychological Reports*, XV (1964), 875–882.

2   STEELE, R. B. "Non-Recurrence in Vocabulary as a Test of Author-
    ship," *PQ*, IV (1925), 267–280.

3   STONE, PHILIP J., DEXTER C. DUNPHY, MARSHALL S. SMITH, AND
    DAVID M. OGILVIE. *The General Inquirer: A Computer Approach to
    Content Analysis*. Cambridge, Mass., and London, 1966.
    See especially Allan B. Ellis and F. André Favat, "From Computer
    to Criticism: An Application of Automatic Content Analysis to Lit-
    erature," pp. 628–637.

4   ŚWIECZKOWSKI, WALERIAN. "On the Margin of Syntax and Style
    (A Quantitative Study)," in *Poetics*, pp. 463–469.
    The author is concerned with the frequency of pronoun reference both
    within and across sentence boundaries. After an examination of texts
    by Kipling, J. B. Priestley, Virginia Woolf, and Llewelyn Tipping
    (*A Higher English Grammar*), he offers an expanded definition of style
    to include structures larger than the sentence.

5   TANNENBAUM, P. H., AND R. K. BREWER. "Consistency of Syntactic
    Structure as a Factor of Journalistic Style," *Journalism Quarterly*,
    XLII (1965), 273–275.

6   TASMAN, P. "Literary Data Processing," *IBM Journal of Research
    and Development*, I, iii (1957), 249–256.
    "Abstract: A Method is presented for rapid compilation of analytical
    indexes and concordances of printed works, using either a conventional
    punched-card system or an electronic data processing machine. A
    detailed description of the procedures used in automatically analyzing
    and indexing the *Summa Theologica* of St. Thomas Aquinas is given.
    Reference is also made to the indexing of the Dead Sea Scrolls using
    an IBM 705" (p. 249).

7   TAYLOR, W. "The Prose Style of Johnson," *University of Wisconsin
    Studies in Language and Literature*, II (1918), 22–56.

8   THAVENIUS, JAN. "Kvantitativa metoder i stilistiken," in *Litteratur-
    vetenskap: Nya mål och metoder* (Stockholm: Natur och Kultur, 1966),
    pp. 37–62.

9   TODOROV, TZVETAN. "Procédés mathématiques dans les études
    littéraires," *Annales*, III (1965), 503–510.

10 ULLMANN, STEPHEN. "New Bearings in Stylistics," in his *Language
    and Style* (New York, 1964), pp. 118–121.
    Ullmann claims that stylostatistics: misses subtle nuances, provides a
    "spurious kind of precision on data too intricate or too fluid to admit
    of such treatment" (p. 119), makes no provision for context, and
    records the obvious. Stylostatistics can, he says, settle cases of disputed

authorship and give rough ideas about density and distribution of stylistic features.

1   ULRICH, NORBERT. "Über ein mathematisches Modell zur Bestimmung literarischer Stilkomponenten," in *Mathematik und Dichtung*, pp. 185–192.

2   USHER, S. "Some Observations on Greek Historical Narrative from 400–1 B.C.: A Study in the Effect of Outlook and Environment on Style," *American Journal of Philology*, LXXXI (1960), 358–372. Usher employs stylostatistical methods in his study of such writers as Xenophon, Polybius, Thucydides, and Diodorus Siculus.

3   VINCENT, E. R. "Mechanical Aids for the Study of Language and Literary Style," in *Literature and Science: Proceedings of the Sixth Triennial Congress of the International Federation for Modern Languages and Literatures* (Oxford, 1955), pp. 56–60.

4   WACHAL, ROBERT S. "On Using a Computer," in *The Computer and Literary Style*, ed. Jacob Leed (Kent, Ohio, 1966), pp. 14–37.

5   WELLS, FREDERIC L. "A Statistical Study of Literary Merit," *Archives of Psychology*, VII (August 1907), 5–30.

6   WILLIAMS, C. B. "A Note on the Statistical Analysis of Sentence-Length as a Criterion of Literary Style," *Biometrika*, XXXI (1939), 356–361.

7   ———. "Statistics as an Aid to Literary Studies," *Science News* (Penguin), XXIV (1952), 99–106.

8   ———. "Studies in the History of Probability and Statistics IV: A Note on an Early Statistical Study of Literary Style," *Biometrika*, XLIII (1956), 248–256. Williams discusses the two papers by Mendenhall (*q.v.*).

9   WIMSATT, W. K., JR. *The Prose Style of Samuel Johnson*. New Haven, 1941 and 1963. Like Ullmann, Wimsatt is critical of methods that involve mere counting: "In considering philosophic words we have of course the the same problem of context as with the specific and sensory. We must proceed, not by statistics, but by examining the function of such words as may securely be called Johnsonian" (p. 61).

10 WINTER, WERNER. "Relative Häufigkeit syntaktischer Erscheinungen als Mittel zur Abgrenzung von Stilarten," *Phonetica*, VII (1961), 193–216. Abstract: "On the basis of rich data from two centuries of German letters, an attempt is made to use the relative frequency of certain syntactic features as a criterion for the delimitation of styles; German primarily spoken and German primarily written are isolated as basic categories" (p. 216).

1   ———. "Styles as Dialects," in *Ninth Congress Papers*, pp. 324–330. Winter describes his work in analyzing syntax by the methods of stylostatistics. "A style may be said to be characterized by a pattern of recurrent selections from the inventory of optional features of a language."

2   WORONCZAK, JERZY. "Statistische Methoden in der Verslehre," in *Poetics*, pp. 607–624.

3   YASUMOTO, B. "The Construction of Style Psychology," *Mathematical Linguistics*, No. 30 (1964), 1–16, and No. 31 (1964), pp. 1–15. In Japanese.

4   YULE, GEORGE UDNY. "On Sentence-Length as a Statistical Characteristic of Style in Prose, with Application to Two Cases of Disputed Authorship," *Biometrika*, XXX (1938), 363–390.

5   ———. *The Statistical Study of Literary Vocabulary*. Cambridge, 1944. Yule considers the problem of the identity of the author of *De Imitatione Christi* and determines, on the basis of vocabulary parameters, that Thomas à Kempis and not Jean Gerson is the author of the book. "The words *distinctive* of the *Imitatio* and Thomas à Kempis are largely words relating to simple personal (not institutional) religion" (p. 267).

6   ZIERNER, E. "Algunas características matemáticas del estilo," *Lenguaje y Ciencias*, V (1962).

7   ZIPF, GEORGE KINGSLEY. *Selected Studies of the Principle of Relative Frequency in Language*. Cambridge, Mass., 1932.

8   ———. *The Psycho-Biology of Language*. Boston, 1935.

9   ———. "The Repetition of Words, Time-Perspective, and Semantic Balance," *The Journal of General Psychology*, XXXII (1945), 127–148.
Zipf tests his length-frequency formula on Joyce's *Ulysses*.

10   ———. "The Meaning-Frequency Relationship of Words," *The Journal of General Psychology*, XXXIII (1945), 251–256.

11   ———. *Human Behavior and the Principle of Least Effort*. Cambridge, Mass., 1949.

12   ZUBRZYCKI, S. "Concerning Yule's Characteristic of Style," *Zastosowania Matematyki*, IV (1959), 328–331.

PROBLEMS IN TRANSLATION

13   ABERNATHY, ROBERT. "The Problems of Linguistic Equivalence," in *Proceedings of the Twelfth Symposium on Applied Mathematics: On the Structure of Language*, ed. Roman Jakobson (Providence, R.I., 1961), pp. 95–98.

1   ALEGRIA, FERNANDO. "How Good Is a Translation," *Américas*, VI
    (1954), 36–38.

2   ALEKSEEV, M. "Problema khudozhestvennogo perevoda" ["The
    Problem of Artistic Translation"], *Sbornik Trudov Irkutskogo Gos.
    Universiteta*, XVIII (1931), 149–196.

3   AMOS, F. R. *Early Theories of Translation.* New York, 1920.

4   ANDREYEV, N. D. "Linguistic Aspects of Translation," in *Ninth
    Congress Papers*, pp. 625–634.

5   ARROWSMITH, WILLIAM, AND ROGER SHATTUCK (eds.). *The Craft
    and Context of Translation: A Critical Symposium.* Garden City, N.Y.,
    1964.

6   BATES, ERNEST S. *Modern Translation.* Oxford, 1936.

7   BISHOP, JOHN PEALE. "On Translating Poets," *Poetry*, LXII (1943),
    111–115.

8   BOOTH, ANDREW D. "The History and Recent Progress of Machine
    Translation," in *Aspects of Translation*, ed. Leonard Foster (London:
    Communications Research Centre Studies in Communication II,
    1958), pp. 88–104.

9   BRANDWOOD, LEONARD. "Previous Experiments in Mechanical
    Translation," *Babel*, II (1956), 125–127.

10 BROWER, REUBEN A. "Seven Agamemnons," *Journal of the History
    of Ideas*, VIII (1947), 383–408; reprinted in *On Translation*, pp. 173–
    195.

11 ———. "Poetic and Dramatic Structure in Versions and Trans-
    lations of Shakespeare," in *Poetics*, pp. 655–674.

12 CARY, EDMOND. "Théories soviétiques de la traduction," *Babel*,
    III (1957), 179–189.

13 ———. "Prolegomena for the Establishment of a General Theory
    of Translation," *Diogenes*, XL (1962), 96–121.

14 ———, AND R. W. JUMPELT (eds.). *Quality in Translation.* New
    York, 1963.

15 CASAGRANDE, JOSEPH B. "The Ends of Translation," *IJAL*, XX
    (1954), 335–340.

16 CATFORD, J. C. *A Linguistic Theory of Translation: An Essay in Applied
    Linguistics.* New York, 1965.

17 CHAMBERLAIN, A. F. "Translation: A Study in the Transference of
    Folk-Thought," *Journal of American Folk-Lore*, XIV (1901), 165–171.

1   CHAO, YUEN REN. "Translation without Machine," in *Ninth Congress Papers*, pp. 504–510.

2   DARBELNET, J. "Valeurs sémantiques du verbe en français et en anglais," *Canadian Journal of Linguistics*, IX (1963), 32–39.

3   DELAVENAY, EMILE. *An Introduction to Machine Translation*. New York, 1960.

4   ——, AND K. DELAVENAY. *Bibliography of Mechanical Translation*. The Hague, 1960.

5   DRAPER, JOHN. "The Theory of Translation in the 18th Century," *Neophilologus*, VI (1921), 241–254.

6   EBEL, JULIA GRACIA. "Studies in Elizabethan Translation," *DA*, XXVI (1965), 354.

7   FIRTH, J. R. "Linguistic Analysis and Translation," in *For Roman Jakobson*, ed. Morris Halle (The Hague, 1956), pp. 133–139.

8   FLETCHER, IAN. "Translation," in *The Concise Encyclopedia of English and American Poetry*, eds. Stephen Spender and Donald Hall (New York, 1963), pp. 333–336.

9   FOLEY, JOSEPH, AND JAMES AYER. "Orwell in English and Newspeak: A Computer Translation," *CCC*, XVII (1966), 15–18.

10   FORSTER, LEONARD. "Translation: An Introduction," in *Aspects of Translation*, ed. Leonard Forster (London: Communications Research Centre Studies in Communication II, 1958), pp. 1–28.

11   FRASER, G. S. "On Translating Poetry," *Arion*, V (1966), 129–148.

12   FRENZ, HORST. "The Art of Translation," in *Comparative Literature: Method and Perspective*, eds. Newton P. Stallknecht and Horst Frenz (Carbondale, Ill., 1961).

13   GOUGENHEIM, GEORGES. "Structure grammaticale et traduction automatique," *La Traduction Automatique*, I (1960), 3–10.

14   GUILLÉN, CLAUDIO. "The Art of Translation," *Comparative Literature*, XVII (1965), 340–342.

15   HOCKETT, CHARLES F. "Translation via Immediate Constituents," *IJAL*, XX (1954), 313–315.

16   HOLLANDER, JOHN. "Versions, Interpretations, and Performances," in *On Translation*, pp. 205–231.

17   *International Conference on Machine Translation of Languages and Applied Language Analysis*. 2 vols. London, 1962.

18   JACOBSEN, ERIC. *Translation: A Traditional Craft*. Copenhagen, 1958.

1 JAKOBSON, ROMAN. "O překladu veršu" ["Translation of Verses"], *Plan*, II (1930), 9–11.

2 ———. "On Linguistic Aspects of Translation," in *On Translation*, pp. 232–239.

3 JANSONIENÉ, N. "Theory of Grammar as Applied to Problems of Translation," *Kalbotyra: Lietuvos TSR Aukųtųjų Mokyklūš Mokslo Darbai*, XII (1965), 75–89.

4 KEY, WILSON BRYAN, JR. "Cloze Procedure: A Technique for Evaluating the Quality of Language Translation," *Journal of Communication*, IX (1959), 14–18.

5 KNIGHT, DOUGLAS. "Translation: The Augustan Mode," in *On Translation*, pp. 196–204.

6 KNOX, RONALD ARBUTHNOTT. *On English Translation*. Oxford, 1957.

7 LATTIMORE, RICHMOND. "Practical Notes on Translating Greek Poetry," in *On Translation*, pp. 48–56.

8 LEVENSTON, E. A. "The 'Translation-Paradigm': A Technique for Contrastive Syntax," *International Review of Applied Linguistics in Language Teaching*, III (1965), 221–225.

9 LEWIS, C. DAY. "On Translating Poetry," *Essays by Divers Hands*, XXXII (1963), 18–26.

10 LOCKE, WILLIAM N., AND A. DONALD BOOTH (eds.). *Machine Translation of Languages*. Cambridge, Mass., and New York, 1955.

11 LONGACRE, ROBERT E. "Items in Context: Their Bearing on Translation Theory," *Language*, XXXIV (1958), 482–491.

12 LONGYEAR, CHRISTOPHER RUDSTON. "Linguistically Determined Categories of Meanings: A Comparative Analysis of Meaning in 'The Snows of Kilimanjaro' in English and German," *DA*, XXII (1962), 2381–2382.

13 MATTHIESSEN, F. O. *Translation: An Elizabethan Art*. Cambridge, Mass., 1931.

14 MAYMI, P. "Grammatical Principles and Techniques in Language Translation," *Hispania*, XLII (1958), 233–238.

15 MILLER, WILLIAM E. "Double Translation in English Humanistic Education," *Studies in the Renaissance*, X (1963), 163–174.

16 MORGAN, BAYARD Q. "In Defense of Translation," *Modern Language Journal*, I (1917), 235–242.

17 ———. "The Art of Translation," *Modern Language Journal*, XIII (1928–1929), 80–85.

1   ———. *On Romanticism and the Art of Translation*. Princeton, 1956.

2   ———. "What Is Translation For?" *Symposium*, X (1956), 322–328.

3   ———. "Critical Bibliography," in *On Translation*, pp. 271–293.

4   NEWMARK, PETER. "Standards of Translation," *Journal of Education* (London), LXXXIX (1957), 248–250.

5   NIDA, EUGENE A. *Bible Translating: An Analysis of Principles and Procedures, with Special Reference to Aboriginal Languages*. New York, 1947.

6   ———. "Translation or Paraphrase," *The Bible Translator*, I (1950), 97–109.

7   ———. "Principles of Translation as Exemplified by Bible Translating," in *On Translation*, pp. 11–31.

8   ———. "Bible Translating and the Science of Linguistics," *Babel*, IX (1963), 99–104.

9   ———. *Toward a Science of Translating, with Special Reference to Principles and Procedures Involved in Bible Translating*. Leiden, 1964. See the extensive bibliography, pp. 265–320.

10   OETTINGER, ANTHONY G. "Automatic Transference, Translation, Remittance, Shunting," in *On Translation*, pp. 240–267.

11   ———. "A New Theory of Translation and Its Application," in *Proceedings of the National Symposium on Machine Translation*, eds. H. P. Edmundson (Englewood Cliffs, N.J., 1961), pp. 363–366.

12   PANOV, D. Y. *Automatic Translation*. New York, 1960.

13   PIKE, KENNETH L. "A Training Device for Translation Theory and Practice," *Bibliotheca Sacra*, CXIV (1957), 347–362.

14   PROCHÁZKA, VLADIMÍR. "Notes on Translating Technique," *Slóvo a Slovesnost*, VIII (1942), 1–20; reprinted in *A Prague School Reader on Esthetics, Literary Structure, and Style*, ed. Paul L. Garvin (Washington, D.C., 1964), pp. 93–112.

15   QUINE, WILLARD V. "Meaning and Translation," in *On Translation*, pp. 148–172.

16   RABIN, C. "The Linguistics of Translation," in *Aspects of Translation*, ed. Leonard Forster (London: Communications Research Centre Studies in Communication II, 1958), pp. 123–145.

17   RAFFEL, BURTON. "Music, Poetry and Translation," *Antioch Review*, XXIV (1964–1965), 453–461.

1   RICHARDS, I. A. "Toward a Theory of Translating," in *Studies in Chinese Thought*, ed. Arthur F. Wright (Chicago, 1953), pp. 247–262.

2   SALZMANN, ZDENEK. "Cultures, Languages, and Translations," *Anthropological Linguistics*, II (1960), 43–47.

3   SAVORY, THEODORE. *The Art of Translation*. London, 1957.

4   SCHOLZ, KARL WILLIAM HENRY. *The Art of Translation*. Philadelphia, 1918.

5   STEINER, GEORGE. "To Traduce or Transfigure: Modern Verse Translation," *Encounter*, XXVII, ii (1966), 48–54.

6   SWADESH, MORRIS. "On the Unit of Translation," *Anthropological Linguistics*, II (1960), 39–42.

7   URE, JEAN. "Types of Translation and Translatability," *Babel*, X (1964), 5–11.

8   WINNY, JAMES (ed.). *Elizabethan Prose Translation*. Cambridge, 1960.

9   YOUNG, RICHARD E. "Theories of Translating Poetry in Victorian England," *DA*, XXV (1964), 3587.

PROSE STYLISTICS

Structures of Sound in Prose

10 ABERCROMBIE, DAVID. "Conversation and Spoken Prose," *English Language Teaching*, XVIII (1963), 10–16.

11 ANDERTON, BASIL. "Sir Thomas Browne," in his *Sketches from a Library Window*. New York, 1923. Pp. 135–172.

12 BAUM, PAULL FRANKLIN. . . . *the other harmony of prose; An Essay in English Prose Rhythm*. Durham, N.C., 1952.
    Written in response to Wimsatt's rejection of the notion of prose rhythm, Baum's *Other Harmony* discerns a metrical structure in prose and relates it to the rhetorical and intonational pattern. "In general, prose which we regard as excellent in other respects, as really excellent, is likely to excell in rhythm also" (pp. 204–205).

13 ———. "Prose Rhythm," in *Encyclopedia of Poetry and Poetics*, eds. Alex Preminger *et al*. (Princeton, 1965), pp. 666–667.

14 CLARK, A. C. *Prose Rhythm in English*. Oxford, 1913.

15 CLASSÉ, ANDRÉ. *The Rhythm of English Prose*. Oxford, 1939. Shapiro.

16 COTT, JEREMY. "Structures of Sound: The Last Sentence of *Wuthering Heights*," *TSLL*, VI (1964), 280–289.

1 CROLL, MORRIS W. "The Cadence of English Oratorical Prose," *SP*, XVI (1919), 29–54; reprinted in *Style, Rhetoric, and Rhythm: Essays by Morris W. Croll*, ed. J. Max Patrick, et al. (Princeton, 1966), pp. 303–359.

2 DAHL, THORSTEN. "Alliteration in English Prose," *English Studies* (Amsterdam), XL (1959), 449–454.

3 VAN DRATT, P. FIJN. "Rhythm in English Prose," *Anglia*, XXXVI (1912), 1–58.

4 ———. "The Place of the Adverb: A Study in Rhythm," *Neophilologus*, VI (1921), 56–88.

5 ELTON, OLIVER. "English Prose Numbers," *Essays and Studies*, IV (1913), 29–54; reprinted in his *A Sheaf of Papers*. London, 1922. Pp. 130–163.

6 EMDEN, CECIL S. "Rhythmical Features in Dr. Johnson's Prose," *RES*, XXV (1949), 38–54.

7 FOSTER, F. M. K. "Cadence in English Prose," *JEGP*, XVI (1917), 456–462.

8 FOWLER, ROGER. " 'Prose Rhythm' and Metre," *Essays on Style and Language*, pp. 82–99.

9 GRIFFITH, HELEN. *Time Patterns in Prose*. Princeton, 1929.

10 HART, CLIVE. "Musical Qualities in Joyce's Late Prose," *Australasian Universities Language and Literature Association, Proceedings*, II (1964), 32–33.

11 HONAN, PARK. "Metrical Prose in Dickens," *Victorian Newsletter*, No. 28 (1965), 1–3.

12 LIPSKY, ABRAM. "Rhythm as a Distinguishing Characteristic of Prose Style," *Archives of Psychology*, IV (1907), 1–44.

13 MALONEY, MICHAEL F. "Meter and *Cursus* in Sir Thomas Browne's Prose," *JEGP*, LVIII (1959), 60–67.

14 MORGAN, M. M. "A Treatise in Cadence," *MLR*, XLVII (1952), 152–164.

15 MORIER, HENRI. *Dictionnaire de Poétique et de Rhétorique*. Paris, 1961. See Morier's treatment of "Prose cadencée, prose poétique, et poème en prose," pp. 313–333.

16 PATTERSON, WILLIAM MORRISON. *The Rhythm of Prose: An Experimental Investigation of Individual Differences in the Sense of Rhythm*. New York, 1916.

1   "Prose Rhythm," *TLS* (September 13, 1957), 547.

A leading article based on remarks on prose rhythm in *The Elements of Style* by William Strunk, Jr., and revised by E. B. White (New York, 1959).

2   SAINTSBURY, GEORGE. *A History of English Prose Rhythm.* London, 1912 and Bloomington, Indiana, 1965. Shapiro.

3   SCOTT, FRED NEWTON. "The Scansion of Prose Rhythm," *PMLA*, XX (1908), 707–728.

4   SCOTT, JOHN HUBERT. "Rhythmic Prose," *University of Iowa Humanistic Studies*, III, i (1925–1927).

Scott gives a brief survey of ancient and modern notions of rhythm and then applies a metrical analysis to examples of selected prose.

5   SHELLY, J. "Rhythmical Prose in Latin and English," *SP*, XVI (1919), 1–55.

6   SONNENSCHEIN, EDWARD A. *What is Rhythm?* Oxford, 1925. Shapiro.

7   TEMPEST, NORTON R. "Rhythm in the Prose of Sir Thomas Browne," *RES*, III (1927), 308–318.

8   ————. *The Rhythm of English Prose.* Cambridge, 1939.

9   WESTERN, AUGUST. *On Sentence-Rhythm and Word-Order in Modern English.* Christiania, 1908.

10   WIMSATT, W. K., JR. *The Prose Style of Samuel Johnson.* New Haven, 1941 and 1963.

" 'Rhythm' as applied to prose is a metaphor. 'Rhythm,' when used literally, means 'measure' or 'regularity,' and since the movement of good prose is precisely *not* regular but varied with the sense, the union of the terms 'prose' and 'rhythm' has been none the happiest" (p. 8).

Other Linguistic Aspects of Prose

11   ADAM, DONALD G. "John Dryden: A Study of His Prose Achievement," *DA*, XXIV (1963), 2025–2026.

12   AITKEN, DAVID. " 'A Kind of Felicity': Some Notes about Trollope's Style," *Nineteenth-Century Fiction*, XX (1966), 337–353.

13   ALBRECHT, ROBERT C. "Content and Style in *The Red Badge of Courage*," *CE*, XXVII (1966), 487–492.

14   ALLEN, WARD S. "The Influence of Greek Rhetorical Structure on the English of the Authorized Version of the New Testament," *DA*, XXIV (1963), 2010.

15   ALLOTT, KENNETH, AND MIRIAM ALLOTT (eds.). "Introduction," *Victorian Prose 1830–1880.* London, 1956.

1   ALY, B. *The Rhetoric of Alexander Hamilton.* New York, 1941.

2   ANDERSON, CHARLES R. "Hemingway's Other Style," *MLN*, LXXVI (1961), 434–442.

3   ———. "Wit and Metaphor in Thoreau's *Walden*," in *USA in Focus: Recent Re-Interpretations*, ed. Sigmund Skard (Oslo, 1966). pp. 70–93.

4   ANTOINE, M. S. *The Rhetoric of Jeremy Taylor's Prose: Ornament of the Sunday Sermons.* Washington, D.C., 1946.

5   ANTRIM, HARRY T. "Faulkner's Suspended Style," *University Review* (Kansas City, Mo.), XXXII (1965), 122–128.

6   ARTHOS, JOHN. "The Prose of Goldsmith," *MLR*, I (1962), 51–55.

7   ASENJO, F. G. "The General Problem of Sentence Structure: An Analysis Prompted by the Loss of Subject in *Finnegans Wake*," *The Centennial Review of Arts and Science*, VIII (1964), 398–408.

8   AURNER, ROBERT R. "Caxton and the English Sentence," *Wisconsin Studies in Language and Literature*, XVIII (1923), 23–59.

9   BAILEY, RICHARD W. "The Public and Private Styles of the Earl of Chesterfield." Unpublished dissertation presented to the University of Connecticut, 1965.
     Bailey notes the use of such words as "simple," "ornamented," "elegant," and "terse" in the criticism of Chesterfield's style. After a survey of the use of modern linguistic techniques in the analysis of prose, he attempts to specify the qualities of Chesterfield's prose that give rise to such critical labels. He concludes with a comparison of the earl's letters and periodical essays.

10   BARISH, JONAS A. "The Prose Style of John Lyly," *ELH*, XXIII (1956), 14–35.
     Barish discusses "the excessive logicality" of Lyly's style and describes "Lyly's zeal for antithetic structure." He introduces his remarks on the style itself with a survey of the literary and philosophical origins of Euphuism.

11   ———. *Ben Jonson and the Language of Prose Comedy.* Cambridge, Mass., 1960.
     "Stylistic studies would seem to need an approach located somewhere between two pillars of unwisdom, between extreme statistic-hunting on the one hand and rank impressionism on the other, one that accepts the subjective basis for judgments of style but places this under conditions of maximum control. The method of Leo Spitzer (*et alia*) . . . may be mentioned, not as models, but as indications of the general direction this study intends to pursue" (pp. 44–45).

12   BARRIÈRE, MARCEL. *Essai sur l'art du roman.* Paris, 1931.

1   BATELY, JANET M. "Dryden's Revisions in the *Essay of Dramatic Poesy:* The Preposition at the End of a Sentence and the Expression of the Relative," *RES*, XV (1964), 268–282.

2   BEACH, JOSEPH WARREN. *The Outlook for American Prose.* Chicago, 1926. See esp. his chapter on Dreiser, "The Naive Style," pp. 177–196.

3   ———. "Style in *For Whom the Bell Tolls*," in *American Fiction, 1920–1940.* Pp. 111–119.

4   BEAUMONT, CHARLES ALLEN. *Swift's Classical Rhetoric.* Athens, Ga., 1961.

5   BECK, WARREN. "William Faulkner's Style," in *William Faulkner: Two Decades of Criticism,* eds. Frederick J. Hoffman and Olga W. Vickery. East Lansing, Mich., 1951. Pp. 147–164.

6   BENNETT, H. S. "Fifteenth Century Secular Prose," *RES*, XXI (1945), 257–263.

7   BENNETT, JOAN. "An Aspect of Seventeenth Century Prose," *RES*, XIX (1943), 33–43.

8   BERGER, MONROE. "Thornstein Veblen's Literary Style," *Cairo Studies in English* (1961–1962), pp. 17–35.

9   BERNARD, F. V. "A Stylistic Touchstone for Johnson's Prose,' *N&Q*, XI (1964), 63–64.

10 BEUM, ROBERT. "The Scientific Affinities of English Baroque Prose," *English Miscellany*, XIII (1962), 59–80.

11 BEVIS, DOROTHY. "*The Waves:* A Fusion of Symbol, Style and Thought in Virginia Woolf," *Twentieth-Century Literature*, II (1956), 5–20.

12 BIESE, Y. M. *Aspects of Expression: Eugene O'Neill's "Strange Interlude' and the Linguistic Presentation of the Interior Monologue.* Helsinki, 1963.

13 ———. *Notes on the Vocabulary in Compton Mackenzie's Novel 'The Lunatic Republic'.* Turku, 1963.

14 BISCHOFF, DIETRICH. *Sir Thomas Browne als Stilkünstler.* Heidelberg' 1943.

15 BLOOMFIELD, MORTON W., AND LEONARD NEWMARK. *A Linguistic Introduction to the History of English.* New York, 1963.
    In Chapter Six, the authors analyze the King James Version of the Lord's Prayer by means of a transformational-generative grammar.

16 BOND, HAROLD L. *The Literary Art of Edward Gibbon.* Oxford, 1960.

17 BOOTH, WAYNE C. *The Rhetoric of Fiction.* Chicago, 1961.

1   BOUGHNER, DANIEL C. "Notes on Hooker's Prose," *RES*, XV (1939), 194–200.

2   BOULTON, JAMES T. "Literature and Politics I: Tom Paine and the Vulgar Style," *EIC*, XII (1962), 18–33.

3   BOULTON, MARJORIE. *The Anatomy of Prose*. New York, 1954.

4   BOWLING, LAWRENCE EDWARD. "What is the Stream of Consciousness Technique?" *PMLA*, LXV (1950), 333–345.

5   BRADBROOK, FRANK W. "Style and Judgment in Jane Austen's Novels," *Cambridge Journal*, IV (1951), 515–537.

6   BRADY, FRANK. "Prose Style and the 'Whig' Tradition," *BNYPL*, LXVI (1962), 455–463.
    Brady adopts W. K. Wimsatt's definition of style as "one plane or level of the organization of meaning . . . the furthest elaboration of the one concept that is the center" (*The Prose Style of Samuel Johnson*, p. 11). He says that he "cannot find sufficient evidence to distinguish a Whig from a Tory prose style in the eighteenth century" (p. 458). Through an examination of Burke's prose style, Brady finds that the "center" of Burke's style is a pragmatic view of world events but that when circumstances conflict with his pragmatism, "Burke characteristically escapes through metaphor or analogy" (p. 460).

7   BREDVOLD, LOUIS I., ROBERT K. ROOT, AND GEORGE SHERBURN. "Introduction," *Eighteenth Century Prose*. New York, 1932.

8   BREWSTER, WILLIAM T. *Studies in Structure and Style, Based on Seven Modern English Essays*. New York, 1911.

9   BRIDGEMAN, RICHARD. *The Colloquial Style in America*. New York, 1966.

10 BROOK, G. L. "The Language of Dickens," *Bulletin of the John Rylands Library*, XLVII (1964), 32–48.

11 BROWN, DAVID D. "John Tillotson's Revisions and Dryden's 'Talent for English Prose,' " *RES*, XII (1961), 24–39.

12 BROWN, HUNTINGTON. *Prose Styles: Five Primary Types*. Minneapolis, 1966.

13 BROWNELL, WILLIAM C. *American Prose Masters*. New York, 1909, and Cambridge, Mass., 1963.
    See esp. chapters on Cooper's style (pp. 103–109), Emerson's (pp. 148–156), Lowell's (pp. 263–269), and Henry James's (pp. 327–332).

14 BUCKLER, WILLIAM E. (ed.). "Introduction," *Prose of the Victorian Period*. Boston, 1958.

15 BUCKLEY, SISTER MARY ANCILLE, F.M.D.M. "Elements of Style in Newman's *Apologia*," *Greyfriar* (Loudonville, N.Y.), IX (1966), 19–30.

1 BURKHARD, ARTHUR. *Conrad Ferdinand Meyer: The Style and the Man.*
   Cambridge, Mass., 1932.

2 CAMBON, GLAUCO. "Stile e percezione del numinoso in un racconto
   di Faulkner," *Studi Americani* (Roma), VII (1961), 147–162.

3 CARROLL, JOHN B. "Vectors of Prose Style," in *Style in Language*,
   pp. 283–293.
   Carroll and his associates chose twenty-nine pairs of adjectives (such
   as *meaningless* and *meaningful*) and asked eight "expert judges" to rate
   one hundred and fifty prose passages in terms of each pair. "Judges
   can often agree in making descriptive classifications of prose passages
   but they agree less often in making general evaluations of style"
   (pp. 288–289). The experimenters found it impossible to separate
   judgments based on style alone from judgments based on the subject
   matter of the prose.

4 CHAMBERS, R. W. *On the Continuity of English Prose from Alfred to
   More and His School.* Part of the introduction to Harpsfield's *Life
   of More*, eds. E. V. Hitchcock and R. W. Chambers. E.E.T.S.,
   No. 185. Reprinted separately, Oxford, 1932 and 1957.
   Chambers examines the critical view of More as the "Father of English Prose" and attempts to describe the "continuity" in prose writing
   from Old English times and its influence on More. "It is in the pos-
   session of this 'plain and open' style, which nevertheless can be varied
   'as matters do rise and fall,' that the excellence of the fourteenth-
   century devotional writers had consisted. In More and his school,
   following them, we find the same excellence" (p. cxx). See article
   by Norman Davis cited below.

5 CHANDLER, ZILPHA EMMA. "An Analysis of the Stylistic Technique
   of Addison, Johnson, Hazlitt, and Pater," *University of Iowa
   Humanistic Studies*, IV, iii (1928). 110 pp.
   Chandler chose 1500 word passages from her four authors and subjected them to intensive analysis based on traditional and *ad hoc*
   grammatical and rhythmical classification. She presents quantitative
   tables on such features as Saxon/classical etymology, type-token pat-
   terning, distribution of parts of speech, and some semantic classifications (e.g., concrete, abstract, sensory, etc.) at the word level. She
   is also concerned with the structure of "phrases" and their function
   at the sentence level. Her treatment of sentence rhythm is based on an
   hierarchy of nested, metrically oriented rhythm classifications. In a
   conclusion to each chapter, she describes the "positive" and "negative"
   qualities of each writer and in an (unpublished) companion volume,
   *A Synopsis of the Stylistic Theory and Practice of Addison, Johnson, Hazlitt,
   and Pater*, relates her findings to the remarks of each writer on prose
   style. Her work is discussed and criticized at length by Wimsatt
   (*The Prose Style of Samuel Johnson*) and Milic (*A Quantitative Approach
   to the Style of Jonathan Swift*).

6 CHISHOLM, WILLIAM S. "Sentence Patterns in *The Sound and the
   Fury*," *DA*, XXV (1965), 7254–7255.

1   CHITTICK, ROGER DALE. "The Augustinian Tradition in Seventeenth Century English Prose," *DA*, XVII (1957), 2606.

2   CHRISTENSEN, FRANCIS. "John Wilkins and the Royal Society's Reform of Prose Style," *MLQ*, VII (1946), 279–290.

3   ———. "Notes Toward a New Rhetoric," *CE*, XXV (1963), 7–18. See Section Two, "A Lesson from Hemingway," (pp. 12–18) for an analysis of style and syntax in "The Undefeated"; reprinted in his *Notes Toward a New Rhetoric* (New York, 1967), pp. 23–38.

4   CLARK, A. C. "Ciceronianism," in *English Literature and the Classics*, ed. George Stewart Gordon. Oxford, 1912.

5   COBAU, WILLIAM WEINSCHENK. "Rhetorical Modes in *The Pilgrim's Progress:* John Bunyan's Quest for Literary Art," *DA*, XXVI (1965), 1037–1038.

6   COHN, DORRIT. "Narrated Monologue: Definition of a Fictional Style," *Comparative Literature*, XVIII (1966), 97–112.

7   COOK, ALBERT S. (ed.). *The Bible and English Prose Style*. Boston, 1892.

8   COPE, JACKSON. "Seventeenth-Century Quaker Style," *PMLA*, LXXI (1956), 725–754.

9   CORDER, JIM W. "Rhetoric and Meaning in *Religio Laici*," *PMLA*, LXXXII (1967), 245–249.

10 CORIN, FERNAND. "Steinbeck and Hemingway—A Study in Literary Economy," *Revue des langues vivantes*, XXIV (1958), 60–75, 153–163.

11 COSTELLO, DONALD P. "The Language of 'The Catcher in the Rye,' " *AS*, XXXIV (1959), 172–181.

12 CRADDOCK, PATRICIA BLAND. "The Style and Construction of Gibbon's Autobiographies," *DA*, XXV (1965), 4684.

13 CRAIG, F. ARMOUR. "On the Style of *Vanity Fair*," in *Style in Prose Fiction*, pp. 87–113.

14 CRANE, WILLIAM G. *Wit and Rhetoric in the Renaissance: The Formal Basis of Elizabethan Prose Style*. New York, 1937.
Basing his discussion on the Aristotelian distinction between figures of thought and figures of expression, Crane describes the influence of classically oriented Renaissance rhetorical theory on the practice of Elizabethan writers.

15 CROLL, MORRIS W. " 'Attic Prose' in the Seventeenth-Century," *SP*, XVIII (1921), 79–128; reprinted in *Style, Rhetoric, and Rhythm: Essays by Morris W. Croll*, eds. J. Max Patrick *et al.* (Princeton, 1966), pp. 51–101.

1   ———. "Muret and the History of 'Attic Prose,'" *PMLA*, XXXIX (1924), 254–309; reprinted in *Style, Rhetoric, and Rhythm: Essays by Morris W. Croll,* eds. J. Max Patrick *et al.* (Princeton, 1966), pp. 107–162.

2   ———. "Attic Prose: Lipsius, Montaigne, Bacon," in *Schelling Anniversary Papers* (New York, 1923), pp. 117–150; reprinted in *Style, Rhetoric, and Rhythm: Essays by Morris W. Croll,* eds. J. Max Patrick *et al.* (Princeton, 1966), pp. 167–202.

3   ———. "The Baroque Style in Prose," in *Studies in English Philology: A Miscellany in Honor of F. Klaeber,* eds. Kemp Malone and Martin P. Ruud (Minneapolis, 1929), pp. 427–456; reprinted in *Style, Rhetoric, and Rhythm: Essays by Morris W. Croll,* eds. J. Max Patrick *et al.* (Princeton, 1966), pp. 207–233; reprinted in Chatman and Levin, pp. 341–361.
     "There are of course several elements of prose technique: diction, or choice of words; the choice of figures; the principle of balance or rhythm; the form of the period, or sentence; and in a full description of baroque prose all of these elements would have to be considered. The last-mentioned of them—the form of the period—is, however, the most important and the determinant of the others; and this alone is to be the subject of discussion in the following pages" (p. 429). Croll gives an extensive description of the two major styles of the anti-Ciceronian or baroque style, the "loose style," and "*stile coupé.*"

4   ———. "The Sources of Euphuistic Rhetoric," the introduction to *Euphues: The Anatomy of Wit; Euphues and his England,* eds. Morris W. Croll and Harry Clemons (London and New York, 1916), pp. xv–lxiv; reprinted in *Style, Rhetoric, and Rhythm: Essays by Morris W. Croll,* eds. J. Max Patrick *et al.* (Princeton, 1966), pp. 241–295.

5   CROW, JOHN C. "The Style of Henry James: *The Wings of the Dove,*" in *Style in Prose Fiction,* pp. 172–179.

6   CULLER, A. DWIGHT. "Method in the Study of Victorian Prose," *Victorian Newsletter,* No. 9 (1957), 1–4.

7   DAHL, THORSTEN. *Linguistic Studies in Some Elizabethan Writings I: An Inquiry into Aspects of the Language of Thomas Deloney.* Copenhagen, 1951.

8   DANIELLS, ROY. "Baroque Form in English Literature," *UTQ,* XIV (1945), 393–408.

9   DANIELS, R. BALFOUR. "The Common Touch," *Forum* (Houston), III, v (1960), 35–39.
     On Woodrow Wilson's prose style.

10   DAVIE, DONALD A. "Berkeley's Style in *Siris,*" *Cambridge Journal,* IV (1951), 427–433.

1 ———. "Irony and Conciseness in Berkeley and Swift," *Dublin Magazine*, N.S. XXVII (Oct.–Dec. 1952), 20–29.

2 ———. "Berkeley and the Style of Dialogue," *The English Mind*, XVIII (1964), 90–106.

3 DAVIES, HUGH SYKES. "Trollope and His Style," *RES*, I (1961), 73–85.

4 DAVIS, HERBERT. "The Conciseness of Swift," *Essays on the Eighteenth Century Presented to David Nichol Smith*, eds. J. R. Sutherland and F. P. Wilson (Oxford, 1945), 15–32.

5 DAVIS, NORMAN. "Styles in English Prose of the Late Middle and Early Modern Period," in *Langue et Littérature*, pp. 165–181.
Davis examines R. W. Chambers' *Continuity* [see above] and his definition of the tradition of English prose in such terms as "simple lucidity," "plainness and openness," and "a certain tone of self-possession." Davis asserts that Chambers' "description is not nearly precise enough to serve as a measure of continuity of style" (p. 173). He de-emphasizes the importance of the devotional writers as an influence on English prose. "In the formation of what seems to us today to be the most successful English prose of the early modern period, I would give much more weight than is commonly allowed to the two factors of French example and conversational use. If pressed, I should hold that conversational use was the more important in providing the essential rhythms, and French example in ordering the construction of sentences" (p. 181).

6 DILL, STEPHEN HORTON. "An Analysis of Some Aspects of Daniel Defoe's Prose Style," *DA*, XXVI (1965), 3922.

7 DOBRÉE, BONAMY. *Modern Prose Style*. Oxford, 1934. Revised edition, New York, 1964.
"Professor Dobrée consistently exhibits his keen sensitivity for good prose, but teachers and students who are seeking to develop a technique for analyzing style are not going to be much enlightened by [his] generalized, subjective commentary." Quoted from a review by Edward P. J. Corbett, *CE*, XXVI (1964), 247.

8 ———. "Some Aspects of Defoe's Prose," in *Pope and His Contemporaries*, eds. J. L. Clifford and L. A. Landa. Oxford, 1949. Pp. 171–184.

9 DOHERTY, G. D. "The Use of Language in S[cience] F[iction]," *SF Horizons*, I (1964), 43–53.

10 DONER, DEAN. "Virginia Woolf: The Service of Style," *Modern Fiction Studies*, II (1956), 1–12.

11 DOUGLAS, WALLACE W. "Drug Store Gothic: The Style of Robert Penn Warren," *CE*, XV (1954), 265–272.

1 DRISKELL, LEON VINSON. "An Evaluation of the Writings of Gilbert Burnet on the Basis of Stylistic Evidence," *DA*, XXVI (1965), 2747.

2 DUFFY, JOHN. "Walter Pater's Prose Style: An Essay in Theory and Analysis," *Style* (Arkansas), I (1967), 45–63.

3 DUNN, RICHARD J. " 'But We Grow Affecting; Let Us Proceed,' " *Dickensian*, LXII (1966), 53–55.
   Dunn discusses Dicken's stylistic self-consciousness.

4 EBLE, KENNETH. "The Craft of Revision: *The Great Gatsby*," *AL*, XXXVI (1964), 315–326.

5 ERÄMETSÄ, ERIK. *A Study of the Word "Sentimental," And Other Linguistic Characteristics of Eighteenth-century Sentimentalism in England.* Helsinki, 1951.

6 ———. "Notes on Richardson's Language," *Neuphilologische Mitteilungen* (Helsinki), LIII (1952), 18–20.

7 ERLICH, VICTOR. "Notes on the Uses of the Monologue in Artistic Prose," *International Journal of Slavic Linguistics and Poetics*, I–II (1959), 223–231.

8 FARRELL, WILLIAM J. "The Style and Action in *Clarissa*," *SEL*, III (1963), 365–375.

9 FIRKINS, OSCAR. *William Dean Howells.* Cambridge, Mass., 1924. See the chapters of Howells' style, pp. 304–321.

10 FISCH, HAROLD. "The Puritans and the Reform of Prose Style," *ELH*, XIX (1952), 220–248.

11 FIXLER, MICHAEL. "George Orwell and the Instrument of Language," *Iowa English Yearbook*, IX (1964), 46–54.

12 FLANAGAN, JOHN T. "Dreiser's Style in *An American Tragedy*," *TSLL*, VII (1965), 285–294.

13 FORSTER, E. M. "English Prose Between 1918 and 1939," *Two Cheers for Democracy*. New York, 1951. Pp. 272–284.

14 FORT, JOSEPH-BARTHELEMY. *Samuel Butler l'Ecrivain: Etude d'un Style.* Bordeaux, 1935.

15 FRANCIS, J. H. *From Caxton to Carlyle: A Study of the Development of Language, Composition and Style in English Prose.* Cambridge, 1957.

16 FRASER, G. S. "Macaulay's Style as an Essayist," *REL*, I (1960), 9–19.

17 FREEMAN, F. BARRON. "Convolutions and Quiddities: Melville's Style," in his *Melville's Billy Budd*. Cambridge, Mass., 1948. Pp. 97–114.

1 FREIMARCK, VINCENT. "The Bible and Neo-Classical Views of Style," *JEGP*, LI (1952), 507–526.

2 FREY, JOHN. "The Historical Present in Narrative Literature, Particularly in Modern German Fiction," *JEGP*, XLV (1946), 43–66.

3 FRIEDMAN, ALAN. "The Stream of Conscience as a Form in Fiction," *Hudson Review*, XVII (1964), 536–546.

4 FRIES, CHARLES C. "One Stylistic Feature of the 1611 English Bible," in *The Fred Newton Scott Anniversary Papers* (Chicago, 1927), pp. 175–187.

5 FULHAM, SISTER MARY VIANNEY, R.S.M. "Some Aspects of the Prose Style of Thomas More in His English Letters," *DA*, XXIII (1963), 4343.

6 GERBER, JOHN C. "The Relation between Point of View and Style in the Works of Mark Twain," in *Style in Prose Fiction*, pp. 142–171.

7 GERWIG, GEORGE WILLIAM. "On the Decrease of Predication and of Sentence Weight in English Prose," *University of Nebraska Studies*, II (1894), 17–44.

8 GIBSON, WALKER. "Behind the Veil: A Distinction Between Poetic and Scientific Language in Tennyson, Lyell, and Darwin," *Victorian Studies*, II (1958), 60–68.

9 GLASGOW, ELLEN. *A Certain Measure: An Interpretation of Prose Fiction.* New York, 1943.
Essays on her own writing.

10 GLENN, ROBERT BRUCE. "Linguistic Class-Indicators in the Speech of Dickens's Characters," *DA*, XXII (1961), 369.

11 GORDON, IAN A. *The Movement of English Prose.* London, 1966.

12 GRAHAM, JOHN. "Ernest Hemingway: The Meaning of Style," *Modern Fiction Studies*, VI (1960), 298–313; reprinted in *Ernest Hemingway*, ed. Carlos Baker (New York, 1962), pp. 183–192.

13 GRAINGER, JAMES M. "Studies in the Syntax of the King James Version," *SP*, II (1907), 1–60.

14 GRAVES, ROBERT, AND ALAN HODGE. *The Reader over Your Shoulder: A Handbook for Writers of English Prose.* London, 1933.
See the chapters on the history of style: "The Ornate and Plain Styles" (pp. 75–85), "Classical Prose" (pp. 86–98), "Romantic Prose" (pp. 99–111), and "Recent Prose" (pp. 112–126).

15 GREENE, DONALD J. "Is There a 'Tory' Prose Style?" *BNYPL*, LXVI (1962), 449–454.
Greene points out some of the difficulties involved in the use of Buffon's

aphorism "the style is the man" as an assumption for stylistic analysis, including the problems of determining the psychology of the "man" and the mechanics of the "style." His intuitive answer to the question posed in his title is "yes."

1   GREGORY, MICHAEL. "Old Bailey Speech in *A Tale of Two Cities*," *REL* (Leeds), VI, ii (1965), 42–55.

2   GRIFFIN, ROBERT J. "Tristram Shandy and Language," *CE*, XXIII (1961), 108–112.

3   GUERARD, ALBERT J. "The Prose Style of John Hawkes," *Critique: Studies in Modern Fiction*, VI, ii (1963), 19–29.

4   GUPTA, RAJ KUMAR. "Form and Style in Herman Melville's *Pierre: Or the Ambiguities*," *DA*, XXVI (1965), 1631–1632.

5   HALL, ROBERT A., Jr. "P. G. Wodehouse and the English Language," *Annali Istituto Universitario Orientale, Napoli, Sezione Germanica*, VII (1964), 103–121.

6   HARKNESS, S. "The Prose of Sir Philip Sidney," *University of Wisconsin Studies in Language and Literature*, II (1918), 57–76.

7   HARRIS, WENDELL V. "Style and the Twentieth-Century Novel," *Western Humanities Review*, XVIII (1964), 127–140.

8   HART, JAMES M. "Rhetoric in the Translation of Bede," in *An English Miscellany Presented to Dr. Furnivall in Honour of His Seventy-fifth Birthday*. Oxford, 1901. Pp. 150–154.

9   HART, JEFFREY. "John Dryden: The Politics of Style," *Modern Age*, VIII (1964), 399–408.

10   HARVEY, J. "The Content Characteristics of Best-Selling Novels," *Public Opinion Quarterly*, XVII (1953), 91–114.

11   HASAN, RUQAIYA. "A Linguistic Study of Contrasting Features in the Style of Two Contemporary English Prose Writers." Unpublished dissertation presented to the Faculty of Arts of the University of Edinburgh, May 1964.
     Hasan employs the system of grammatical description developed by M. A. K. Halliday to analyze and describe random samples from *Free Fall* by William Golding and *Anglo-Saxon Attitudes* by Angus Wilson. "The most important respect in which the present interpretation differs from many others is in insisting a) that 'stylistics' is a study of linguistic patterns alone and that it is not competent to discuss *qua* stylistics the 'emotive' aspect of these patterns and b) that the study of style embraces more than just the 'marked features' of style such as metaphor, simile, trope, inversion and so on" (p. iii).

12   HASHMI, SHAHNAZ. "Indirect Style in *To The Lighthouse*," *Indian Journal of English Studies* (Calcutta), II (1961), 112–120.

1   HASKELL, ANN SULLIVAN. "The Representation of Gullah-Influenced Dialect in Twentieth Century South Carolina Prose: 1922–1930," *DA*, XXV (1964), 3562–3563.

2   HAWKINS, MARION E. "Oliver Goldsmith the Essayist: A Study of Themes and Style," *DA*, XXV (1965), 5904–5905.

3   HAYAKAWA, HIROSHI. "Negation in William Faulkner," in *Studies Otsuka*, pp. 103–116.

4   HAYES, CURTIS W. "A Linguistic Analysis of the Prose Style of Edward Gibbon," *DA*, XXV (1965), 5268.

5   ———. "A Study in Prose Styles: Edward Gibbon and Ernest Hemingway," *TSLL*, VII (1965), 371–386.

6   HEILMAN, ROBERT B. "Hardy's Mayor: Notes on Style," *Nineteenth-Century Fiction*, XVIII (1964), 307–329.

7   HENDRICK, LEO T. "Henry James: The Late and Early Styles (A Stylistics Study)," *DA*, XIII (1953), 808–809.

8   HIGASHIDA, CHIAKI. "On the Prose Style of D. H. Lawrence," *Studies in English Literature* (Tokyo), XIX (1939), 545–556.

9   HIGGINSON, FRED H. "Style in *Finnegans Wake*," Abstract in *Style In Language*, p. 277; expanded in his *Anna Livia Plurabelle: The Making of a Chapter*. Minneapolis, 1960.

10 HIGHET, GILBERT. "Baroque Prose," in his *The Classical Tradition* (New York and London, 1949), pp. 322–354.

11 HIRSCHMAN, JACK A. "The Orchestrated Novel: A Study of Poetic Devices in Novels of Djuna Barnes and Hermann Broch, and the Influences of the Works of James Joyce upon Them," *DA*, XXII (1962), 3220.

12 HNATKO, EUGENE. "Studies in the Prose Style of Laurence Sterne," *DA*, XXIII (1963), 4685.

13 HODGART, MATTHEW. "Politics and Prose Style in the Late Eighteenth Century: The Radicals," *BNYPL*, LXVI (1962), 464–469.
    Hodgart discusses the style of Paine's *The Rights of Man* and Godwin's *Political Justice* and the influence of Burke's style upon them. "Paine's style, though to a lesser degree than Burke's, is metaphoric and analogical. The images are drawn from his experience: they are usually deeply felt yet carefully worked out; like Burke, he seems to think metaphorically" (p. 465). Godwin's "style reflects his abstraction from concrete, sensuous reality; when he does use metaphors they are usually dead ones" (p. 466).

14 HOLLAND, NORMAN N. "Style as Character: *The Secret Agent*," *Modern Fiction Studies*, XII (1966), 221–231.

1   HOLLOWAY, JOHN. *The Victorian Sage: Studies in Argument*. London, 1953.
Holloway analyzes rhetorical structure in the major nineteenth-century prose writers.

2   HOPKINS, VIOLA. "The Ordering Style of *The Age of Innocence*," *AL*, XXX (1958), 345–357.

3   HORNÁT, JAROSLAV. "Some Remarks on Fiction Style, Old and New," *Philologica Pragensia*, VIII (1965), 204–211.

4   HOUGHTON, WALTER. *The Art of Newman's "Apologia."* New Haven, 1945.

5   ———. "The Rhetoric of T. H. Huxley," *UTQ*, XVIII (1949), 159–175.

6   HOWELL, A. C. "*Res et Verba:* Words and Things," *ELH*, XIII (1946), 131–142; reprinted in *Essential Articles for the Study of English Augustan Backgrounds*, ed. Bernard Schelling. Hamden, Conn., 1961. Pp. 53–65.

7   HOWES, R. F. "The Talked and the Written," *QJS*, XXVI (1940), 229–235.

8   HURT, ELLEN LOUISE. "The Prose Style of Robert Burton: The Fruits of Knowledge," *DA*, XXV (1965), 5908.

9   JACK, IAN. "De Quincey Revises His *Confessions*," *PMLA*, LXXII (1957), 122–146.

10   JACKSON, ROBERT SUMNER. "The 'Inspired' Style of the English Bible," *Journal of the Bible and Religion*, XXIX (1961), 4–15.

11   JACOBSON, WILLIAM SPENCER. "The Rhetorical Structure of Fielding's Epic, *Joseph Andrews*," *DA*, XXVII (1966), 1057A–1058A.

12   JAMES, EUSTACE ANTHONY. "Defoe's Many Voices: Aspects of the Author's Prose Style and Literary Method," *DA*, XXVI (1965), 7318–7319.

13   JEFFERSON, D. W. "Introduction," *Eighteenth-Century Prose: 1700–1780*. London, 1956.

14   JEREMY, SISTER, C.S.J. "*The Violent Bear It Away:* A Linguistic Education," *Renascence*, XVII (1964), 11–16.

15   JOHNSON, PAMELA HANSFORD. "The Style," in *Hungry Gulliver: An English Critical Appraisal of Thomas Wolfe*. New York, 1948. Pp. 20–39.

16   JONES, HOWARD MUMFORD. "American Prose Style: 1700–1770," *HLB*, VI (1934), 115–151.

1   JONES, RICHARD FOSTER. "Science and English Prose Style in the
     Third Quarter of the Seventeenth Century," *PMLA*, XLV (1930),
     977–1009; reprinted in *The Seventeenth Century from Bacon to Pope
     . . . by Richard Foster Jones and Others Writing in His Honor* (Stan-
     ford, 1951), pp. 75–110; reprinted in *Essential Articles for the Study
     of English Augustan Backgrounds*, ed. Bernard Schelling (Hamden,
     Conn., 1961), pp. 66–102.

2   ————. "The Attack on Pulpit Eloquence in the Restoration: An
     Episode in the Development of the Neo-Classical Standard Prose,"
     JEGP, XXX (1931), 188–217; reprinted in *The Seventeenth Century
     from Bacon to Pope . . . by Richard Foster Jones and Others Writing in
     His Honor* (Stanford, 1951), pp. 111–142; reprinted in *Essential
     Articles for the Study of English Augustan Backgrounds*, ed. Bernard
     Schelling (Hamden, Conn., 1961), pp. 103–136.

3   ————. "Science and Language in England of the Mid-Seventeenth
     Century," *JEGP*, XXXI (1932), 315–331; reprinted in *The Seven-
     teenth Century from Bacon to Pope . . . by Richard Foster Jones and
     Others Writing in His Honor* (Stanford, 1951), pp. 143–160.

4   KALUŻA, I. "William Faulkner's Subjective Style," *Kwartalnik
     Neofilologiczny*, XI (1964), 13–29.

5   KAPLAN, FRED. "The Development of Dickens' Style," *DA*, XXVII
     (1966), 747A–748A.

6   KAPLAN, HAROLD. *The Passive Voice: An Approach to Modern Fiction*.
     Athens, Ohio, 1966.

7   KAULA, DAVID. "The Low Style in Nashe's *The Unfortunate Trav-
     eller*," *Studies in English Literature, 1500–1900*, VI (1966), 43–57.

8   KEGEL, CHARLES H. "Incommunicability in Salinger's *Catcher in
     the Rye*," *Western Humanities Review*, XI (1957), 188–190.

9   KELLY, JOHN C. "Lawrence Durrell's Style," *Studies* (Irish Quar-
     terly Review), LII (1963), 199–204.

10   KENNEY, WILLIAM. "Addison, Johnson, and the 'Energetick
     Style,'" *Studia Neophilologica*, XXXIII (1961), 103–114.

11   KING, JAMES ROY. "Certain Aspects of Jeremy Taylor's Prose
     Style," *English Studies* (Amsterdam), XXXVII (1956), 197–210.

12   KISSANE, LEEDICE. "Dangling Constructions in Melville's 'Bar-
     tleby,'" *AS*, XXXVI (1961), 195–200.

13   KNIGHTS, L. C. "Elizabethan Prose," *Scrutiny*, II (1934), 427–438;
     reprinted as Appendix A to his *Drama and Society in the Age of Jonson*
     (London, 1937), pp. 301–314.
     Elizabethan English "retained many more of the primitive functions
     of speech than are to be found after the seventeenth century. Not

only was the relation of word and thing, of word and action, far more intimate than in a society that obtains most of its more permanent impressions from books and newspapers, a large number of Elizabethan words and phrases are the direct equivalent of action—gestures of sociability, contempt, or offence (the Elizabethans had a particularly rich vocabulary of abuse)" (pp. 305–306).

1 KNOX, GEORGE. "James's Rhetoric of 'Quotes,' " *CE*, XVII (1956), 293–297.

2 KOCH, WALTER ALFRED. "Contrasts in the Novel," *Acta Linguistica* (Budapest), XVI (1966), 23–27.

3 KRANIDAS, THOMAS. " 'Decorum' and the Style of Milton's Anti-prelatical Tracts," *SP*, LXII (1965), 176–187.

4 ———. "Milton and the Rhetoric of Zeal," *TSLL*, VI (1965)' 423–432.

5 KRAUSE, S. J. "James's Revisions of the Style of *The Portrait of a Lady*," *AL*, XXX (1958), 67–88.

6 KRZYŻANOWSKI, JULIAN. "James Fenimore Cooper and Adam Mickiewicz: A Stylistic Device from Prison Lore," *International Journal of Slavic Linguistics and Poetics*, IV (1961), 75–83.

7 LANNERING, JAN. *Studies in the Prose Style of Joseph Addison*. Uppsala and Cambridge, Mass., 1951.

8 LASCELLES, MARY. *Jane Austen and Her Art*. Oxford, 1939.
See the chapter on Austen's style, pp. 87–116.

9 LAWTON, GEORGE. *John Wesley's English: A Study of His Literary Style*. London, 1962.
See the review in *TLS* (August 3, 1962), 559.

10 LEE, VERNON [pseud. of Violet Paget]. *The Handling of Words and other Studies in Literary Psychology*. New York, 1923.
Includes: "The Syntax of De Quincey," "The Rhetoric of Landor,' and "Carlyle and the Present Tense."

11 LEHAN, RICHARD. "Faulkner's Poetic Prose; Style and Meaning in 'The Bear,' " *CE*, XXVII (1965), 243–247.

12 LENZ, SISTER MARY BAYLON. "A Rhetorical Analysis of Cardinal Newman's *Apologia pro vita sua*," *DA*, XXIII (1963), 2518.

13 LEVIN, HARRY. "Observations on the Style of Ernest Hemingway," *KR*, XIII (1951), 581–609; reprinted as "The Prose of Ernest Hemingway," in his *Contexts of Criticism* (Cambridge, Mass., 1957), pp. 140–167.
"We need make no word-count to be sure that his literary vocabulary, with foreign and technical exceptions, consists of relatively few and

short words. The corollary, of course, is that every word sees a great deal of hard use. Furthermore, his syntax is informal to the point of fluidity, simplifying as far as possible the already simple system of English inflections" (p. 596).

1   ———. *The Power of Blackness: Hawthorne, Poe, Melville.* New York, 1953.

2   LEVINE, GEORGE. "The Prose of the *Apologia Pro Vita Sua,*" *Victorian Newsletter,* No. 27 (1965), 5–8.

3   LEVY, LEO B. "Picturesque Style in *The House of the Seven Gables,*" *New England Quarterly,* XXXIX (1966), 147–160.

4   LEWIS, EDWIN H. *The History of the English Paragraph.* Chicago, 1894.

5   LIEBLICH, HYMAN. "Matthew Arnold as Prose Stylist," *DA,* XXV (1964), 453.

6   LINDBERG, JOHN. "The Decadence of Style: Symbolic Structure in Carlyle's Later Prose," *Studies in Scottish Literature,* I (1964), 183–195.

7   LODGE, DAVID. *Language of Fiction: Essays in Criticism and Verbal Analysis.* New York, 1966.

8   LOWENHERZ, ROBERT J. "The Beginning of 'Huckleberry Finn,' " *AS,* XXXVIII (1963), 196–201.

9   LOWES, JOHN LIVINGSTON. "The Noblest Monument of English Prose," in *Essays in Appreciation.* Boston, 1936.

10   LUTWACK, LEONARD. "Melville's Struggle with Style: The Plain, the Ornate, the Reflective," *Forum* (Houston), III (1962), 11–17.

11   LYONS, JOHN O. "The Romantic Style in Salinger's 'Seymour: An Introduction,' " *Wisconsin Studies in Contemporary Literature,* IV, i (1963), 62–69.

12   MACDONALD, HUGH. "Another Aspect of Seventeenth-Century Prose," *RES,* XVII (1941), 281–297.
       See the article by Joan Bennett above.

13   MAJDIAK, DANIEL THOMAS. "The Prose Style of William Hazlitt," *DA,* XXVI (1965), 6698–6699.

14   MAJOR, JOHN CAMPBELL. "Matthew Arnold and Attic Prose Style," *PMLA,* LIX (1944), 1086–1103.

15   MARTIN, HAROLD C. "The Development of Style in Nineteenth-Century American Fiction," in *Style in Prose Fiction,* pp. 172–179.

16   MARX, LEO. "The Pilot and the Passenger: Landscape Conventions and the Style of *Huckleberry Finn,*" *AL,* XXVIII (1956), 129–146.

1 McFarlane, J. W. "Plasticity in Language: Some Notes on the Prose Style of Ernst Barlach," *MLR*, XLIX (1954), 451–460.

2 Mégroz, R. L. "Conrad's Craftsmanship," *This Quarter*, IV (1931), 130–141.

3 Mercier, Vivian. "James Joyce and the Macaronic Tradition," in *Twelve and a Tilly: Essays on the Occasion of the 25th Anniversary of Finnegans Wake* (London and Evanston, Ill., 1965), pp. 26–35.

4 Miller, Henry Knight. "Some Functions of Rhetoric in *Tom Jones*," *PQ*, XLV (1966), 209–235.

5 Minter, David Lee. "The Interpreted Design: A Study in American Prose," *DA*, XXVI (1965), 4667.

6 Minto, William. *A Manual of English Prose Literature*. Boston, 1901.

7 Mitchell, W. Fraser. *English Pulpit Oratory from Andrewes to Tillotson*. New York, 1932.

8 Mohanty, Jatindra Mohan. "*Walden*: Style Considered as Vision of Life," *Literary Criterion* (Mysore, India), VII, ii (1966), 78–85.

9 Moore, Harry T. "The Prose Style of D. H. Lawrence," in *Langue et Littérature*, pp. 317–318.
Moore outlines the varieties of "heightened and incantatory language" (p. 317) characteristic of four periods of Lawrence's artistic career.

10 Morgan, Raleigh, Jr. "Stylistic Devices and Levels of Speech in the Works of Hemingway," in *Sprache und Literatur Englands und Amerikas: III. Die wissenschaftliche Erschliessung der Prosa*. Tübingen, 1959. Pp. 145–154.

11 Morrissette, Bruce. "Narrative 'You' in Contemporary Literature," *Comparative Literature Studies*, II (1965), 1–24.

12 Morse, J. Mitchell. "The Mephistophelian Style of James Joyce," in *Langue et Littérature*, p. 308.
Morse points out that in all his work, Joyce was concerned with "etymological allusiveness and unobtrusive references to historical events or literary works, both so carefully subordinated to the narrative as to be invisible to the hasty or casual eye" (p. 309).

13 Munson, Gorham B. *Style and Form in American Prose*. New York, 1927.

14 Natanson, Maurice. "The Privileged Moment: A Study in the Rhetoric of Thomas Wolfe," *QJS*, XLIII (1957), 143–150.

15 Nejdefors-Frisk, Sonja. *George Moore's Naturalistic Prose*. Uppsala, 1952.

1   NOSEK, JIŘÍ. "Studies in Post-Shakespearean English: Prose Style," *Universitas Carolina: Philologica* (Prague), III (1957), 101–144.

2   OHMANN, RICHARD M. "Prolegomena to the Analysis of Prose Style," in *Style in Prose Fiction*, pp. 1–24; Bobbs-Merrill Reprint, *Language-70*; reprinted in Chatman and Levin, pp. 398–411.

The study of style, says Ohmann, attempts to discover an author's "habitual kinds of choice" (p. 15) from his confrontation with the universe. "In these multifarious *ur*-choices, these preverbal and verbal pigeon-holings, style has its beginnings" (p. 9). But the critic must be careful not to attribute the gestalten of language or of style register, norm, or genre of the writing to the free choice of the writer. The study of style, then, merges with the study of psychology, just as "emotion enters prose not only as disguises for slipping into the reader's confidence, but as sheer expression of self" (p. 21).

3   ————. *Arnold, Shaw, Wilde: Studies in Prose Style.* Unpublished dissertation presented to Harvard University, 1960.

Ohmann's dissertation must be consulted at the Harvard Archives (call number: HU 90.7826) or obtained on inter-library loan since it is not on microfilm.

4   ————. *Shaw: The Style and the Man.* Middletown, Conn., 1962.

Following the outline of his "prolegomena," Ohmann is concerned both "with style as a way of knowing and . . . with the rhetorical and emotional uses to which that way of knowing is put" (p. 73). His main concern is to use the results of his stylistic analysis to illuminate our knowledge of Shaw's world-view and to explain the emotive characteristics of Shaw's writing. Appendix I is an exposition of Ohmann's structural analysis of 2600 words from Shaw and like samples from five contemporaries of Shaw. In Appendix II, he tests his conclusions against the choices (and rejections) evidenced by four Shaw-corrected typescripts in the Houghton Library.

5   ————. "Generative Grammars and the Concept of Literary Style," *Word*, XX (1964), 423–439.

Ohmann discusses the rendering into form of literary content and the use of syntactic analysis to reveal an author's style. Hemingway and Faulkner are the subject of illustrative analysis.

6   ————. "Literature as Sentences," *CE*, XXVII (1966), 261–267; reprinted in Chatman and Levin, pp. 231–238.

Ohmann reasserts his critical theory with illustrations from Conrad and Dylan Thomas. "Since critical understanding follows and builds on an understanding of sentences, generative grammar should eventually be a reliable assistant in the effort of seeing just how a given literary work sifts through a reader's mind, what cognitive and emotional process it sets in motion, and what organization of experience it encourages" (p. 267).

7   ————. "Mentalism in the Study of Literary Language," to appear in *Studies in Psycholinguistics*, eds. Bever and Weksel.

Ohmann supposes a "nonce intuition" on the part of an author; just as a native speaker knows that certain sentences are English sentences, so too an author knows that certain utterances "belong" to the work he is writing. Gibbon, Bellow, and Henry James are examined in this light. Ohmann concludes his article with an examination of literary images.

1   OLIVER, H. J. "Izaak Walton's Prose Style," *RES*, XXI (1945), 280–288.

2   OLIVER, ROBERT T. "The Bible and Style," *The Sewanee Review*, XLII (1934), 350–355.

3   ORDOÑEZ, ELMER ALINDOGAN. "The Early Development of Joseph Conrad: Revisions and Style," *DA*, XXIII (1963), 4362.

4   OSINSKI, SISTER MARY LUCILLA, O.S.F. "A Study of the Structures of Coordination in a Representative Sample of the *Biographia Literaria*," *DA*, XXIV (1964), 3731–3732.

5   PAGE, NORMAN. "Standards of Excellence: Jane Austen's Language," *REL*, VII, iii (1966), 91–98.

6   PETERSON, R. G. "A Picture Is a Fact: Wittgenstein and *The Naked Lunch*," *Twentieth Century Literature*, XII (1966), 78–86.

7   PORIER, RICHARD. *A World Elsewhere: The Place of Style in American Literature*. New York, 1966.

8   POUND, LOUISE. "The Dialect of Cooper's Leatherstocking," *AS*, II (1927), 479–488.

9   POWELL, JOCELYN. "John Lyly and the Language of Play," in *Elizabethan Theatre* (= Stratford-upon-Avon Studies, VI) (London and New York, 1965), pp. 147–167.

10   PRAGER, LEONARD. "The Language of Shakespeare's Low Characters: An Introductory Study," *DA*, XXVII (1966), 751A–752A.

11   PRESCOTT, JOSEPH. "The Language of James Joyce's *Ulysses*," in *Langue et Littérature*, pp. 306–307.
    Prescott gives a brief outline of the variety and multiplicity of styles in *Ulysses*.

12   ———. "Stylistic Realism in Joyce's *Ulysses*," in *Stil- und Formprobleme*, pp. 339–343.

13   PRETZER, WALLACE LEONARD. "Eighteenth-Century Literary Conventions in the Fictional Style of John Pendleton Kennedy," *DA*, XXIV (1963), 731–732.

14   PRICE, MARTIN. *Swift's Rhetorical Art: A Study in Structure and Meaning*. New Haven, 1953.
    Price relates Swift's stylistic predilictions to his attitudes toward the

New Science, the eighteenth-century social structure, and organized religion. Simplicity, for Swift, "is the norm from which man departs through perversity and which he must work to regain or restore. It is similar to the ideal of the primitive church to which Swift constantly alludes as an ecclesiastical standard . . ." (p. 15).

1   PRINS, A. A. *"The Booke of Common Prayer"* (1549): *An Inquiry into its Language.* Amsterdam, 1933.

2   QUIRK, RANDOLPH. *Charles Dickens and Appropriate Language.* Durham, 1959. 26 pp.

3   ———. "The Language of Dickens," in *Langue et Littérature*, pp. 322–323.
Quirk suggests a re-evaluation of Dickens' prose in terms of the artistic purposes it serves. He lists four aspects of style for consideration: "individualizing, typifying, structural, and experimental" (p. 322).

4   ———. "Some Observations on the Language of Dickens," *REL*, II, iii (1961), 19–28.

5   RAHV, PHILIP. "Fiction and the Criticism of Fiction," *KR*, XVIII (1956), 276–299.

6   RALEIGH, JOHN HENRY. "Style and Structure in Defoe's *Roxana*," *University of Kansas City Review*, XX (1953), 128–135.

7   RAMSAY, WILLIAM. "The Claims of Language: Virginia Woolf as Symbolist," *English Fiction in Transition (1880–1920)* (Purdue), IV, i (1961), 12–17.

8   RANDOLPH, GERALD RICHARD. "An Analysis of Form and Style in the Prose Works of Thomas Nashe," *DA*, XXIII (1963), 3890–3891.

9   RANSOM, JOHN CROWE. "The Understanding of Fiction," *KR*, XII (1950), 189–218.

10   RANTAVAARA, IRMA. *"Ing*-Forms in the Service of Rhythm and Style in Virginia Woolf's 'The Waves,' " *Neuphilologische Mitteilungen* (Helsinki), LXI (1960), 79–97.

11   ———. "Language and Style," in her *Virginia Woolf's "The Waves."* Helsinki, 1960. Pp. 36–91.

12   RATNER, MARC L. "Style and Humanity in Malamud's Fiction," *Massachusetts Review*, V (1964), 663–683.

13   RAYBOULD, EDITH. "Of Jane Austen's Use of Expanded Verb Forms: One More Method of Approach to the Problem Presented by these Forms," in *Studies in English Language and Literature: Presented to Professor Dr. Karl Brunner on the Occasion of his Seventieth Birthday*, ed. Siegfried Korninger. Wien und Stuttgart, 1957. Pp. 175–190.

1 READ, HERBERT. *English Prose Style*. New York, 1928. Revised edition, New York, 1952.
Read divides his book into sections on "Composition" and "Rhetoric" and quotes extensive passages from English prose writers for analysis and discussion. "The prose style of Swift," he says, "is a unique, an irrefrangible instrument of clear, animated, animating and effective thought" (p. xiii). "Nothing, in the end, is so wearisome as idiosyncrasy and waywardness; the universal alone is stable, and a universal style is an impersonal style" (p. 193).

2 ———. "The Style of Criticism," in *English Studies Today: Second Series*, ed. G. A. Bonnard. Bern, 1961. Pp. 29–41.

3 REISS, H. S. "Style and Structure in Modern Experimental Fiction," in *Stil- und Formprobleme*, pp. 419–424.

4 RIEDEL, F. C. "Faulkner as Stylist," *South Atlantic Quarterly*, LVI (1957), 462–479.

5 RIEGER, JAMES HENRY. "*Au pied de la lettre:* Stylistic Uncertainty in *Vathek*," *Criticism*, IV (1962), 302–312.

6 RINGLER, W. "The Immediate Source of Euphuism," *PMLA*, LIII (1938), 678–686.

7 ROELLINGER, FRANCIS X., JR. "The Early Development of Carlyle's Style," *PMLA*, LXXII (1957), 926–951.

8 ROONEY, WILLIAM J. J. "John Donne's 'Second Prebend Sermon'— a Stylistic Analysis," *TSLL*, IV (1962), 24–34.

9 RUSSELL, JOHN. "From Style to Meaning in 'Araby,' " *CE*, XXVIII (1966), 170–171.
See the reply by Richard Ohmann, *ibid.*, 171–173.

10 SACKTON, ALEXANDER H. *Rhetoric as Dramatic Language in Ben Jonson*. New York, 1948.

11 SANKEY, BENJAMIN. "Hardy's Prose Style," *Twentieth Century Literature*, XI (1965), 3–15.

12 SATTERWHITE, JOSEPH N. "The Tremulous Formula: Form and Technique in Godey's Fiction," *American Quarterly*, VII (1956), 99–114.

13 SAYCE, R. A. *Style in French Prose: A Method of Analysis*. Oxford, 1953.

14 SCHMIDT, H. *Der Prosastil Samuel Johnsons*. Marburg, 1905.

15 SCHORER, MARK. "The Background of a Style," *Kenyon Review*, III (1941), 101–105.

1 SCHWEIK, R. C. "Method in the Study of Victorian Prose: A Criticism," *Victorian Newsletter*, No. 11 (1957), 1–5.

2 SCOTT, JOHN H., AND ZILPHA E. CHANDLER. *Phrasal Patterns in English Prose*. New York, 1932.

3 SHACKFORD, JOHN B. "Sterne's Use of Catachresis in *Tristram Shandy*," *Iowa English Yearbook*, VIII (1963), 74–79.

4 SHANNON, EDGAR F., JR. "The Present Tense in *Jane Eyre*," *Nineteenth-Century Fiction*," X (1955), 141–145.

5 SHELDON, ESTHER K. "Boswell's English in the 'London Journal,' " *PMLA*, LXXI (1956), 1067–1093.
   Sheldon compares Boswell's linguistic habits in the *London Journal* with the prescriptions of eighteenth-century grammarians.

6 SHKLOVSKY, VICTOR. "Sterne's *Tristram Shandy:* Stylistic Commentary," in *Russian Formalist Criticism: Four Essays*, tr. and with an introduction by Lee T. Lemon and Marion J. Reis. Lincoln, Neb., 1965. Pp. 25–57.

7 SHIMIZU, MAMORU. "On Some Stylistic Features, Chiefly Biblical, of *The Good Earth*," *Studies in English Literature* (English number for 1964), 117–134.

8 SHORT, R. W. "The Sentence Structure of Henry James," *AL*, XVIII (1946), 71–88.

9 SIMON, IRÈNE. "Dryden's Prose Style," *Revue des Langues Vivantes*, XXXI (1965), 506–530.

10 SLABEY, ROBERT M. "*The Turn of the Screw:* Grammar and Optics," *College Language Association Journal*, IX (1965), 68–72.

11 SLATOFF, WALTER J. "The Edge of Order: The Pattern of Faulkner's Rhetoric," *Twentieth-Century Literature*, III (1957), 107–127.

12 SLEDD, JAMES. "Applied Grammar: Some Notes on English Prose Style," in his *A Short Introduction to English Grammar*. Chicago, 1959. Pp. 260–334.
   Sledd writes on some of the means that a student might employ in writing effective prose. He emphasizes the fact that "style in language is choice of structural patterns as well as choice of words" (p. 274).

13 SMITH, COLIN. "Aspects of Destutt de Tracy's Linguistic Analysis as Adopted by Stendhal," *MLR*, LI (1956), 512–521.

14 SMITH, WILLIAM R. "The Rhetoric of the Declaration of Independence," *CE*, XXVI (1965), 306–309.

15 SÖDERLIND, JOHANNES. *Verb Syntax in John Dryden's Prose*. 2 vols. Cambridge, Mass., 1951–1958.

1   SPILLER, ROBERT E. "Cooper's Notes on Language," *AS*, IV (1929), 294–300.
    Spiller presents some of Cooper's remarks on the American language and its dialects and briefly relates them to Cooper's practice in his fiction.

2   SPINUCCI, PIETRO. "Ernest Hemingway: Lo stile e la vita," *Humanitas* (Brescia), XVI (1961), 937–944.

3   STANLIS, PETER. "Burke's Prose Style," *Burke Newsletter*, IV (1962–1963), 181–184.

4   STATON, WALTER F. "Characters of Style in Elizabethan Prose," *JEGP*, LVII (1958), 197–207.
    Staton discusses the pervasive Elizabethan doctrine of "high," "middle," and "low" styles and relates them to the prose of Lyly, Greene, Sidney, and Nashe. "The plain writing of the 1590's is to be explained by the doctrine of the characters of style rather than by a major change in literary taste" (p. 198).

5   STAUFFER, DONALD B. "Prose Style in the Fiction of Edgar A. Poe," *DA*, XXIV (1964), 2912.

6   STENERSON, DOUGLAS C. "Mencken's Early Newspaper Experience: The Genesis of a Style," *AL*, XXXVII (1965), 153–166.

7   STEVENSON, LIONEL. "Meredith and the Problem of Style in the Novel," *Zeitschrift für Anglistik und Amerikanistik*, VI (1958), 181–189.

8   STONE, ROBERT K. "Middle English Prose Style: Margery Kempe and Julian of Norwich," *DA*, XXIV (1963), 288–289.

9   STRAINCHAMPS, ETHEL. "Nabokov's Handling of English Syntax," *AS*, XXXVI (1961), 234–235.

10 STRAUSS, ALBRECHT B. "On Smollett's Language: A Paragraph in *Ferdinand Count Fathom*," in *Style in Prose Fiction*, pp. 25–54.

11 SUMMERSGILL, TRAVIS L. "The Influence of the Marprelate Controversy on the Style of Thomas Nashe," *SP*, XLVIII (1951), 145–160.

12 SUTHERLAND, JAMES. "Some Aspects of Eighteenth-Century Prose," in *Essays on the Eighteenth Century: Presented to David Nichol Smith in Honour of His Seventieth Birthday*. Oxford, 1945. Pp. 94–110.
    Sutherland discusses some major English prose writers, sometimes with the aid of an elegant metaphor: "The writer does not tyrannize over his sentences; he controls them rather as a shepherd walking behind his sheep, satisfied if they are moving in the right direction, but not troubling about the changing pattern of their movement" (p. 99).

1   ———. *On English Prose*. Toronto, 1957.
     Sutherland's style lectures survey the history of English prose. "What it is that we recognize when we say, 'That is Swift,' would be hard to define; but I suspect that in the final analysis what is most personal to a prose writer is an individual rhythm, a rhythm of both thought and language" (pp. 77–78).

2   SUTHERLAND, ROBERT D. "Language and Lewis Carroll," *DA*, XXV (1964), 2522–2523.

3   SVAGLIC, MARTIN J. "Method in the Study of Victorian Prose: Another View," *Victorian Newsletter*, No. 11 (1957), 1–5.

4   SYKES, ROBERT H. "Ernest Hemingway's Style: A Descriptive Analysis," *DA*, XXIV (1964), 2043.

5   TANNER, TONY. "Samuel Clemens and the Progress of a Stylistic Rebel," *British Association for American Studies Bulletin*, N.S. III (1961), 31–42.

6   TARSELIUS, RUT. "*All Colors will Agree in the Dark*": A Contribution to the Syntax of Francis Bacon," *Studia Neophilologica* (Uppsala), XXV (1952–1953), 155–160.

7   TARTELLA, VINCENT P. "Charles Dickens's *Oliver Twist:* Moral Realism and the Uses of Style," *DA*, XXII (1961), 1616–1617.

8   TEETS, BRUCE E. "Two Faces of Style in Renaissance Prose Fiction," in *Sweet Smoke of Rhetoric: A Collection of Renaissance Essays*, eds. Natalie Grimes Lawrence and J. A. Reynolds (Coral Gables, Fla., 1964), pp. 69–81.

9   THOMPSON, ELBERT N. S. "Milton's Prose Style," *PQ*, XIV (1935), 1–15.

10   THOMSON, JAMES ALEXANDER KER. *Classical Influences on English Prose*. London, 1956, and New York, 1962.
     Thomson discusses both the generic and structural influences of Greek and Latin literature on prose from the Renaissance to the nineteenth century.

11   THORPE, PETER. "Content and Style in *The Red Badge of Courage*," *CE*, XXVII (1966), 487–492.

12   TILLOTSON, GEOFFREY. "Trollope's Style," *Ball State Teachers College Forum*, II, ii (1961), 3–6.

13   TILLYARD, E. M. W. "Scott's Linguistic Vagaries," *Etudes Anglaises*, XI (1958), 112–118.

14   TOMASHEVSKY, BORIS. "Thematics," in *Russian Formalist Criticism: Four Essays*, tr. and with an introduction by Lee T. Lemon and Marion J. Reis. Lincoln, Neb., 1965. Pp. 62–95.

1 Toor, David Sydney. "Euphuism in England before John Lyly," *DA*, XXVI (1966), 4642.

2 Townsend, F. G. "Newman and the Problem of Critical Prose," *Victorian Newsletter*, No. 11 (1957), 22–25.

3 Traschen, I. "Henry James and the Art of Revision," *PQ*, XXXV (1956), 39–47.

4 Troy, William. "Virginia Woolf: The Poetic Method," *Symposium*, III (1932), 53–63.

5 ———. "Virginia Woolf: The Poetic Style," *Symposium*, III (1932), 153–156.

6 Tucker, W. J. "Irish Masters of Prose," *Catholic World*, CXLIV (1937), 712–717.

7 Uhrhan, E. Esther. "Linguistic Analysis of Góngora's Baroque Style," in *Descriptive Studies in Spanish Grammar*, eds. H. R. Kahane and A. Pietrangeli. Urbana, Ill., 1954. Pp. 177–214.

8 Ullmann, Stephen. *Style in the French Novel*. Cambridge, 1957. See the review by Michael Riffaterre, *Word*, XV (1959), 404–413.

9 Umbach, Herbert M. "The Merit of the Metaphysical Style in Donne's Easter Sermons," *ELH*, XII (1945), 108–129.

10 Uve, Peter. "Introduction," *Seventeenth-Century Prose, 1620–1700*. London, 1956.

11 Valdes, Helen Joyce Merrill. "Style in the Novels of Susan Ferrier," *DA*, XXII (1961), 19.

12 Van Ghent, Dorothy. *The English Novel: Form and Function*. New York, 1953.

13 Visser, F. T. *A Syntax of the English Language of St. Thomas More*. 2 vols. Louvain, 1946–1952.

14 Visser, G. J. "James Joyce's *Ulysses* and Anglo-Irish," *English Studies* (Amsterdam), XXIV (1942), 45–56, 79–90.

15 Wagner, Vern. "The Maligned Style of Theodore Dreiser," *Western Humanities Review*, XIX (1965), 175–184.

16 Wall, Carey G. "Faulkner's Rhetoric," *DA*, XXV (1965), 5947.

17 Walpole, Hugh. *The Art of James Branch Cabell*. New York, 1920.

18 Wanning, Andrews. "Some Changes in the Prose Style of the Seventeenth Century." Unpublished Ph.D. dissertation presented to the University of Cambridge, 1938.
"The consideration of style is a consideration of complete meanings

and there is little of any importance that can be studied that is not a consideration of meanings" (p. 20; quoted by Ohmann, "Prolegomena," q.v.).

1   WARNER, ALAN. "English Without Bones," *English* (Oxford), XIII (1961), 136–139.
Warner discusses the decline in present-day prose style.

2   WARREN, AUSTIN. "The Style of Sir Thomas Browne," *KR*, XIII (1951), 674–687.
Warren discusses the three levels of style to be found in Browne (see articles by Staton and Croll above). "In terms of the two rival traditions of prose style, the Ciceronian (or oratorical), and the Senecan (or philosophical), the tropes, or thought-figures, like metaphor and paradox, belong to the latter; the schemes or sound figures, under which the *cursus*—like rhymed alliteration—was classified, belong to the oratorical, or ornate tradition" (p. 680).

3   WATANABE, H. "Past Perfect Retrospection in the Style of Henry James," *AL*, XXXIV (1962), 165–181.

4   WATKINS, FLOYD C. "Rhetoric in Southern Writing: Wolfe," *Georgia Review*, XII (Spring 1958), 79–82.

5   WATT, IAN. "The First Paragraph of *The Ambassadors:* An Explication," *EIC*, X (1960), 250–274.

6   WEBB, HOWARD W. "The Development of a Style: The Lardner Idiom," *American Quarterly*, XII (1960), 482–492.

7   WEBBER, JOAN. "The Prose Style of John Donne's *Devotions upon Emergent Occasions*," *Anglia*, LXXIX (1962), 138–152.

8   ———. *Contrary Music: The Prose Style of John Donne.* Madison, Wis., 1963.

9   ———. "Celebration of Word and World in Lancelot Andrewes' Style," *JEGP*, LXIV (1965), 255–269.

10 WENDELL, CHARLES W. "Narrative Style in Rabelais and Sterne," *DA*, XXV (1965), 4711–4712.

11 WHALLON, WILLIAM. "Hebraic Synonymy in Sir Thomas Browne," *ELH*, XXVIII (1961), 335–352.
Whallon relates Browne's prose style to the structure of Old Testament language (especially the Psalter). "On purely speculative grounds, the Bible must be held a potential stylistic influence upon writers of the seventeenth century; on empirical grounds it was an influence upon Browne, whose works may contain more examples of identifiably Hebraic synonymy than does all of Western antiquity" (p. 344).

12 WHEELER, THOMAS. "The New Style of the Tudor Chroniclers," *Tennessee Studies in Literature*, VII (1962), 71–77.

1WHITE, MOTHER ELIZABETH STUYVESANT, R.S.C.J. "A Study of the Symmetrical and Asymmetrical Tendencies in the Sentence Structure of Sir Thomas Browne's *Urne Buriall*," *DA*, XXIV (1963), 733.

2WHITLEY, EILEEN. "Contextual Analysis: Swift's 'Little Language' in the *Journal to Stella*," in *In Memory of J. R. Firth*, ed. C. E. Bazell *et al*. London, 1966.

3WILLEY, BASIL. "Sir Thomas Browne," in his *The Seventeenth Century Background*. London, 1934. Pp. 44–57.

"Browne's 'style' is the incarnation of his sensibility, and we can trace, I think, even in some of its details, his sense of the proximity of the different worlds of thought and feeling, and his desire to exploit the resources of them all" (p. 48).

4WILLIAMSON, GEORGE. "The Restoration Revolt against Enthusiasm," *SP*, XXX (1933), 571–603.

5————. "The Rhetorical Pattern of Neo-Classic Wit," *MP*, XXXIII (1935), 55–81; reprinted in his *Seventeenth-Century Contexts* (London, 1960), pp. 240–271.

6————. "Senecan Style in the Seventeenth Century," *PQ*, XV (1936), 321–351; reprinted in *Essential Articles for the Study of English Augustan Backgrounds*, ed. Bernard Schelling (Hamden, Conn., 1961), pp. 137–172.

7————. *The Senecan Amble: A Study in Prose from Bacon to Collier*. London and Chicago, 1951.

Williamson studies the influence of classical writers—especially Isocrates, Gorgias, and their Roman imitators—on the prose of the seventeenth century. "For the accurate definition of a prose style, it is necessary to determine not only what figures are used but how they are used" (p. 31).

8WILSON, F. P. *Seventeenth Century Prose: Five Lectures*. Berkeley, 1960.

Wilson discusses the prose of the character writers and historians, Burton, Browne, and such sermon writers as Lancelot Andrewes and Jeremy Taylor.

9WILSON, R. M. "On the Continuity of English Prose," in *Mélanges de linguistique et de philologie: Ferdinand Mossé in memoriam*. Paris, 1959. Pp. 486–494.

10WIMSATT, W. K., JR. *The Prose Style of Samuel Johnson*. New Haven, 1941 and 1963.

After a discussion of the parallelism, antithesis, diction, and other qualities characteristic of Johnson's style, Wimsatt describes Johnson's theory and relates it to his practice. The introductory essay, "Style as Meaning," contains a survey of the questions that stylistic critics have asked in the past and a justification for Wimsatt's method of study. ". . . the analysis of elements of style cannot be a blind experiment by which we discover some quality in the writing which we could not discover by reading. Analysis can be only a corroboration and detailed appraisal of some quality perceived by the reader as part of meaning" (p. 81). "Style as Meaning" is reprinted in Chatman and Levin, pp. 362–373.

1   WINBURNE, JOHN NEWTON. "Sentence Sequence in Discourse," in *Ninth Congress Papers*, pp. 1094–1098.

2   WINSHIP, GEORGE PARKER, JR. "Style," in his "A Study of the Essay Journal *The World* (1753–1757)." Unpublished dissertation presented to the University of North Carolina, 1948. Pp. 324–335. Winship examines the prose of seven of the thirty-seven known contributors to *The World* and compares them to short samples from Bacon, Dryden, Shaftesbury, Swift, and Johnson according to their scores on the readability scale developed by Rudolph Flesch (*The Art of Plain Talk* [New York, 1946]. Flesch explains the most recent manifestation of his readability formula in "How to Test Readability," in *How to Write, Speak, and Think More Effectively* [New York, 1963], pp. 298–318). Winship finds that the contributors to *The World* fall into the "Difficult" and "Very Difficult" categories on Flesch's scale, but he discounts his results on the basis of Flesch's equation of easy readability with short sentences. "*The World* is written in an easy rambling prose, characterized by long sentences and short words" (p. 335).

3   WINTEROWD, WALTER ROSS. "The Poles of Discourse: A Study of Eighteenth-Century Rhetoric in *Amelia* and *Clarissa*," *DA*, XXVI (1965), 360–361.

4   WOODRING, CARL. "Introduction," *Prose of the Romantic Period*. Boston, 1961.

5   WORKMAN, S. K. *Fifteenth-Century Translations as an Influence on English Prose*. Princeton, 1940.

6   ZANDVOORT, R. W. "What is Euphuism?" in *Mélanges de linguistique et philologie: Ferdinand Mossé in memoriam*. Paris, 1959. Pp. 508–517.

7   ZICKGRAF, GERTRAUT. *Swifts Stilforderungen und Stil*. Marburg, 1940.

8   ZOELLNER, ROBERT H. "Faulkner's Prose Style in *Absalom, Absalom!*," *AL*, XXX (1959), 486–502.

STYLE IN POETRY

Structures of Sound in Poetry

9   ABERCROMBIE, DAVID. "A Phonetician's View of Verse Structure," *Linguistics*, VI (1964), 5–13; reprinted in his *Studies in Phonetics and Linguistics* (London, 1965), pp. 16–25.

The English language, says Abercrombie, is stress-timed and organized into isochronous feet (in the sense employed by Daniel Jones and other British phoneticians). "A foot, in this usage, may be defined as the space in time from the incidence of one stress-pulse up to, but not including, the next stress-pulse" (p. 10). All feet are isochronous or of equal quantity and silence may replace a stress-pulse in the perception of the hearer. "The rhythmic unit of both prose and verse is the foot; the metrical unit of verse is the line. This is the crucial difference between the two modes: in prose the feet are not organized into a higher metrical unit" (p. 12).

1   ABERCROMBIE, LASCELLES. *Principles of English Prosody*. London, 1923. Shapiro.

2   ADLER, JACOB. "Pope and the Rules of Prosody," *PMLA*, LXXVI (1961), 218–226.

3   ———. *The Reach of Art: A Study in the Prosody of Pope*. Gainesville, Fla., 1964.

4   ALDEN, RAYMOND MACDONALD. *English Verse: Specimens Illustrating its Principles and History*. New York, 1903. Shapiro.
    Alden's collection is particularly valuable for its full catalogue of the varieties of line lengths and metrical combinations in English poetry. The last section contains an anthology of comments on meter from Aristotle to 1896.

5   ALLEN, C. "Cadenced Free Verse," *CE*, IX (1948), 195–199.

6   ALLEN, GAY WILSON. *American Prosody*. New York, 1935. Shapiro.

7   ALLEN, W. S. "On Quantity and Quantitative Verse," *In Honor of Daniel Jones: Papers on the Occasion of His Eightieth Birthday*, eds. David Abercrombie *et al*. London, 1964. Pp. 3–15.

8   ANDERSON, JOHANNES CARL. *The Laws of Verse*. Cambridge, 1928. Shapiro.

9   BAKER, SHERIDAN. "English Meter *Is* Quantitative," *CE*, XXI (1960), 309–315.

10 BARKAS, PALLESTER. *A Critique of Modern English Prosody, 1880–1930*. Halle, 1934.

11 BARRY, SISTER M. M. *An Analysis of the Prosodic Structure of Selected Poems of T. S. Eliot*. Washington, D.C., 1948.

12 BATESON, F. W. Comment on Hawkes's "The Matter of Metre" (q.v.), *EIC*, XII (1962), 421–423; also *EIC*, XIII (1963), 200–201.

13 BAUM, PAULL FRANKLIN. *The Principles of English Versification*. Cambridge, Mass., 1922. Shapiro.

14 BAYFIELD, MATTHEW ALBERT. *The Measures of Poets*. Cambridge, 1919. Shapiro.

1   BELOOF, ROBERT LAWRENCE. "E. E. Cummings: The Prosodic Shape of His Poems," *DA*, XIV (1954), 2342–2343.

2   ———. "Strength in the Exquisite; A Study of John Crowe Ransom's Prosody," *Annali Istituto Universitario Orientale, Napoli, Sezione Germanica*, IV (1961), 215–222.

3   BERG, SISTER MARY GRETCHEN, O.S.F. *The Prosodic Structure of Robert Bridges' "Neo-Miltonic Syllabics."* Washington, D.C., 1962.

4   BERNARD, JULES EUGENE. *The Prosody of the Tudor Interlude*. New Haven, 1939.

5   BERRY, FRANCIS. "The Poet's Voice: The Influence of the Poet's Physical Voice on His Work, Especially its Typical Grammatical Forms," in *Poetics*, pp. 453–461.

6   ———. *Poetry and the Physical Voice*. New York, 1962.
    Berry asserts that readers can detect "the physical voice" of poets in their poems and even trace the changes in that voice from puberty to senility. He discusses Shakespeare, Milton, Shelley, and Tennyson and uses biographical evidence whenever possible to support his intuitions about their voices. Experimental evaluation of reader's responses might be interesting to support some of his remarks, but a real difficulty in his approach is in separating phonological and semantic levels in poetry.

7   ———. "The Sound of Personification in Gray's 'Elegy,' " *EIC*, XII (1962), 442–445.

8   BEUM, ROBERT. "The Rhyme in *Samson Agonistes*." *TSLL*, IV (1962), 177–182.

9   ———. "Some Observations on Spenser's Verse Forms," *Neuphilologische Mitteilungen*, LXIV (1963), 180–196.

10 ———. "Yeats the Rhymer," *Papers on English Language and Literature*, I (1965), 338–350.

11 BLACKMUR, R. P. "Lord Tennyson's Scissors," in his *Form and Value in Modern Poetry*. Garden City, N.Y., 1957. Pp. 369–388.

12 BOLINGER, DWIGHT L. "Rime, Assonance, and Morpheme Analysis," *Word*, VI (1950), 117–136.

13 BREWER, ROBERT FREDERICK. *Orthometry: The Art of Versification*. Edinburgh, 1908. Shapiro.

14 ———. *The Art of Versification and the Technicalities of Poetry*. Edinburgh, 1923.

15 BRIDGES, ROBERT. *Milton's Prosody*. Oxford, 1921. Shapiro.

16 BROOKE-ROSE, CHRISTINE. "Notes on the Meter of Auden's 'The Age of Anxiety,' " *EIC*, XIII (1963), 253–264.

1   BROWN, CALVIN S. "Can Musical Notation Help English Scansion?" *JAAC*, XXIII (1965), 329–334.

2   BROWN, WARNER. *Time in English Verse Rhythm*. New York, 1908.

3   BROWNELL, BAKER. "Kinaesthetic Verse," *Poetry*, XXII–XXIII (1923), 36–40. Shapiro.

4   BRUNHUMER, ANNE BUTLER. "Metrical Principles of English Poetry: A Course of Lectures by Professor Ruth Wallerstein," *DA*, XXI (1961), 3087.

5   BURKE, FIDELIAN. *Metrical Roughness in Marston's Formal Satire*. Washington, D.C., 1957.

6   BURKE, KENNETH. "On Musicality in Verse," *Poetry*, LVII (1940), 31–40. Shapiro.

7   BURKLUND, CARL E. "Melody in Verse," *QJS*, XXXIX (1953), 57–60.

8   BURNSHAW, STANLEY. "Vers-libre in Full Bloom," *Poetry*, XXXII (1928), 277–282, 334–341.

9   CANNON, GARLAND. "Linguistics and the Performance of Poetry," *CCC*, XVI (1965), 20–26.

10   CHALKER, JOHN. "Aspects of Rhythm and Rhyme in Eliot's Early Poems," *English* (London), XVI (1966), 84–88.

11   CHATMAN, SEYMOUR. "Robert Frost's 'Mowing': An Inquiry into Prosodic Structure," *KR*, XVIII (1956), 421–438; Bobbs-Merrill Reprint, *Language-97*.
     "Far from abandoning the older two-valued metrics of alternating stresses, [Chatman's method] tries to account for the phonological complexity of verse by envisaging a tension between two systems: the abstract metrical pattern, as historical product of the English verse tradition, and the ordinary stress-pitch-juncture system of spoken English, determined as it is by requirements of meaning and emphasis" (p. 422). Chatman illustrates his thesis with a comparison of eight readings of Frost's sonnet.

12   ———. "Mr. Stein on Donne," *KR*, XVIII (1956), 443–451; Bobbs-Merrill Reprint, *Language-97*.
     Chatman claims that "textual ambiguities" must be resolved in performance and that the metrical complexities claimed for Donne's "Elegy X" by Arnold Stein ("Donne's Prosody," q.v.) are in part "paper ambiguities."

13   ———. "Linguistics, Poetics, and Interpretation: The Phonemic Dimension," *QJS*, XLIII (1957), 248–256; Bobbs-Merrill Reprint, *Language-13*.
     Chatman discusses some of the ways in which a phonemic analysis

of poems might be of use to literary critics. He evaluates the problems of phonetic symbolism and of the configurational pattern of segmental phonemes (assonance, alliteration, etc.). The study of suprasegmentals, he says in a well-illustrated commentary, is illuminating and "demonstrates the incapacity of conventional metrics to show significant meaning contrasts" (p. 254). See the reply by John C. McLaughlin, and comments by Wimsatt and Beardsley, and Kellog and Steele (q.v.).

1 ———. "Comparing Metrical Styles," in *Style in Language*, pp. 149–172; reprinted in Chatman and Levin, pp. 132–155.

Chatman's "chief purpose is to devise and test an application of strictly descriptive techniques to prosodic style" (p. 150). He tests his method by contrasting Pope's imitations of two of Donne's satires with the originals. In addition to discussing the two "metrical styles," Chatman considers run-on lines, and rhyme and other patterns of segmental sounds. For satiric purposes, he concludes, "Pope prefers a stiletto to Donne's blunderbuss" (p. 172).

2 ———. "New Directions in Metrics," in *The Concise Encyclopedia of English and American Poetry*, eds. Stephen Spender and Donald Hall (New York, 1963), pp. 229–233.

3 ———. *A Theory of Meter*. The Hague, 1965.

4 CLARK, ARTHUR MELVILLE, AND HAROLD WHITEHALL. "Rhyme," in *Encyclopedia of Poetry and Poetics*, eds. Alex Preminger *et al.* (Princeton, 1965), pp. 705–710.

5 COLLIER, S. J. "Max Jacob and the 'Poème en Prose,'" *MLR*, LI (1956), 725–754.

6 CONE, EDWARD T. "Words into Music: The Composer's Approach to the Text," in *Sound and Poetry*, pp. 3–15.

7 CONRAD, PHILIP. "Visual Poetry," *Poetry*, XXXII (1928), 112–114. Shapiro.

8 CORSON, HIRAM. *A Primer of English Verse*. Boston, 1892. Shapiro.

9 CORY, ROBERT E. "The Prosody of Walt Whitman," *North Dakota Quarterly*, XXVIII (1960), 74–79.

10 CRAPSEY, ADELAIDE. *A Study in English Metrics*. New York, 1918.

11 CREEK, HERBERT L. "Rising and Falling Rhythm in English Verse," *PMLA*, XXXV (1920), 76–90. Shapiro.

12 CROLL, MORRIS W. "The Rhythm of English Verse," in *Style, Rhetoric, and Rhythm: Essays by Morris W. Croll*, ed. J. Max Patrick *et al.* (Princeton, 1966), pp. 365–429.

13 ———. "Music and Metrics: A Reconsideration," *SP*, XX (1923), 388–394; reprinted in *Style, Rhetoric, and Rhythm: Essays by Morris W. Croll*, ed. J. Max Patrick (Princeton, 1966), pp. 430–436. Shapiro.

1 CUMMINGS, DONALD WAYNE. "Towards a Theory of Prosodic Analysis for English Metrical Verse," *DA*, XXVII (1966), 177A.

2 DABNEY, JULIA PARKER. *The Musical Basis of Verse*. New York, 1901. Shapiro.

3 DAVIE, DONALD. "Syntax and Music in 'Paradise Lost,' " in *The Living Milton*, ed. Frank Kermode. New York, 1961. Pp. 70–84.

4 DAVIES, A. TALFON. "William Barnes, Gerard Manley Hopkins, Dylan Thomas: The Influence of Welsh Prosody on Modern English Poetry," in *Proceedings of the Third Congress of the International Comparative Literature Association*. The Hague, 1962. Pp. 90–122.

5 DAVIS, WALTER R. "Melodic and Poetic Structure: The Examples of Campion and Dowland," *Criticism*, IV (1962), 89–107.

6 DAY-LEWIS, C. *Poetry for You*. Oxford, 1944. Shapiro.

7 DE GROOT, A. WILLEM. "Phonetics and its Relations to Aesthetics," in *Manual of Phonetics*, ed. L. Kaiser. Amsterdam, 1957. Pp. 385–400.

8 DOBRÉE, BONAMY. "Prosody, Forms of Verse, and Some Usages," in *The Concise Encyclopedia of English and American Poetry*, eds. Stephen Spender and Donald Hall (New York, 1963), pp. 247–269.

9 DRAPER, JOHN W. "The Origin of Rhyme," *Revue de Littérature Comparée*, XXXI (1957), 74–85.

10 ———. "The Origin of Rhyme: A Supplement," *Revue de Littérature Comparée*, XXXIX (1965), 452–453.

11 EPSTEIN, EDMUND L., AND TERENCE HAWKES (WITH AN INTRODUCTION BY HENRY LEE SMITH, JR.). *Linguistics and English Prosody*. Buffalo: *Studies in Linguistics, Occasional Paper VII*, 1959.

12 EVANS, ROBERT O. "Some Aspects of Wyatt's Metrical Technique," *JEGP*, LIII (1954), 197–213.

13 FOWLER, ROGER. " 'Prose Rhythm' and Metre," *Essays on Style and Language*, pp. 82–99.

14 ———. "Structural Metrics," *Linguistics*, No. 27 (1966), 49–64; reprinted in Chatman and Levin, pp. 156–170.

15 FRYE, NORTHROP. "Lexos and Melos," in *Sound and Poetry*, pp. ix–xxvii.

16 ———. "The Rhythm of Recurrence: Epos," in his *Anatomy of Criticism*. Princeton, 1957. Pp. 251–262.

17 FUSSELL, PAUL, JR. *Theory of Prosody in Eighteenth-Century England*. New London, Conn., 1955.

1   ———. "Meter," in *Encyclopedia of Poetry and Poetics*, eds. Alex Preminger *et al.* (Princeton, 1965), pp. 496–499.

2   ———. *Poetic Meter and Poetic Form*. New York, 1965.

3   GARDNER, HELEN L. *Four Quartets: A Commentary*. London, 1947. Shapiro.

4   GEIGER, DON. *The Sound, Sense, and Performance of Poetry*. Chicago, 1963.

5   GOLDSMITH, U. K. " 'Words out of a Hat?' Alliteration and Assonance in Shakespeare's Sonnets," *JEGP*, XLIX (1950), 33–48.

6   GREW, SIDNEY. *A Book of English Prosody*. London, 1924. Shapiro.

7   GROSS, HARVEY. "The Aesthetic Function of Prosody," *The Centennial Review of Arts and Sciences* (Michigan State Univ.). VII (1963), 204–218.

8   ———. *Sound and Form in Modern Poetry: A Study of Prosody from Thomas Hardy to Robert Lowell*. Ann Arbor, 1964.

9   ———. "T. S. Eliot and the Music of Poetry," abridged from his *Sound and Form in Modern Poetry*, and reprinted in his *The Structure of Verse* (Greenwich, Conn., 1966), pp. 202–217.

10   GROSS, HARVEY (ed.). *The Structure of Verse: Modern Essays on Prosody*. Greenwich, Conn., 1966.
      Fourteen essays on the theory of meter and prosodic analysis by twentieth-century critics.

11   GUIRAUD, PIERRE. *Langage et versification d'après l'oeuvre de Paul Valéry*. Paris, 1953.

12   HALPERN, MARTIN. "On the Two Chief Metrical Modes in English," *PMLA*, LXXVII (1962), 177–186.
      Halpern refines the distinction proposed by Wimsett and Beardsley ("The Concept of Meter," q.v.) between the isoaccentual "strong-stress" meter of the native or Old English tradition and the iambic tradition introduced into English by Chaucer. The former can be regarded as both isoaccentual and isochronic, but the latter "is not patterned in terms of a uniform recurrence of heavily stressed syllables, and will not usually lend itself to oral renderings in which equal time-intervals occur between each major syllable" (p. 186).

13   HAMER, ENID. *The Metres of English Poetry*. London, 1930. Shapiro.

14   HAMM, VICTOR M. "Meter and Meaning," *PMLA*, LXIX (1954), 695–710.

15   HAMMOND, MAC. "A New Theory of Meter," *Sewanee Review*, LXX (1962), 688–691.
      Review article of Thompson's *The Founding of English Metre*.

1 HANLEY, MILES L. *Index to Rimes in American and English Poetry, 1500–1900.* Madison, Wis.: Microcard Foundation, 1959.

2 HARTWIG, JOAN. "The Principle of Measure in 'To His Coy Mistress,'" *CE*, XXV (1964), 572–575.

3 HAVENS, RAYMOND D. "Structure and Prosodic Pattern in Shelley's Lyrics," *PMLA*, LXV (1950), 1076–1087.

4 HAWKES, TERENCE. "The Problems of Prosody," *REL*, III, ii (1962), 32–49.

5 ———. "The Matter of Metre," *EIC*, XII (1962), 413–421, and *EIC*, XIII (1963), 198–199.
Review article of Thompson's *The Founding of English Metre*.

6 ———. "New Prosodists for Old?" *EIC*, XVI (1966), 258.
See the reply by Laurence Michel, *ibid.*, 259.

7 HELLENBRECHT, H. *Das Problem der freien Rhythmen mit Bezug auf Nietzsche.* Bern: *Sprache und Dichtung*, vol. 48, 1931.

8 HEMPHILL, GEORGE. "The Meters of the Intermediate Poets," *KR*, XIX (1957), 37–55.

9 HEMPHILL, GEORGE (ed.). *Discussions of Poetry: Rhythm and Sound.* Boston, 1961.
Hemphill's anthology contains remarks on meter by the following authors: Gascoigne, Jonson, Milton, Marvell, Dryden, Johnson, Jefferson, Coleridge, Blake, Poe, Lanier, Hopkins, Saintsbury, Young, Bridges, Winters, Wellek and Warren, Shapiro, Whitehall, Chatman, Stein, and Ransom.

10 HENDREN, JOSEPH W. *A Study of Ballad Rhythm.* Princeton, 1936.

11 ———. "Time and Stress in English Verse," *Rice University Pamphlet*, XLVI (1959).

12 ———. "A Word for Rhythm and a Word for Meter," *PMLA*, LXXVI (1961), 300–305.
Hendren replies to Wimsatt and Beardsley's "The Concept of Meter" (q.v.): "I wonder if the authors are aware that to reject measured time as an integral character of metrical structure is to deny the existence of verse rhythm" (p. 300). He presents a precise measurement of the time taken by each syllable in several poetic lines according to the system developed by William Thomson (q.v.). Wimsatt and Beardsley reply to his criticism of their theory, *ibid.*, pp. 305–308.

13 HENDRICKSON, G. L. "Elizabethan Quantitative Hexameters," *PQ*, XXVIII (1949), 237–260.

14 HILLYER, ROBERT SILLMAN. *First Principles of Verse.* Boston, 1938. Shapiro.

1   HOLLANDER, JOHN. "The Music of Poetry," *JAAC*, XV (1956), 232–244.

2   ——. "Musica Mundana and *Twelfth Night*," in *Sound and Poetry*, pp. 55–82.

3   ——. "The Metrical Emblem," abstract in *Style in Language*, pp. 191–192; published in full in *KR*, XXI (1959), 279–296; reprinted in Chatman and Levin, pp. 115–126.
Hollander argues that certain features in poetry such as meter, typographical format, and some types of enjambment serve an "emblematic function" in recalling a poem's "family tree by appeal to those resemblances which connect it, in some ways with one, in some ways with another kind of poem that may, historically, precede or follow it" (p. 294).

4   ——. "Experimental and Pseudo-Experimental Metrics in Recent American Poetry," *Poetics*, pp. 127–135.
Hollander examines both the critical remarks of the followers of Pound and W. C. Williams who feel that traditional meters are "no longer a viable form of poetic discourse" and those of current writers of metrical verse.

5   ——. "Blake and the Metrical Contract," in *From Sensibility to Romanticism: Essays Presented to Frederick A. Pottle*, New York, 1965. Pp. 293–310.

6   HOLLOWAY, SISTER MARCELLA MARIE. *The Prosodic Theory of Gerard Manley Hopkins*. Washington, D.C., 1947.

7   HOWARTH, HERBERT. "Metre and Emphasis: A Conservative Note," *Essays on Shakespeare*, ed. Gordon Ross Smith. London, 1965. Pp. 211–227.

8   HRUSHOVSKI, BENJAMIN. "On Free Rhythms in Modern Poetry: Preliminary Remarks toward a Critical Theory of Their Structures and Functions," in *Style in Language*, pp. 173–191.
"By free rhythms I mean poems which (1) have no consistent metrical scheme, that is, in tonic syllabic poetry have a freedom from the prevalent, predetermined arrangement of stressed and unstressed syllables: but (2) do have a poetic language organized so as to create impressions and fulfill functions of poetic rhythm" (p. 183).

9   HUNTER, W. B., JR. "The Sources of Milton's Prosody," *PQ*, XXVIII (1945), 125–144.

10   HYMAN, LAWRENCE W. "*Paradise Lost:* The Argument and the Rhythmic Pattern," *Minnesota Review*, V (1965), 223–228.

11   HYMES, DELL H. "Phonological Aspects of Style: Some English Sonnets," in *Style in Language*, pp. 109–131; reprinted in Chatman and Levin, pp. 33–53.

Hymes tests and develops the method proposed by J. J. Lynch ("The Tonality of Lyric Poetry," *q.v.*) for scrutinizing the role of sound and sound symbolism in poems. He examines ten sonnets by Wordsworth and ten by Keats: "The sonnet was examined for a word or words fulfilling three criteria: (1) on the level of sound, containing sounds dominant in the poem and/or much higher in rank than usual; (2) on the level of meaning, expressing the theme of the poem (or octet or sestet); (3) regarding position, placed so as to have a culminating effect. When all three criteria were met, the result has been termed a *summative* word. When only the first two criteria were met, the result has been termed a *key* word" (p. 118). These two concepts should be compared to the notion of *coupling* developed by Samuel R. Levin, *Linguistic Structures in Poetry* (*q.v.*).

1 ING, CATHERINE. *Elizabethan Lyrics: A Study of the Development of English Metrics and Their Relation to Poetic Effect.* London, 1951.

2 JACOB, CARY FRANKLIN. *The Foundations and Nature of Verse.* New York, 1918. Shapiro.

3 JAKOBSON, ROMAN. "O lingwistycznej analizie rymu," [On the linguistic analysis of rhyme] *Prace filologiczne,* XVIII (1963), 47–52.

4 JESPERSEN, OTTO. "Notes on Metre" (1900) and "Postscript" (1933), in his *Linguistica* (Copenhagen, 1933), pp. 249–274; both reprinted in Chatman and Levin, pp. 71–90.

5 KAPLAN, ROBERT B. "An Analysis of Contemporary Poetic Structure, 1930–1955," *DA,* XXIV (1964), 3749–3750.
The authors uses an oscilloscope to study the meter of modern poems and claims that his analysis is more precise and valuable than either traditionally or linguistically oriented scansions.

6 KELL, RICHARD. "A Note on Versification," *British Journal of Aesthetics,* III (1963), 341–345.

7 KELLOG, GEORGE A. "Bridges' 'Milton's Prosody' and Renaissance Metrical Theory," *PMLA,* LXVIII (1953), 268–285.

8 KELLOG, ROBERT L., AND OLIVER L. STEELE. "On the Punctuation of Two Lines in *The Faerie Queene,*" *PMLA,* LXXVIII (1963), 147–148.
The authors object to the analysis suggested by Chatman ("Linguistics, Poetics, and Interpretation," *q.v.*) and approved by Wimsatt and Beardsley ("The Concept of Meter," *q.v.*) of Spenser's lines: "And like a *Persian* mitre on her hed/Shee wore, with crowns and owches garnished" (*FQ,* I, ii, 13, 4–5). "A phonemic analysis of misunderstood syntax," they claim, "results in bad criticism and inaccurate texts" (p. 147).

9 KIBÉDI VARGA, A. "Rythme et signification poétique," *Revue d'esthétique,* III–IV (1965), 265–286.

1 KINSLEY, JAMES. "The Music of the Heart," *Renaissance and Modern Studies*, VIII (1964), 6–52.

2 KOMMERELL, M. *Gedanken über Gedichte*. Frankfurt am Main, 1943.

3 KOPCZYŃSKA, ZDZISLAWA. "Le Rôle de l'Intonation dans la Versification," *Poetics*, pp. 215–224.
The author proposes the use of various mechanical devices, particularly the oscilloscope, in recording the sound pattern of the performance of a poem.

4 LACHMANN, E. *Hölderlins Hymnen in freien Strophen: eine metrische Untersuchung*. Frankfurt am Main, 1937.

5 LADRIÈRE, J. CRAIG. "Structure, Sound and Meaning," in *Sound and Poetry*, pp. 85–108.

6 ———. "The Comparative Method in the Study of Prosody," in *Proceedings of the Second Congress of the International Comparative Literature Association*. Chapel Hill, N.C., 1959. Vol. I, pp. 160–175.

7 ———. "Prosody," in *Encyclopedia of Poetry and Poetics*, eds. Alex Preminger *et al.* (Princeton, 1965), pp. 669–677.

8 LANIER, SIDNEY. *The Science of English Verse*. New York, 1880. Shapiro.

9 LANZ, H. *The Physical Basis of Rime*. Stanford and London, 1931.

10 LEATHES, STANLEY. *Rhythm in English Poetry*. London, 1935. Shapiro.

11 LEE, CHARLOTTE I. "The Line as a Rhythmic Unit in the Poetry of Theodore Roethke," *Speech Monographs*, XXX (1963), 15–22.

12 LEVIN, SAMUEL R. "Suprasegmentals and the Performance of Poetry," *QJS*, XLVIII (1962), 366–372; Bobbs-Merrill Reprint, *Language-1*.
Levin considers the role of performance in resolving structural ambiguities. Performance, says Levin, is the best way to bring such cruxes out into the open; it makes them available for discussion. He contrasts two readings of a Dylan Thomas poem and shows what assumptions about the poem's structure and meaning are manifested in both.

13 LEVÝ, JIŘÍ. "Rhythmical Ambivalence in the Poetry of T. S. Eliot," *Anglia*, LXVII (1949), 54–64.

14 ———. "A Contribution to the Typology of Accentual-Syllabic Versifications," *Poetics*, pp. 177–188.
Through the examination of Czech and English examples, Levý defines and discusses accentual, accentual-syllabic, and syllabic patterns in poetry.

1   LIDDELL, MARK HARVEY. *An Introduction to the Scientific Study of English Poetry*. New York, 1902.

2   LIGGINS, E. M., AND H. W. PIPER. "Sound and Sense in a Shakespeare Sonnet," in *Langue et Littérature*, p. 417.

The authors claim that there is a relation between the position of the articulation of sounds and the meaning of a poem. In examining Shakespeare's "Sonnet II," they found, for example, that "in line 3, the lip-rounding is pushed into a representation of the young man's pout" (p. 417).

3   LIGHTFOOT, MARJORIE J. "T. S. Eliot's *The Cocktail Party:* An Experiment in Prosodic Description," *DA*, XXV (1965), 6630.

4   ———. "Poetry and Performance," *QJS*, LIII (1967), 61–66.

5   LOESCH, KATHERINE TAYLOR. "Prosodic Patterns in the Poetry of Dylan Thomas," *DA*, XXII (1962), 3295.

6   LOTSPEICH, C. M. "The Metrical Technique of Pope's Illustrative Couplets," *JEGP*, XXVI (1927), 471–474.

7   LOTZ, JOHN. "Notes on Structural Analysis in Metrics," *Helicon*, IV (1943), 119–146.

8   ———. "A Notation for the Germanic Verse Line," *Lingua*, VI (1956–1957), 1–7.

9   ———. "Metric Typology," in *Style in Language*, pp. 135–149; another version, "Metrics and Linguistics," *Georgetown Monographs 12* (1960), 129–137.

Lotz attempts to set up a framework for describing the variables that constitute the basis of metrical organization in various languages. He sees "metric analysis as a sub-domain of linguistics, and [claims that] all metric phenomena must be describable in linguistic terms" ("Metrics and Linguistics," p. 136).

10   LOWELL, AMY. "Vers libre and Metrical Prose," *Poetry*, III (1914), 213–220. Shapiro.

11   LÜDTKE, HELMUT. "Der Vergleich metrischer Schemata hinsichtlich ihrer Redundanz," in *Mathematik und Dichtung*, pp. 233–242.

12   LUKANITSCH, RUTH M. "The Relationship of Figures of Sound to the Rhythm in Certain Poems of Gerard Manley Hopkins." Unpublished dissertation presented to Northwestern University, 1963. See the abstract in *Speech Monographs*, XXXI (1964), 261.

13   LYNCH, J. J. "The Tonality of Lyric Poetry: An Experiment in Method," *Word*, IX (1953), 211–224.

14   ———. "The Sounds of Lyric Poetry," in *Langue et Littérature*, pp. 415–416.

A combination of laboratory study of sound and statistics may help to determine the "tonal predilections of the writer" and "contribute objective evidence for poetic interpretations that have been reached by subjective reading and intuition, and even suggest new readings" (p. 416).

1 MAEDA, CANA. "On a Method of Prosodic Analysis and Its Relevance to Style," *Essays and Studies* (Tokyo Woman's Christian College), XVI (1966), 73–96.

2 MAEDER, H. "Hölderlin und das Wort: zur Problem der freien Rhythmen in Hölderlins Dichtung," *Trivium*, II (1944), 42–59.

3 MALOF, JOSEPH. "The Native Rhythm of English Meters," *TSLL*, V (1964), 580–594.

4 ———. "The Artifice of Scansion," *English Journal*, LIV (1965), 857–860, 871.

5 MALONEY, M. F. "Donne's Metrical Practice," *PMLA*, LXV (1950), 232–239.

6 MANIERRE, WILLIAM READ. "Versification and Imagery in *The Fall of Hyperion*," *TSLL*, III (1961), 264–279.

7 MASSON, DAVID I. "Vowel and Consonant Patterns in Poetry," *JAAC*, XII (1953), 213–227; reprinted in Chatman and Levin, pp. 3–18.

8 ———. "Wilfred Owen's Free Phonetic Patterns: Their Style and Function," *JAAC*, XIII (1955), 360–369.

9 ———. "Thematic Analysis of Sounds in Poetry," in *Proceedings of the Leeds Philosophical and Literary Society*, IX, iv (1960), 133–147; reprinted in Chatman and Levin, pp. 54–68.

10 ———. "Sound and Sense in a Line of Poetry," *British Journal of Aesthetics*, III (1963), 70–72.
Masson discusses line 117 of "The Wreck of the Deutschland": "And frightful a nightfall folded rueful a day."

11 ———. "Sound-Repetition Terms," in *Poetics*, pp. 189–199.
Masson believes that such traditional terms for sound-repetition as assonance, consonance, alliteration, and so forth are inadequate for dealing with the complexities of sound patterns in poetry. He then proposes a series of terms to specify echoic functions and to relate them to larger structures in verse.

12 MATTHEWS, BRANDER. *A Study of Versification.* New York, 1911. Shapiro.

13 MAYNARD, THEODORE. *A Preface to Poetry.* New York, 1933. Shapiro.

14 MAYOR, JOSEPH B. *Chapters on English Meter.* London, 1886. Shapiro.

1   ———. *A Handbook of Modern English Meter*. Cambridge, 1903. Shapiro.

2   McAULEY, JAMES. "Metrical Accent and Speech Stress," *Balcony: The Sydney Review*, No. 4 (1966), 21–31.

3   McFADDEN, GEORGE. "Dryden and the Numbers of His Native Tongue," *Essays and Studies in Language and Literature*, XXIII (1964), 87–109.

4   McLAUGHLIN, JOHN C. "Linguistics and Literary Analysis: A Reply to Chatman," *QJS*, XLIV (1958), 175–178; Bobbs-Merrill Reprint, *Language-13*.
     McLaughlin objects to Chatman's ("Linguistics, Poetics, and Interpretation," *q.v.*) excerpting /š t b r/ from Keats's [ənrævišt brayd əv kwayitnes] to illustrate Keats's method of "striving to slow the reader down," since, he claims, there is no "unusual density of low-frequency consonant clusters" (p. 176). McLaughlin then remarks some of the "subjective, controversial and especially deficient aspects" of the Smith-Trager method of marking suprasegmentals and calls for a consideration of syntax to delimit some of the possibilities that might occur in performance.

5   McNAUGHTON, WILLIAM. "Ezra Pound's Meters and Rhythms," *PMLA*, LXXVIII (1963), 136–146.

6   MÉGROZ, RODOLPHE LOUIS. *Modern English Poetry, 1882–1932: Technical Developments*. London, 1933. Shapiro.

7   MESCHTER, CHARLES K. "Orchestral Poetry," *Poetry*, XXIV (1924), 327–330. Shapiro.

8   MOHR, W. "Freie Rhythmen," in P. Merker and W. Stammler, *Reallexikon der deutschen Literaturgeschichte*, eds. W. Kohlschmidt and W. Mohr. Berlin, 1955. Pp. 479–481.

9   MONROE, HARRIET. *Poets and Their Art*. New York, 1926. Shapiro.

10   MORGAN, EDWIN. " 'Strong Lines' and Strong Minds," *Cambridge Journal*, IV (1951), 481–491.

11   MORIER, HENRI. *Le Rhythme du vers libre symboliste*. 3 vols. Genève, 1943–1944.

12   MUKAŘOVSKÝ, JAN. "Intonation comme facteur du rhythm poétique," *Archives néerlandaises de phonétique experimentale*, VIII–IX (1932), 153–165.

13   ———. "La Phonologie et la Poétique," *Travaux du Cercle Linguistique de Prague*, IV (1935), 278–288.

14   MURDY, THELMA LOUISE BAUGHAN. "Sound and Meaning in Dylan Thomas's Poetry," *DA*, XXIII (1963), 3382–3383.

1   ———. *Sound and Meaning in Dylan Thomas's Poetry*. The Hague, 1966.

2   MUSSULMAN, JOSEPH A. "A Descriptive System of Musical Prosody," *The Centennial Review of Arts & Science*, IX (1965), 332–347.

3   NABOKOV, VLADIMIR. *Notes on Prosody*. New York, 1964. Nabokov's *Notes* were first published as an appendix to his translation of Pushkin's *Eugene Onegin*. He decries the poverty of metrical analysis in English and proposes "a simple little terminology of my own" (p. 4). Before entering on a comparative discussion of Russian meter, Nabokov presents a metrical typology of English verse.

4   NIST, JOHN. "Gerard Manley Hopkins and Textual Intensity: A Linguistic Analysis," *CE*, XXII (1961), 497–500.

5   ———. "Sound and Sense: Some Structures of Poetry," *CE*, XXIII (1962), 291–295.

6   ———. "The Word-group Cadence: Basis of English Metrics," *Linguistics*, VI (1964), 73–82.

7   OLDING, WILLIAM. *The Technic of Versification*. Oxford, 1916. Shapiro.

8   OLSON, ELDER. *General Prosody*. Chicago, 1938. Shapiro.

9   OMOND, THOMAS STEWART. *English Metrists: Being a Sketch of English Prosodical Criticism from Elizabethan Times to the Present Day*. Oxford, 1921. Shapiro.

10   ———. *Some Thoughts about Verse*. Oxford, 1923. Shapiro.

11   ORAS, ANTS. "Surrey's Technique of Phonetic Echoes: A Method and its Background," *JEGP*, L (1951), 289–308.

12   ———. "Echoing Verse Endings in *Paradise Lost*," in *South Atlantic Studies for Sturgis E. Leavitt*, eds. Thomas B. Stroup and Sterling A. Stoudemire. Washington, D.C., 1953. Pp. 175–190.

13   ———. "Spenser and Milton: Some Parallels and Contrasts in the Handling of Sound," in *Poetry and Sound*, pp. 109–133; reprinted in Chatman and Levin, pp. 19–32.

14   ———. *Verse Patterns in Elizabethan Drama*. Gainesville, Fla., 1960.

15   OSTRIKER, ALICIA. "Song and Speech in the Metrics of George Herbert," *PMLA*, LXXX (1965), 62–68.

16   ———. "The Three Modes of Tennyson's Prosody," *PMLA*, LXXXII (1967), 273–284.

17   PACE, GEORGE B. "The Two Domains: Meter and Rhythm," *PMLA*, LXXVI (1961), 413–420.

Pace attempts to make a *rapprochement* between traditional metrists and linguistically oriented critics.

1   PARTRIDGE, A. C. *Orthography in Shakespeare and Elizabethan Drama: A Study of Colloquial Contractions, Elision, Prosody and Punctuation.* Lincoln, Neb., 1964.

2   PERLOFF, MARJORIE. "Rhyme and Meaning in the Poetry of Yeats," *DA*, XXVI (1965), 6721–6722.

3   PERRY, JOHN O. "The Relationships between Rhythm and Meaning," *Criticism*, VII (1965), 373–378.

4   PIERSON, ROBERT M. "The Meter of 'The Listeners,' " *English Studies*, XLV (1964), 373–381.

5   POGGIOLI, RENATO. "Poetics and Metrics," in *Proceedings of the Second Congress of the International Comparative Literature Association.* Chapel Hill, N.C., 1959. Pp. 192–204.

6   POUND, EZRA. "A Few Don'ts by an Imagiste," *Poetry*, I (1913), 200–206. Shapiro.

7   ———. "Treatise on Meter," in his *ABC of Reading.* Norfolk, Conn., n.d.

8   PRALL, D. W. "Temporal Patterns," in his *Aesthetic Analysis.* New York, 1936. Pp. 93–134.
     "It is hard to believe that any adequate account of verse form will be built up by either misapplied classical terms or loose musical analogies. What seems to be required is an attempt first to discern the temporal pattern itself and the constituents of verse form as temporally integrated, and only then to consider other aspects of the form of verse, all of which together will be required to understand the nature of concrete rhythmical structure, the rich, subtle, patterned flow of English poetry" (p. 118).

9   PRINCE, F. T. *The Italian Element in Milton's Verse.* Oxford, 1954.
     See the chapters on "Milton's Blank Verse: The Diction," "Milton's Blank Verse: The Prosody," and "The Choruses of *Samson Agonistes*." "It is clear, then, that the systematic deformation of 'logical' word-order, as it is applied to Milton, is made to serve the poetic effect both in a narrowly technical and in a more general aesthetic manner. By means of the phrasing the sense is suspended and diffused throughout a larger block of words than could otherwise be built into a unity; verses and sentences are thus bound together and brought into animated movement" (p. 122).

10   RANSOM, JOHN CROWE. "The Strange Music of English Verse," *KR*, XVIII (1956), 460–470; Bobbs-Merrill Reprint, *Language-97*.
     Ransom discusses Chatman's contributions to the *Kenyon Review* symposium and considers the value of Trager-Smith suprasegmental analysis in the analysis of poetry. He lists the four most common

"exceptions" to the ideal metrical pattern of iambic verse. "Pure empty meter, the truant, has abandoned the dignity of its primal estate, where it dwelt in real, unchanging, and eternal being, and attached itself to a bride whose circumstances were only 'seeming' and 'becoming,' who was herself only—mortal. And on this earth, with these circumstances and this bride, it has stayed, for a long time" (p. 475).

1   REESE, JACK E. "Sound and Sense: The Teaching of Prosody," *CE*, XXVII (1966), 368–373.

2   RICHARDS, I. A. "Rhythm and Meter," in his *Principles of Literary Criticism*. London, 1926. Pp. 134–146.

"Rhythm and its specialized form, metre, depend upon repetition, and expectancy" (p. 134). Richards' treatment of rhythm rests on his concern for the emotive aspects of art and the psychology of the beholder. "In prose, the influence of past words extends only a little way ahead. In verse, especially when stanza-form and rime co-operate to give a larger unit than the line, it may extend far ahead" (p. 140).

3   ———. "Poetic Form" in his *Practical Criticism: A Study in Literary Judgment* (first ed., 1929). New York: Harcourt, Brace and Company, n.d. Pp. 214–222.

"The rhythm which we admire, which we seem to detect actually *in* the sounds, and which we seem to respond to, is something which we only *ascribe* to them and is, actually, a rhythm of the mental activity through which we apprehend not only the sound of the words but their sense and feeling" (New York edition, p. 217). Richards' idea of rhythm as a compound of sound, "sense and feeling," and his rejection of rigid and systemized rules for meter are discussed by Wimsatt and Beardsley, "The Concept of Meter" (*q.v.*), pp. 590–591.

4   RICHARDSON, CHARLES. *A Study of English Rhyme*. Hanover, N.H., 1909.

5   RIDLAND, J. M. "The Matter of Metre," *EIC*, XIV (1964), 102–104.

Reply by F. W. Bateson, 104–106.

6   RILEY, JOSEPH RAYMOND. "George Crabbe's Prosodic Theory and Practice," *DA*, XXIII (1962), 1370–1371.

7   RYDER, FRANK G. "How Rhymed Is a Poem?" *Word*, XIX (1963), 310–321.

8   SAINTSBURY, GEORGE. *A History of English Prosody from the Twelfth Century to the Present Day*. 3 vols. New York and London, 1906–1910. Shapiro.

9   ———. *Some Recent Studies in English Prosody*. London, 1919. Shapiro.

1   SAUL, GEORGE BRANDON. "On English Metrics—and Certain Absurdities," *CE*, V (1943), 157–159.

2   SCHILLER, ANDREW. "An Approach to Whitman's Metrics," *Emerson Society Quarterly*, No. 22 (1961), pp. 23–25.

3   SCHIPPER, JAKOB. *A History of English Versification*. London, 1910. Shapiro.

4   SCHNEIDER, ELISABETH W. "Sprung Rhythm: A Chapter in the Evolution of Nineteenth-Century Verse," *PMLA*, LXXX (1965), 237–253.

5   SCHOLL, E. H. "English Meter Once More," *PMLA*, LXIII (1948), 293–326.

6   SCHWARTZ, ELIAS. "Rhythm and 'Exercises in Abstraction,'" *PMLA*, LXXVII (1962), 668–670, 671–674.
    Schwartz attempts to improve on the objections raised by Hendren ("A Word for Rhythm and a Word for Meter," *q.v.*) to Wimsatt and Beardsley's "Concept of Meter" (*q.v.*). He defines rhythm as "a psychological phenomenon insofar as it takes place in the reader or observer. It is something felt, though it is virtually existent—embodied *in potentia*—in some kind of sensuous material" (p. 669). Wimsatt and Beardsley reply that Schwartz seems to be in essential agreement with them if he, in fact, believes that "meter is both a public feature of the poem as linguistic object and a phenomenally objective quality of it as auditory object" (p. 671). But Schwartz rejects such an interpretation of his view and disowns the notion of meter as a "phenomenally objective quality." "In psychological terms," he says, "the rhythm involves what has been called 'double audition.' The listener is simultaneously aware of the actual sound of the poem and of its ideal norm (its meter), which is 'heard' by the mind's ear" (p. 673). Wimsatt and Beardsley agree with the idea of "double audition," but they re-assert the "phenomenally objective quality" of meter and reject Schwartz's "realism" which "seems to place meter safely beyond verifiable public discussion, where we have no wish to follow" (p. 674).

7   ———. "The Meter of Some Poems of Wyatt," *SP*, LX (1963), 155–165.

8   ———. "Rhythm and Meaning in English Verse," *Criticism*, VI (1964), 246–255.

9   SCOTT, JOHN HUBERT. "Rhythmic Verse," *University of Iowa Humanistic Studies*, III, ii (1925–1927).
    Scott recognizes the "rhythmic phrase" as the essential unit of English verse and discounts the idea of the foot. "The true poet allows us only such outcroppings and shadowings-forth of meter as will enable us to keep our place, as it were, in the lines, within whose limits the rhythmic modulations of the voice are accustomed variously to accommodate their onward movement" (pp. 48–49).

1   SECKEL, D. *Hölderlins Sprachrythmus*. Leipzig, 1937.

2   SELLERS, W. H. "Wordsworth and Spenser: Some Speculations on the Use of Rhyme," *SEL*, V (1965), 641–650.

3   SHAPIRO, KARL JAY. "English Prosody and Modern Poetry," *ELH*, XIV (1947), 77–92; published separately, Baltimore, 1947.

4   ———. "Prosody as the Meaning," *Poetry*, LXIII (1949), 336–351.

5   SHAPIRO, KARL, AND ROBERT BEUM. *A Prosody Handbook*. New York, 1965.

6   SKINNER, B. F. "The Alliteration in Shakespeare's Sonnets: A Study in Literary Behavior," *The Psychological Record*, III (1939), 186–192.

7   ———. "A Quantitative Analysis of Certain Types of Sound-Patterning in Poetry," *The American Journal of Psychology*, LIV (1961), 64–79.

8   SMITH, EGERTON. *The Principles of English Metre*. London, 1923. Shapiro.

9   SMITH, HENRY LEE, JR. "Toward Redefining English Prosody," *SIL*, XIV (1959), 68–76.

10   SNELL, ADA L. F. *Pause: A Study of its Nature and its Rhythmical Function, in Verse, Especially Blank Verse*. Ann Arbor, 1918.
     Snell employed an elaborate apparatus designed to record both oral and nasal air-flow during an audible reading. By studying her kymograph record, she was able to analyze pauses in readings from *Paradise Lost* (for the most part) made by readers with varying experience of poetry. "A phrase rhythm once established in the mind undoubtedly will produce pauses at points where they would not occur in non-rhythmical discourse. The rhythm of the line also, once established, may produce a pause at the end of a line when a pause is possible. Variations among readers in the placing of pauses seem to depend to some extent upon whether readers respond more sensitively to the phrase or to the line rhythm" (pp. 82–83).

11   ———. "An Objective Study of Syllabic Quantity in English Verse," *PMLA*, XXXIII (1918), 396–408, and XXXIV (1919), 416–435.

12   SONNENSCHEIN, EDWARD ADOLPH. *What is Rhythm?* Oxford, 1925. Shapiro.
     "Rhythm is that property of a sequence of events in time which produces in the mind of an observer the impression of proportion between the durations of the several events or groups of events of which the sequence is composed" (p. 16). See the discussion and criticism of this view by I. A. Richards, *Practical Criticism* (*q.v.*), pp. 340–342.

1 SPROTT, S. ERNEST. *Milton's Art of Prosody*. Oxford, 1953.

2 STAUFFER, DONALD A. *The Nature of Poetry*. New York, 1946. Shapiro.

3 STEIN, ARNOLD. "Donne's Prosody," *KR*, XVIII (1956), 440–443; Bobbs-Merrill Reprint, *Language-97*.
Stein's analysis (which first appeared in *KR*, XIII [1951]) of two lines from Donne's "Elegy X" attracts the attention of Chatman in his "Mr. Stein on Donne" (*q.v.*). Stein outlines the possibilities for performance inherent in the two lines and says: "Hesitating among alternatives, as one must, one becomes aware that the metrical ambiguity is a functional part of the larger ambiguity carefully balanced in the whole complex metaphor. . . . The metrical structure, then, is a kind of key metaphor within a larger metaphor that deals with a problem in reality" (p. 442).

4 ———. "A Note on Meter," *KR*, XVIII (1956), 451–460; Bobbs-Merrill Reprint, *Language-97*.
Stein discusses the interaction of meter and rhythm. "In the process of the poem meter, the ideal metronomic pattern, creates, or becomes, rhythm. This happens, our first and most general observation tells us, by means of the external interaction between meter and the way the words have to be emphasized" (p. 451). Context and meaning, he says, also play a part in the manifestation of rhythm.

5 STEWART, GEORGE R., JR. "The Meter of the Popular Ballad," *PMLA*, XL (1925), 933–962. Shapiro.

6 ———. *The Technique of English Verse*. New York, 1930.

7 STOKES, EDWARD. "The Metrics of *Maud*," *Victorian Poetry*, II (1964), 97–110.

8 STONE, WILLIAM JOHNSON. *On the Use of Classical Meters in English*. London, 1899. Shapiro.

9 STROHEKER, FR. *Doppelformen und Rhythmus bei Marlowe und Kyd*. Heidelberg, 1913.

10 SUTHERLAND, RONALD. "Structural Linguistics and English Prosody," *CE*, XX (1958), 12–17; in *Readings II*, pp. 492–499.
Sutherland contrasts the traditional scansion of Yeats's "After Long Silence" provided by Brooks and Warren (*Understanding Poetry*, pp. 116–121) with his own rendering of the poem by the use of the Trager-Smith system of recording suprasegmentals. He concludes: "We were not able, except in one minor case, to arrive at a *greater* understanding of how the language pattern of the poem reinforced its effect and meaning; however, I venture to say that we did achieve a *clearer* understanding" (*Readings II*, p. 499). His remark that "much of the information accumulated by this new science is inconsequential to English prosody" is eagerly absorbed by Wimsatt and Beardsley, "The Concept of Meter" (*q.v.*), p. 586, Note 3.

1   SWALLOW, ALAN. "The Pentameter Lines in Skelton and Wyatt,"
    MP, XLVIII (1950), 1–11.

2   SWANN, ROBERT, AND FRANK SIDGWICK. *The Making of Verse.*
    London, 1934. Shapiro.

3   SWETT, MARGERY. "Free Verse Again," *Poetry*, XXV (1924), 153–
    159. Shapiro.

4   *Syllabics as an Organizing Principle in English Verse:* Letter from
    Zulfikar Ghose in response to reviews of George MacBeth's *The
    Broken Places*, *TLS* (January 16, 1964), p. 53; Letter from R. J.
    Baker, *TLS* (February 13, 1964), p. 127; Letters from Thom Gunn
    and John Mountford, *TLS* (March 12, 1964), p. 215; Letter from
    Martin Seymour-Smith, *TLS* (March 19, 1964), p. 235; Letters
    from Robert Conquest, Tom Scott, and Bonamy Dobrée, *TLS*
    (April 2, 1964), p. 277; Letter from C. A. Ladd, *TLS* (April 30,
    1964), p. 381; Letter from Tom Scott, *TLS* (May 14, 1964), p. 415.

5   SYMONDS, JOHN ADDINGTON. *Blank Verse.* New York, 1895. Shapiro.

6   TAYLOR, CLYDE R. "Developments in English Prosody," *Revue de
    l'Université de Sherbrooke* (Quebec), IV (October 1962), 9–20.

7   THOMPSON, JOHN. "The Iambic Line from Wyatt to Sidney," *DA*,
    XVIII (1958), 1040.

8   ———. "Linguistic Structure and the Poetic Line," *Poetics*, pp.
    167–175.
    Thompson discusses such methods of organizing the meter of English
    poetry as syllabics, strong-stress verse, and traditional meters. In his
    discussion of the interaction between meter and intonation, he remarks
    that "metrical tension is greatest when the metrical pattern is strict
    and the language is colloquial, and when the mutual relation is
    strongly indicated by a readily-recognized convention or all the more
    important individual sound-relations" (p. 174).

9   ———. *The Founding of English Metre.* New York and London, 1961.
    Thompson traces the developing concept of meter and its relation to
    the rhythm of intonation from Wyatt, Tottel's *Miscellany*, and Surrey
    to Sir Philip Sidney. His introductory chapter is particularly valuable
    for its analysis of "the three separate sound patterns of metrics, first,
    the abstract metrical pattern, second, the pattern of normal speech,
    and third, the pattern of the line of verse" (p. 4, n. 1).

10 THOMSON, WILLIAM. *The Rhythm of Speech.* Glasgow, 1923. Shapiro.

11 UNDERDOWN, MARY I. "Sir Philip Sidney's 'Arcadian' *Eclogues:*
    A Study of his Quantitative Verse," *DA*, XXV (1964), 1222.

12 VERHEUL, K. "Music, Meaning and Poetry in 'Four Quartets' by
    T. S. Eliot," *Lingua*, XVI (1966), 279–291.

1   VERRIER, PAUL. *Essai sur les principes de la métrique anglaise.* 3 vols. Paris, 1909.

2   WALLERSTEIN, RUTH C. "The Development of the Rhetoric and Meter of the Heroic Couplet, Especially in 1625–1645," *PMLA*, L (1935), 166–209; reprinted in *Essential Articles for the Study of English Augustan Backgrounds*, ed. Bernard Schelling (Hamden, Conn., 1961), pp. 198–250.

3   WELLECK, ALBERT. "The Relationship between Music and Poetry," *JAAC*, XXI (1962), 149–156.

4   WELLEK, RENÉ, AND AUSTIN WARREN. "Euphony, Rhythm and Meter," in their *Theory of Literature*. New York, 1956. Pp. 146–162. The authors consider the difficulties of describing poetic meter in terms of traditional scansion, musical notation, and acoustic metrics (i.e., the recording of certain features of readings of poetry with a kymograph or other instrument). "The pattern of verse," they conclude, "is inaccessible and incomprehensible to merely acoustic or musical methods. The meaning of verse simply cannot be ignored in a theory of metrics" (p. 158). They endorse (with some reservations) the consideration of sound and meaning in the criticism of the Russian Formalists.

5   WHALER, JAMES. *Counterpoint and Symbol: An Inquiry into the Rhythm of Milton's Epic Style.* Copenhagen: *Anglistica VI*, 1956.

6   WHITEHALL, HAROLD. "Sprung Rhythm," *KR*, VI (1944), 333–354; reprinted in *Gerard Manley Hopkins, by the Kenyon Critics*. Norfolk, Conn., 1945. Pp. 33–57.

7   ⸻, AND ARCHIBALD A. HILL. "A Report on the Language-Literature Seminar," in *Readings I*, pp. 294–297; in *Readings II*, pp. 488–492. The authors report on a seminar concerned with "re-examining English metrics in the light of phonemic theory" (*Readings II*, p. 489). They discuss the four varieties of English stress and relate them to metrical points, and introduce the reader to the notions of terminal junctures and isochronism. Both traditional metrical theory and musical scansion, they conclude, "are pre-phonemic, and both attempt to explain English verse by extraneous material" (p. 492).

8   ⸻. "From Linguistics to Criticism," *KR*, XIII (1951), 710–714; reprinted in *KR*, XVIII (1956), 411–421; reprinted in *Readings I*, pp. 389–410; Bobbs-Merrill Reprint, *Language-97*. Whitehall's essay, a review of the Trager-Smith *Outline of English Structure*, contains a discussion of the value of the recording of stress and juncture in metrics and metric typology as well as a brief treatment of isochronism in English. "Yet as no science can go beyond mathematics, no criticism can go beyond its linguistics" (*KR* [1956], 415).

1 ———. "From Linguistics to Poetry," in *Sound and Poetry*, pp. 134–145.

2 WHITELEY, M. "Verse and its Feet," *RES*, IX (1958), 268–279. See remarks by Ernest Schanzer, *RES*, X (1959), 191–192; reply to Schanzer by Whiteley, *RES*, XI (1960), 191–192; further note by Schanzer, *ibid.*, 192; remarks on Schanzer by John Buxton, *ibid.*, 305.

3 WHITMORE, CHARLES. "A Proposed Compromise in Metrics," *PMLA*, XLI (1926), 102–143. Shapiro.

4 WILLIAMSON, GEORGE. "Strong Lines," in his *Seventeenth Century Contexts*. London, 1960. Pp. 120–131.

5 WILSON, KATHERINE M. *Sound and Meaning in English Poetry*. London, 1930. Shapiro.

6 WIMSATT, W. K., JR., AND MONROE C. BEARDSLEY. "The Concept of Meter: An Exercise in Abstraction," abstract in *Style in Language*, pp. 193–196; printed in full in *PMLA*, LXXIV (1959), 585–598; reprinted in Chatman and Levin, pp. 91–114.

The authors attack both the equation of meter and intonation by the "linguists" and the performative notations of the temporal or musical scanners. They argue that the meter "inheres in the language of the poem." "We hold that it inheres in aspects of the language that can be abstracted with considerable precision, isolated, and even preserved in the appearance of an essence—mummified or dummified" (p. 390). In the course of argument, they distinguish "two kinds of stress— strong stress (the Old English, the *Piers Plowman* tradition) and syllable stress (the Chaucer-Tennyson tradition)" (p. 388). "Scanning a line is reading it in a special, more or less forced, way, to bring out the meter *and* any definite deviations or substitutions" (p. 596).

7 ———. "A Word for Rhythm and a Word for Meter," *PMLA*, LXXVI (1961), 305–308.

Wimsatt and Beardsley reply to Joseph W. Hendren's attack on their "Concept of Meter." They criticize the temporal or musical scansion Hendren employs for its supposed indecision between syllable quantity as an immutable fact of the English language or as a variable feature of poetic language subject to manipulation by the poet. "Two basic requirements for a specific and linguistically objective meter," they claim, are 1) recurrence, and 2) "a capacity in the linguistic features to be manipulated by the poet" (p. 307).

8 ———. "Rhythm and 'Exercises in Abstraction,'" *PMLA*, LXXVII (1962), 670–671, 674.

Wimsatt and Beardsley reply to the criticisms of their "Concept of Meter" made by Elias Schwartz. See the discussion of their arguments above (*s.v.* Schwartz).

9 WINTERS, YVOR. *Primitivism and Decadence*. New York, 1937. Shapiro.

1 ————. "The Audible Reading of Poetry," *Hudson Review*, IV (1951), 433–447.

2 ————. *The Function of Criticism*. Denver, 1957.
"Meter is an arithmetic norm, the purely theoretical structure of the line; rhythm is controlled departure from the norm" (p. 82).

3 WRIGHT, ELIZABETH. *Metaphor, Sound and Meaning in Bridges' The Testament of Beauty*. Philadelphia, 1951.

4 WYLD, H. C. *Studies in English Rhymes from Surrey to Pope*. London, 1923.

5 YOUNG, GEORGE. *An English Prosody on Inductive Lines*. London, 1928. Shapiro.

6 ZHIRMUNSKIJ, VICTOR. *Introduction to Metrics*, eds. Edward Stankiewicz and Walter Vickery. New York, 1966.

7 ZILLMAN, LAWRENCE JOHN. *The Elements of English Verse*. New York, 1935. Shapiro.

Other Linguistic Aspects of Poetry

8 ABBOT, CHARLES DAVID. "Poetry in the Making," *Poetry*, LV (1940), 259–266. Shapiro.

9 ABERNATHY, ROBERT. "Mathematical Linguistics and Poetics," *Poetics*, pp. 563–569.
Abernathy considers the role of "unexpectedness" in the information channel of poetry.

10 ABRAMS, M. H. "Structure and Style in the Greater Romantic Lyric," in *From Sensibility to Romanticism: Essays Presented to Frederick A. Pottle*, eds. Frederick W. Hilles and Harold Bloom. New York, 1965. Pp. 527–560.

11 ALONSO, DAMASO. "Poesia correlativa Inglesa en los siglos XVI y XVII," *Filologia Moderna*, I, ii (1960), 1–47.

12 ARTHOS, JOHN. *The Language of Natural Description in Eighteenth-Century Poetry*. Ann Arbor: University of Michigan Publications in Language and Literature, XXIV, 1949.

13 AUSPRICH, HENRY. "A Rhetorical Analysis of the Restoration Prologue and Epilogue." Unpublished dissertation presented to Michigan State University, 1963.

14 BABB, HOWARD S. "The 'Epitaph to Elizabeth, L. H.' and Ben Jonson's Style," *JEGP*, LXII (1963), 738–744.

15 BABCOCK, SISTER MARY DAVID, O.S.B. "Cummings' Typography: An Ideogrammic Style," *Renascence*, XV (1963), 115–123.

1 BAKER, WILLIAM E. "The Syntax of English Poetry: 1870–1930," *DA*, XXV (1965), 4123.

2 ———. *Syntax in English Poetry, 1870–1930*. Berkeley and Los Angeles, 1967.

3 BALLIET, CONRAD A. "The History and Rhetoric of the Triplet," *PMLA*, LXXX (1965), 528–534.

4 BARTEL, ROLAND. "Byron's Respect for Language," *Papers on English Language and Literature* (So. Ill. Univ.), I (1965), 373–378.

5 BATE, WALTER JACKSON. *The Stylistic Development of John Keats*. New York and London, 1945.
Bate discusses the stylistic development of Keats's poetry in terms of syntax, stanza forms, sound, rhyme, and rhetorical strategy. In addition, he traces the literary antecedents which influenced Keats's stylistic experimentation.

6 BATESON, F. W. *English Poetry and the English Language*. Oxford, 1934.
"I suggest that poetry develops *pari passu* with the words it uses, that its history is a part of the general history of the language, and that its changes of style and mood are merely the reflection of changing tendencies in the uses to which the language is put" (p. 25). Bateson surveys the history of English poetry.

7 BEARDSLEY, MONROE, AND SAM HYNES. "Misunderstanding Poetry: Notes on Some Readings of Dylan Thomas," *CE*, XVI (1960), 315–322.

8 BELMORE, H. W. *Rilke's Craftsmanship: An Analysis of his Poetic Style*. Oxford, 1954.

9 BERRY, FRANCIS. *The Poet's Grammar*. London, 1958.
Berry investigates the "poetic function of certain grammatical forms and their variation through English literature." He gives particular attention to verb tense and mood, prepositions, and pronouns.

10 BEUM, ROBERT. "Yeats's Idealized Speech," *Michigan Quarterly Review*, IV (1965), 227–233.

11 BOGGS, W. ARTHUR. "A Linguistic Definition of Poetry," *BNYPL*, LXVI (1962), 117–136.

12 BØGHOLM, N. "On the Spenserian Style," *Travaux du Cercle Linguistique de Copenhague*, I (1945), 5–21.

13 BONAZZA, BLAZE O. *Shakespeare's Early Comedies: A Structural Analysis*. The Hague, 1966.

14 BROOKS, CLEANTH, AND ROBERT PENN WARREN. *Understanding Poetry*. New York, 1938. Shapiro. Third edition, 1960.

1   Brown, Calvin S. "Monosyllables in English Verse," *SEL*, III (1963), 473–491.

2   Burton, Dolores M. "*To Keep Decorum:* A Stylistic Analysis of Shakespeare's *Richard II* and *Antony and Cleopatra.*" Unpublished dissertation presented to Harvard University, 1968.

3   Cooper, Sherod Monroe, Jr., "A Stylistic Study of the Sonnets of *Astrophel and Stella*," *DA*, XXIV (1963), 1612–1613.

4   Davie, Donald. *Articulate Energy: An Enquiry into the Syntax of English Poetry.* New York, 1958.
    Davie considers the poetic theories of T. E. Hulme, Susanne Langer, and Ernest Fenollosa and then discusses the function and modulation of syntax in several English poets.

5   ———. "The Relation between Syntax and Music in Some Modern Poems in English," in *Poetics*, pp. 203–214.

6   De Groot, A. Willem. *Algemen Versleer.* The Hague, 1946.
    See the review (with a summary in English) by C. F. P. Stutterheim, *Lingua*, I (1947), 104–117.

7   ———. "The Description of A Poem," in *Ninth Congress Papers*, pp. 294–300.
    De Groot discusses the problem of "how to describe poems on the basis of an acceptable theory of structural poetics." After a survey of several critical theories, he asserts: "Stylistics may be defined as the theory of the use of a language for aesthetic purposes, including the study of aesthetic language products."

8   Donoghue, Denis. "A Mode of Communication: Frost and the 'Middle' Style," *Yale Review*, LII (1962), 205–219.

9   Draper, John W. "Patterns of Style in *Romeo and Juliet*," *Studia Neophilologica* (Uppsala), XXI (1948–1949), 195–210.

10 ———. "Stylistic Contrast in Shakespeare's Plays," *West Virginia University Philological Papers*, XIII (1961), 11–24.

11 Drechsler, W. *Der Stil des Macphersonschen Ossian.* Berlin, 1904.

12 Dunn, Thomas A. *Philip Massinger.* London, 1957.
    Dunn compares the syntactic aspects of Shakespeare's and Massinger's styles. He praises Shakespeare's "colloquial" syntax, which "runs to principal clauses or their phrasal equivalents, to loose and accumulative rather than to periodic sentences and to simple constructions." Massinger does not write colloquial dialogue but rather elaborate periodic sentences.

13 Dyboski, R. *Tennysons Sprache und Stil.* Wien und Leipzig: Wiener Beiträge zur englischen Philologie, 1907.

14 Eastman, Max. *The Enjoyment of Poetry.* New York, 1939. Shapiro.

1 ECKMAN, FREDERICK WILLIAM. "The Language of American Poetry, 1900–1910," *DA*, XX (1959–1960), 2798–2800.

2 EKHTIAR, MANSUR. *From Linguistics to Literature*. Tehran, 1962. In his first section, Ekhtiar discusses the problem of separating form and content as well as the relation of literature to the "norms" of language. In Section Two, he discusses some of the phonological and morphological aspects of Emerson's poetry. The book is based on his Indiana University Ph.D. dissertation: "Emerson's Poetic Language: A Linguistic and Literary Investigation," *DA*, XXI (1960–61), 884.

3 EMBLEN, D. L. "A Comment on 'Structural Patterns in the Poetry of Emily Dickinson,' " *AL*, XXXVII (1965), 64–65.
Emblen disputes the conclusion reached by Suzanne Wilson (*q.v.*) that Emily Dickinson's poems show the influence of American Calvinist sermons. The "structural patterns" Miss Wilson finds, he says, are common to *all* expository prose.

4 EMMA, RONALD D. *Milton's Grammar*. The Hague, 1964.
See the abstract in *DA*, XXI (1961), 2286.

5 ESCH, ARNO. "Structure and Style in Some Minor Epics of the Seventeenth Century," *Anglia*, LXXVIII (1960), 40–54.

6 EVANS, B. IFOR. *The Language of Shakespeare's Plays*. Bloomington, Indiana, 1952.

7 FENOLLOSA, ERNEST. *The Chinese Written Character as a Medium for Poetry: An ars poetica*, ed. Ezra Pound. Washington, D.C.: The Square Dollar Press, n.d. Printed in part in *Prose Keys to Modern Poetry*, ed. Karl Shapiro. Evanston, Ill., 1962. Pp. 136–155.
Fenollosa presents a theory of how "things" are (or ought to be) represented in poetry. "The moment we use the copula, the moment we express subjective inclusions, poetry evaporates. The more concretely and vividly we express the interaction of things the better the poetry. We need in poetry thousands of active words, each doing its utmost to show forth the motive and visual forces" (p. 78).

8 FISH, STANLEY E. "Aspects of Rhetorical Analysis: Skelton's *Philip Sparrow*," *Studia Neophilologica*, XXXIV (1962), 216–238.

9 FITZGERALD, ROBERT P. "The Style of Ossian," *Studies in Romanticism*, VI (1966), 22–33.

10 FÓNAGY, IVAN. "Communication in Poetry," *Word*, XVII (1961), 194–218.

11 FRANCIS, HENRY ELLSWORTH. "The Adjectives of Donne and Wordsworth: The Key to a Poetic Quality," *DA*, XXV (1964), 1891.

1 FRANKE, W. *Der Stil in den epischen Dichtungen Walter Scotts*. Berlin, 1909.

2 FREEMAN, DONALD C. " 'Brave To Be A King': A Stylistic Analysis of Christopher Marlowe's Dramatic Poetry," *DA*, XXVII (1966), 5411.

3 FRIEDMANN, ANTHONY EDWARD. "The Description of Landscape in Spenser's *Faerie Queene:* A Study of Rhetorical Tradition," *DA*, XXVI (1965), 6039–6040.

4 FRIEND, JOSEPH H. "Teaching the 'Grammar of Poetry,' " *CE*, XXVII (1966), 361–367.

5 GREENE, DONALD J. "Logical Structure in Eighteenth-Century Poetry," *PQ*, XXI (1952), 315–336.

6 GRENNEN, JOSEPH E. "Grammar as Thaumaturgy: Hopkins' 'Heraclitean Fire,' " *Renascence*, XV (1963), 208–211.

7 GRIFFITH, ROBERT J. "Notes on Structural Devices in Whitman's Poetry," *Tennessee Studies in Literature*, VI (1961), 15–24.

8 GUIRAUD, PIERRE. "Pour une sémiologie de l'expression poétique," in *Langue et Littérature*, pp. 124–134.

9 HAAS, CHARLES E. "A Structural Analysis of Selected Sonnets of Gerard Manley Hopkins," *DA*, XXV (1965), 5443.

10 HAMMOND, MAC. "On the Grammar of Wallace Stevens," *The Act of the Mind: Essays on the Poetry of Wallace Stevens*, eds. Roy Harvey Pearce and J. Hillis Miller. Baltimore, 1965. Pp. 179–184.

11 ———. "Poetic Syntax," in *Poetics*, pp. 475–482.
Hammond examines and criticizes the emphasis on the mimetic function of poetic syntax described by Donald Davie in *Articulate Energy*. "Syntax is poetic when grammatically equivalent constituents in connected speech are juxtaposed by coordination or parataxis, or are otherwise prominently accumulated" (p. 482).

12 HAUSER, WILLIAM R. "An Analysis of the Structure, Influence, and Diction of Christopher Smart's *A Song to David*," *DA*, XXIV (1963), 2012–2013.

13 HEMPHILL, GEORGE. "Dryden's Heroic Line," *PMLA*, LXXII (1957), 863–879.

14 HENSLEY, DON HARPER. "Wordsworth and a New Mythology: A Stylistic Analysis of *The Excursion*," *DA*, XXV (1964), 1914–1915.

15 HERMAN, B. "The Language of Hart Crane," *Sewanee Review*, LVIII (1950), 237–260.

1   HILL, ARCHIBALD A. "A Sample Literary Analysis," *Georgetown Monographs 4* (1953), 87–93.

Hill uses Tennyson's lyric, "Now sleeps the crimson petal," as an heuristic device to show some of the possibilities of linguistic-literary analysis. He catalogues the imagery into the semiotic framework maleness-femaleness and tests this "segmentation" by appeal to a more comprehensive "design" of the poem in terms of the "diversity-unity theme . . . which has been one of the major motives in all our literature" (p. 92).

2   ———. "An Analysis of *The Windhover:* An Experiment in Structural Method," *PMLA*, LXX (1955), 968–978; Bobbs-Merrill Reprint, *Language-44*.

Hill proposes an analysis of Hopkin's poem that will, like linguistics, "work from formal and observable characteristics toward meanings" (p. 969). He is concerned with the strict separation of the micro-literary (structures in the poem) and metaliterary ("all those patterned activities and objects which are outside the poem" [p. 973]) levels of analysis. Using the probability techniques of discourse analysis, Hill attempts to choose among alternative interpretations: "There are instances in this poem where multiple meanings must be recognized, but these occur only when there is positive evidence for more than one interpretation. Multiple meaning is not acceptable when there is merely a choice between two meanings which are both formally and structurally satisfactory" (p. 971). See the criticism by Matchett (below).

3   ———. "Poetry and Stylistics." Charlottesville, Va.: The Peters Rushton Seminar in Contemporary Prose and Poetry, 1956. Reprinted in *Essays on the Language of Literature*, eds. Seymour Chatman and Samuel R. Levin (Boston, 1967), pp. 385–397.

4   ———. "Pippa's Song: Two Attempts at Structural Criticism," *Texas Studies in English*, XXV (1956), 51–56; in *Readings I*, pp. 402–406.

Hill contrasts his analysis by means of structural criticism of Browning's poem with the interpretation proposed by John Crowe Ransom. "In contrast, the analysis given here rests on one of the most basic assumptions in linguistics, that it is form which gives meaning and not meaning which gives form. Ransom's assumptions are commonly used by critics, those used here by linguists" (*Readings I*, p. 406).

5   ———. " 'The Windhover' Revisited: Linguistic Analysis of Poetry Reassessed," *TSLL*, VII (1965), 349–359.

6   HINDUS, MILTON. "Notes Toward the Definition of a Typical Poetic Line in Whitman," *Walt Whitman Review*, IX (1963), 75–81.

7   HOLLAND, JOANNE N. FIELD. "The Language of the *Faerie Queene*." Unpublished dissertation presented to Harvard University, 1965.

This dissertation is not on microfilm, but it can be consulted at the Harvard Archives (call number: HU 90.8772.5) or obtained on inter-library loan.

1   HOLLOWAY, JOHN. "Style and World in *The Tower*," in *An Honoured Guest: New Essays on W. B. Yeats*, eds. Denis Donoghue and J. R. Mulryne. London, 1965. Pp. 88–105.

2   HORSMAN, E. A. "The Language of *The Dynasts*," *Durham University Journal*, IX (1948), 11–16.

3   HYMAN, STANLEY EDGAR. "The Language of Scottish Poetry," *KR*, XVI (1954), 20–37.

4   JAKOBSON, ROMAN, AND CLAUDE LÉVI-STRAUSS. "*Les Chats* de Baudelaire," *L'Homme*, III (1962), 5–21.
     In a brief introduction, Lévi-Strauss suggests that the techniques used by literary-linguists to discover structures in poems are analogous to those used by ethnologists to extract structures from myths. In his analysis of *Les Chats*, Jakobson finds that the poet manipulates grammatical structures in such a way as to establish unexpected equivalents. A static view of the cat is combined with a view of potent action in a synthesis of the two contrary states. See the criticism of their method by Riffaterre, 69:4.

5   JAKOBSON, ROMAN. "The Grammatical Texture of a Sonnet from Sir Philip Sidney's *Arcadia*," in *Studies in Language and Literature in Honour of Margaret Schlauch*, eds. Mieczyslaw Brahmer, Stanislaw Helsztyński, and Julian Krzyżanowski (Warsaw, 1966), pp. 165–173.

6   ——. *Poetry of Grammar and Grammar of Poetry* (Vol. III of his *Selected Writings*). The Hague, forthcoming.

7   ——. *Verse and Its Masters* (Vol. V of his *Selected Writings*). The Hague, forthcoming.

8   JESPERSEN, OTTO. "Shakespeare and the Language of Poetry," in his *Growth and Structure of the English Language*. First published in 1908. Garden City, N.Y., n.d. Pp. 224–248.
     Jespersen discusses the size and range of Shakespeare's vocabulary, his use of words in characterization, and the influence of his literary style on later writers. "As for the technical *grammar* of modern poetry, the influence of Shakespeare is not very strong, in fact not so strong as that of the Authorized Version of the Bible" (p. 244).

9   JINDRA, V. *Syntactic Analysis of Ben Jonson's Plays*. Prague, 1930.

10   JOSEPH, SISTER MIRIAM, C.S.C. *Shakespeare's Use of the Arts of Language*. New York, 1947.
     Sister Miriam's first two sections deal with the general theory of composition in Shakespeare's day and his use of grammatical and

rhetorical figures derived from it. Her third section (pp. 293–399) is a catalogue of the figures, supported by definitions from the Tudor handbook writers.

1   JOSHI, B. N. "Hopkins and T. S. Eliot—A Study in Linguistic Innovation," *Osmania Journal of English Studies* (Osmania University, Hyderabad), I (1961), 13–16.

2   JUMPER, WILL C. "The Language of Wallace Stevens," *Iowa English Yearbook*. No. 6 (1961), pp. 23–24.

3   JUNGNELL, TORE. "Notes on the Language of Ben Jonson," *Studier i Modern Språkvetenskap* (Stockholm), n.s. I (1960), 86–110.

4   KALLICH, MARTIN. "Unity and Dialectic: The Structural Role of Antithesis in Pope's *Essay on Man*," Papers on *English Language and Literature* (So. Ill. Univ.), I (1965), 109–124.

5   KAYSER, WOLFGANG. "Zur Frage von Syntax und Rhythmus in der Vers-sprache," *Trivium*, V (1947), 283–292.

6   KING, ARTHUR H. *The Language of Satirized Characters in 'Poetaster': A Socio-Stylistic Analysis*. Lund: Lund Studies in English X, 1941.

7   KROEBER, KARL. *The Artifice of Reality: Poetic Style in Wordsworth, Foscolo, Keats and Leopardi*. Madison, 1964.

8   LANGWORTHY, CHARLES A. "Verse-Sentence Patterns in English Poetry," *PQ*, VII (1928), 283–298.
     Langworthy studies the relationship of syntax to enjambment in poems.

9   LASKI, MARGHANITA. "The Language of the Nightingale Ode," *Essays and Studies*, XIX (1966), 60–73.

10   LAVERTY, CARROL D. "Structural Patterns in Emily Dickinson's Poetry," *Emerson Society Quarterly*, No. 44 (1966), 12–17.

11   LE COMTE, EDWARD S. *Yet Once More: Verbal and Psychological Pattern in Milton*. New York, 1953.

12   LEECH, CLIFFORD. "The Dramatic Style of John Fletcher," in *English Studies Today: Second Series*, ed. G. A. Bonnard. Bern, 1961. Pp. 143–157.

13   LEECH, GEOFFREY. " 'This bread I break'— Language and Interpretation," *REL*, VI (1965), 66–75.

14   LEVIN, SAMUEL R. *Linguistic Structures in Poetry*. The Hague, 1962.
     Levin discusses the ways in which various aspects of linguistic structure (including meaning) "reinforce" one another in poems. By means of a "coupling" (technical term), the poet brings words and concepts to the "foreground" of his composition. He describes the ways in which rhyme, meter, alliteration, syntax, and other features contribute to

this effect. See the reviews by Louis G. Heller, *AS*, XXXVIII (1963), 137–140; L. Zgusta, *Archiv Orientalni*, XXXI (1963), 686; and William O. Hendricks, *Language*, XLII (1966), 639–649.

1 LEVÝ, JIŘÍ. "On the Relation of Language and Stanza Pattern in the English Sonnet," in *Worte und Werte: Bruno Markwardt zum 60. Geburtstag*, eds. Gustav Erdmann and Alfons Eichstaedt. Berlin, 1961. Pp. 214–231.

2 LOGAN, JOHN F. "The Blue Guitar: A Semantic Study of Poetry," *DA*, XIII (1962), 1741.

3 MACINTYRE, JAMES MALCOLM. "Marlowe's Use of Rhetorical Figures," *DA*, XXIII (1963), 2518–2519.

4 MALTBY, JOSEPH. "The Effect of Irony on Tone and Structure in Some Poems of Dryden," *DA*, XXIV (1963), 2463–2464.

5 MANIERRE, WILLIAM P. 2ND. "Verbal Patterns in the Poetry of Edward Taylor," *CE*, XXII (1962), 296–299.

6 MATCHETT, WILLIAM H. "An Analysis of *The Windhover*," *PMLA*, LXX (1955), 310–311; Bobbs-Merrill Reprint, *Language-44*.
Matchett objects to Hill's desire to limit interpretations of poems in places where they show formal and constructional homonymy (see above, *s.v.* Hill). "Surely criticism must not insist on a single meaning, need not view multiple meaning as an unfortunate aberration which occasionally 'must be recognized,' " says Matchett (p. 310). It is important to note that Hill is willing to recognize multiple meaning when "there is positive evidence for more than one interpretation" (Hill, p. 971).

7 McCoy, DOROTHY SCHUCHMAN. *Tradition and Convention: A Study of Periphrasis in English Pastoral Poetry from 1557–1715*. The Hague, 1965.

8 McINTOSH, ANGUS, AND COLIN WILLIAMSON. "*King Lear*, Act I, Scene i: A Stylistic Note," *RES*, XIV (1963), 54–58.

9 McINTOSH, ANGUS. "*As You Like It:* A Grammatical Clue to Character," *REL*, IV (April, 1963), 68–81; reprinted in *Patterns of Language: Papers in General, Descriptive and Applied Linguistics*, by Angus McIntosh and M. A. K. Halliday (London, 1966), pp. 70–82.

10 McMICHAEL, JAMES LEE. "Rhetoric and the Skeptics' Void: A Study of the Influence of Nominalism on Some Aspects of Modern American Poetic Style," *DA*, XXVII (1966), 1061A.

11 MEYER, SAM. "The Figures of Rhetoric in Spenser's *Colin Clout*," *PMLA*, LXXIX (1964), 206–218.

1   MILES, JOSEPHINE. "The Sweet and Lovely Language," in *Gerard Manley Hopkins, by the Kenyon Critics*. Norfolk, Conn., 1945. Pp. 58–73.

2   ———. "Major Adjectives in Poetry: From Wyatt to Auden," *University of California Publications in English*, XII, iii (1946), 305–426.

3   ———. "The Primary Language of Poetry in the 1640's," *University of California Publications in English*, XIX, i (1948), 1–160; "The Primary Language of Poetry in the 1740's and 1840's," *ibid.*, XIX, ii (1948), 161–382; "The Primary Language of Poetry in the 1940's," *ibid.*, XIX, iii (1948), 383–542.

4   ———. "The Language of William Blake," in *English Institute Essays 1950*. New York, 1951. Pp. 141–169.

5   ———. "The Language of Ballads," *Romance Philology*, VII (1953–1954), 1–9.

6   ———. "The Language of the Donne Tradition," *KR*, XIII (1951), 37–49.

7   ———. "Eras in English Poetry," *PMLA*, LXX (1955), 853–875; reprinted in Chatman and Levin, pp. 175–196.

8   ———. *Eras and Modes in English Poetry*. Berkeley and Los Angeles, 1957.

9   ———. *Renaissance, Eighteenth-Century, and Modern Language in English Poetry: A Tabular View*. Berkeley and Los Angeles, 1960.

10 MILLER, CLARENCE H. "The Styles of *The Hind and the Panther*," *JEGP*, LXI (1962), 511–527.

11 MOLES, ABRAHAM A. "L'Analyse des Structures du Message Poétique aux Différents Niveaux de la Sensibilité," in *Poetics*, pp. 811–826.

12 MONTGOMERY, ROBERT L. *Symmetry and Sense in the Poetry of Sir Philip Sidney*. Austin, Texas, 1961.
    Montgomery is particularly concerned with the influence of Renaissance rhetorical and stylistic theory on Sidney's poems. He includes a brief glossary of rhetorical figures (pp. 123–124).

13 MOSS, LEONARD. "The Rhetorical Style of *Samson Agonistes*," *MP*, LXII (1965), 296–301.

14 MOYNIHAN, WILLIAM T. "Dylan Thomas and the 'Biblical Rhythm,'" *PMLA*, LXXIX (1964), 631–647.

15 MURRAY, ROGER N. "The Blending of Perception: Aspects of Style in Wordsworth's *Lyrical Ballads* of 1800," *DA*, XXVI (1965), 6025–6026.

1 O'BRIEN, A. P. "Structure Complex of Hopkins' Words," *Indian Journal of English Studies* (Calcutta), I (1960), 48–56.

2 OSTRIKER, ALICIA. *Vision and Verse in William Blake*. Madison, Wis., 1965.

3 PARKER, MARION HOPE. *Language and Reality: A Course in Contemporary Criticism*. London, 1949.
Parker examines aspects of diction and syntax in recent poetry and relates her analysis to the dislocation of values felt by some modern poets.

4 PARTRIDGE, A. C. *The Accidence of Ben Jonson's Plays, Masques, and Entertainments*. Cambridge, 1953.

5 ———. *Studies in the Syntax of Ben Jonson's Plays*. Cambridge, 1953.

6 PEARCE, DONALD R. "The Style of Milton's Epic," *Yale Review*, LII (1963), 427–444.

7 PENNANEN, ESKO V. *Chapters on the Language in Ben Jonson's Dramatic Works*. Turku, 1951.

8 PEROSA, SERGIO. "Il linguaggio di Whitman," in *Il Simbolismo nella letteratura Nord-Americana: Atti del Symposium tenuto a Firenze 27–29 novembre 1964*, eds. Mario Praz et al. (Firenze, 1965), pp. 315–341.

9 PETERS, W. A. M. *Gerard Manley Hopkins: A Critical Essay Towards the Understanding of His Poetry*. Oxford, 1948.

10 PREYER, ROBERT. "Two Styles in the Verse of Robert Browning," *ELH*, XXXII (1965), 62–84.

11 PRIESTLEY, F. E. L. "Control of Tone in Tennyson's *The Princess*," in *Langue et Littérature*, pp. 314–315.
Priestley argues that Tennyson had a serious and complex purpose in mixing comic, heroic, idyllic, and romantic elements in *The Princess*.

12 READ, HERBERT. "The Intangibility of Poetic Style," *Style* (Arkansas), I (1967), 15–28.

13 REDIN, MATS. *Word-Order in English Verse from Pope to Sassoon*. Uppsala: Uppsala Universitets Årsskrift, 1925.

14 RICKS, CHRISTOPHER. *Milton's Grand Style*. London, 1963.

15 RIDENOUR, GEORGE M. *The Style of Don Juan*. New Haven, 1960.

16 RIESE, TEUT ANDREAS. "Emily Dickinson und der Sprachgeist amerikanischer Lyrik," *Die Neueren Sprachen*, XII (1963), 145–159.

17 ROBILLARD, RICHARD H. "The Rhetoric of Wallace Stevens: He That of Repetition is Most Master," *DA*, XXIV (1964), 3757.

1   ROBINSON, FRED C. "Verb Tense in Blake's 'The Tyger,' " *PMLA*, LXXIX (1964), 666–669.
    A discussion of John E. Grant's "The Art and Argument of 'The Tyger,' " in Grant's *Discussions of William Blake* (Boston, 1961), pp. 64–82. See Grant's reply and Robinson's rejoinder: "Tense and the Sense of Blake's 'The Tyger,' " *PMLA*, LXXXI (1966), 596–603.

2   RODWAY, ALAN. "By Algebra to Augustanism," in *Essays on Style and Language*, pp. 53–67.

3   RUS, LOUIS C. "Structural Ambiguity: A Note on Meaning and the Linguistic Analysis of Literature, with Illustrations from E. E. Cummings," *Language Learning*, VI (1955), 62–67.

4   RUWET, NICOLAS. "L'analyse structurale de la poésie," *Linguistics*, No. 2 (1963), 38–59.

5   ———. "Analyse structurale d'un poème français," *Linguistics*, No. 3 (1964), 62–83.

6   RYAN, FRANK L. "A Wordsworth Sonnet: One Phase of a Structural Linguistic Analysis," *Studies in English Literature*, XLII (1965), 65–69.

7   ST. GEORGE, PRISCILLA P. "The Styles of Good and Evil in 'The Sensitive Plant,' " *JEGP*, LXIX (1965), 479–488.

8   SASAKI, TATSU. *On the Language of Robert Bridges' Poetry*. Tokyo, 1930.

9   SCHLAUCH, MARGARET. *Modern English and American Poetry: Techniques and Ideologies*. London, 1956.
    See especially: "Poetic Language: Words, Images, Symbols," pp. 24–50; "Simple Statements and Larger Themes," pp. 51–76; "The Sounds of Poetry Today," pp. 129–149; and "Rhythms, Dynamics, Harmonies," pp. 150–175.

10 ———. "Linguistic Aspects of Emily Dickinson's Style," *Prace Filologiczne*, XVIII (1963), 201–215.

11 SERIGHT, ORIN DALE. "Syntactic Structures in Keats' Poetry," *DA*, XXVI (1965), 1033–1034.

12 SERNER, G. *On the Language of Swinburne's Lyrics and Epics*. Lund, 1910.

13 SINCLAIR, JOHN McH. "When is a Poem like a Sunset?" *REL*, VI, ii (1965), 76–91.

14 ———. "Taking a Poem to Pieces," in *Essays on Style and Language*, pp. 68–81.
    Sinclair analyzes the structure of a short lyric in terms of the grammatical system developed by M. A. K. Halliday.

1 SLOAN, THOMAS O., JR. "The Rhetoric in the Poetry of John Donne," *DA*, XXI (1961), 1557.

2 SPITZER, LEO. "*Explication de Texte* Applied to Whitman's Poem 'Out of the Cradle Endlessly Rocking,' " *ELH*, XVI (1949), 229–249; reprinted in his *Essays on English and American Literature*, ed. Anna G. Hatcher. Princeton, 1962. Pp. 14–36.

3 ———. "On Yeats's Poem 'Leda and the Swan,' " *MP*, LI (1954), 271–276; reprinted in his *Essays on English and American Literature* (see above), pp. 3–13.

4 ———. "The 'Ode on a Grecian Urn'; or, Content vs. Metagrammar," *Comparative Literature*, VII (1955), 203–225; reprinted in his *Essays on English and American Literature* (see above), pp. 67–97.

5 ———. "Marvell's 'Nymph Contemplating the Death of her Faun': Source vs. Meaning," *MLQ*, XIX (1958), 231–243; reprinted in his *Essays on English and American Literature* (see above), pp. 98–115.

6 STANKIEWICZ, EDWARD. "Poetic and Non-Poetic Language in their Interrelation," in *Poetics*, pp. 11–23.
"Poetic language is the message oriented towards itself, the message is an autonomous structure" (p. 14).

7 STAUFFER, DONALD B. "Style and Meaning in 'Ligeia' and 'William Wilson,' " *Studies in Short Fiction*, II (1965), 316–330.

8 STEIN, ARNOLD. *John Donne's Lyrics: The Eloquence of Action.* Minneapolis, 1962.

9 ———. "Plain Style, Plain Criticism, Plain Dealing, and Ben Jonson," *ELH*, XXX (1963), 306–316.
Review of Trimpi's *Ben Jonson's Poems: A Study of the Plain Style* (see below).

10 STEIN, JACK M. "Poetry for the Eye," *Monatshefte*, LV (1963), 361–366.

11 STOEHR, TAYLOR. "Syntax and Poetic Form in Milton's Sonnets," *English Studies*, XLV (1964), 289–301.

12 STUTTERHEIM, C. F. P. "Poetry and Prose: Their Interrelations and Transitional Forms," *Poetics*, pp. 225–237.
Stutterheim considers the function of the typographical line and other strategic devices in defining poetry.

13 SUGDEN, H. W. "The Grammar of Spenser's 'Faerie Queene,' " *Language Dissertations*, XXII (1936).

14 SUMMERS, MIMOSA FAYE. "Style in Selected Poems of Arthur Hugh Clough," *DA*, XXVI (1966), 4677.

1   TAYLOR, EDMUND DENNIS. "The Rhetoric of Hardy's Poetry,"
    DA, XXVII (1966), 189A.

2   THOMSON, JAMES ALEXANDER KER. *Classical Influences on English
    Poetry*. New York, 1951.
    Thomson discusses not only epic and dramatic poetry, but such forms
    as the lyric, the elegy, the pastoral, satire, and the epigram.

3   TRIMPI, WESLEY. "Jonson and the Neo-Latin Authorities for the
    Plain Style," *PMLA*, LXXVII (1962), 21–26.

4   ———. *Ben Jonson's Poems: A Study of the Plain Style*. Stanford, 1962.

5   TUNBERG, JACQUELINE DUFFIÉ. "British and American Verse
    Drama, 1900–1965: A Survey of Style, Subject Matter, and Tech-
    nique," *DA*, XXVI (1965), 2226–2227.

6   WARFEL, HARRY. "The Mathematics of Poe's Poetry," *CEA Critic*,
    XXI (1959), 1, 5–6.

7   WELLS, HENRY W. *New Poets from Old*. London, 1964.
    Wells investigates the influence of style and language in the English
    literary tradition.

8   WHEELWRIGHT, PHILIP. "On the Semantics of Poetry," *KR*, II
    (1940); reprinted in Chatman and Levin, pp. 250–263.
    See the reply by Josephine Miles, "More Semantics of Poetry," *KR*,
    II (1940); reprinted in Chatman and Levin, pp. 264–268.

9   WHITCOMB-HESS, M. "The Language of Poetry," *Philosophical Re-
    view*, LIII (1944), 484–492.

10 WILLIAMS, WILLIAM CARLOS. "The Work of Gertrude Stein,"
    Pagany, I (1930), 41–46.

11 WILLIAMSON, GEORGE. *The Proper Wit of Poetry*. Chicago, 1962.

12 WILSON, SUZANNE M. "Structural Patterns in the Poetry of Emily
    Dickinson," *AL*, XXV (1963), 53–59.

13 WIMSATT, W. K., JR. "One Relation of Rhyme to Reason," *MLQ*,
    V (1944), 323–338; reprinted in his *Verbal Icon*. Lexington, Ky.,
    1954, and New York, 1958. Pp. 153–166.
    Wimsatt considers the relation of syntactic and semantic parallel to
    the artificial parallel created by rhyme and other sound links. He
    discusses effects that range from homoeoteleuton (repetition of the
    same morpheme or inflectional morpheme) to extreme difference in
    etymology (e.g., Byron's rhyme of "mahogany" and "philogyny")
    or syntactic function.

14 ———. "Rhetoric and Poems: Alexander Pope," in *English Insti-
    tute Essays 1948* [New York, 1949]; reprinted in his *Verbal Icon*
    (see above), pp. 169–185.

Wimsatt discusses the effect of Renaissance rhetorical theory and the use of "figures of thought and speech" in Pope.

1   WRENN, C. L. "The Language of Milton," in *Studies in English Language and Literature: Presented to Professor Dr. Karl Brunner on the Occasion of his Seventieth Birthday*, ed. Siegfreid Korninger. Vienna and Stuttgart, 1957. Pp. 252–267.

2   WRIGHT, KEITH. "Rhetorical Repetition in T. S. Eliot's Early Verse," *REL*, VI (1965), 93–100.

3   ———. "Word-Repetition in T. S. Eliot's Early Verse," *EIC*, XVI (1966), 201–206.

INDEX: STYLES UNDER SCRUTINY

INDEX: CRITICS OF STYLE

The following index is an alphabetical listing of all the authors whose works appear in the bibliography. If the page and item number appear in italics, the reader will find that the item is annotated. Major discussions of a critic's work may be found following the abbreviation DISC.